· THE VIOLENT SEX ·

Male Psychobiology
and the
Evolution of Consciousness

LAUREL HOLLIDAY

BLUESTOCKING BOOKS

Published by Bluestocking Books
Box 475
Guerneville, California 95446

Distributed by Bookpeople
2940 Seventh Street
Berkeley, California 94710

and Women in Distribution, Inc.
Box 8858
Washington, D. C. 20003

Designed by Gina Covina and Laurel Holliday
Manufactured in the U. S. A.
ISBN 0-931458-01-3

1 2 3 4 5 6 7 8 9

Library of Congress Cataloging in Publication Data

Holliday, Laurel, 1946-
   The violent sex.

   Includes bibliographical references.
   1. Men--Psychology. 2. Psychobiology.
3. Violence. 4. Consciousness. I. Title.
BF692.5.H64   155.3'32   78-7344
ISBN 0-931458-01-3

Bluestocking:
1. a woman with considerable scholarly, literary, or intellectual
ability or interest. 2. a member of a mid-18th century London
literary circle (so called from the informal attire, esp. blue
woolen instead of black silk stockings, worn by some women of
the group).   *(Random House Dictionary)*

To the Power of Love

With Special Appreciation

for Gina

CONTENTS

CHAPTER TWO - 95

Violence Begets Violence

CHAPTER THREE - 109

The Evolution of the Sexes

CHAPTER FOUR - 143

Man's Dominion: The Hunter Today

CHAPTER FIVE - 183
Home Remedies

CHAPTER SIX - 209
New Paths

APPENDIX I - 215
How to Have a Girl

APPENDIX II - 221
Female Primacy & the Male Mutation

PREFACE

In the summer of 1974 I moved to Somerville, Massachusetts, an Irish Catholic/poor student suburb of Cambridge, and discovered that I lived only a few blocks from Tufts University. My partner, Gina, and I had come from Berkeley seeking a more intellectual, "cultural" atmosphere, but as the leaves began to turn and fall and the monotonous gray-shingled houses began to be matched by a daily monochromatic sky, we found ourselves isolated, uninspired by Cambridge "culture," and hungering to do something with our restless brains. Nearly every day, we hiked up the hill to Tufts to feed our cerebral cells at the library.

At the time, we were editing and publishing a women's magazine, *Amazon Quarterly*, which we had brought with us from California. In addition to supporting us while we wrote, it *required* us to keep finding new topics to write about in order to fill its pages. Gina began working on an article she called "Rosy Rightbrain's Exorcism/Invocation" and I took on the task of researching sex differences in brain lateralization for her at Tufts library. The collection was limited on this precise topic, but I found enough scientific articles about hemispheric differences in male and female brain function to excite *my* detective, bloodhound, left brain to really go to work on the ques-

9

tion.

I borrowed a card for Harvard's library of medicine, and so began a search which would go far beyond brain lateralization. For the next two years, I spent most of my waking hours in libraries--first Tufts and Harvard, and later U. C. Berkeley, after the Boston climate (meteorological, sociological, cultural) had induced us to return to California.

WHAT MAKES A MAN A MAN?

My nearly total preoccupation at this time was the question of the physiological differences between males and females which influence our obvious behavioral differences, particularly the sex difference in aggressiveness. For some reason this had been a verboten line of inquiry; no one wanted to hear that behavior might be under genetic control, and feminists in particular were bending over backwards to deny any biological influence on sex-differentiated behavior. Kate Millett, among others, had firmly rejected the notion that sex roles were derived from anything more than different social conditioning:

> It is time that we realized that the whole structure of male and female personality is entirely imposed by social conditioning. The possible traits of human personality have in this conditioning been arbitrarily assigned into two categories: thus aggression is masculine, passivity feminine. [1]

After a few months of research, I knew that this was a limited perspective. The scientific position is concisely summarized by two Oxford professors of psychology, Dr. J. A. Gray and Dr. A. W. H. Buffery:

> ...any purely cultural account of the relevant human sex differences is extremely implausible. [2]

Since I have never been able to understand or empathize with much of male behavior, I felt a personal calling to find out what lay behind it. What in the world, for example, would induce so many of them to want to spend hours each week watching those human hulks kicking a ball down a field and piling on top of each other to try to get

it? What could possibly induce a man to rape a woman?
to hunt and kill the creatures I love in the woods? to
murder their own kind by the millions? What was the
payoff? Until I could understand all this I would have a
hard time empathizing with men, and thus there would always be a part of me which would live in fear of them.
For myself, then, I wanted to come to terms with and
really understand male psychobiology. I wanted to know
why, for example, sex is the most reliable predictor of
how violent a person will be in all cultures, races and
classes in recorded history. And why are 90% of all violent crimes committed by men? Why *are* males the violent sex? Because Daddy encouraged them to be tough and
play with guns, because teacher said they were stronger
and faster than girls and didn't cry, because Mommy took
away their dolls? What "makes a man a man"? At the
time I had no idea just how big a question I was asking.
The more I researched, the larger the scope of my ignorance became. What had begun as a few references for
Gina's article on brain hemispheres was becoming a book.

I BECOME AN ANDROLOGIST?

None of us, as yet, can claim to be certified "andro-
logists," for in order to answer the question of what
makes a man a man we must explore everything from
psychology to paleoanthropology, from sociology and criminology to anatomy, biochemistry, genetics, art and literature. In fact, there is hardly any discipline which does
not have some bearing on the study of maleness.
　　This book is an attempt to bring together what various
disciplines currently have to tell us about the nature of
masculinity. A glance through the table of contents will
give you an idea of the scope which I felt was necessary
to understand male behavior. After a year of documenting
the surprising number of psychobiological differences between males and females, I went on to try to discover how
we inherited such disparate genetic potentials from our pre-
decessors, a search which took me back millions of years
through the theoretical labyrinths of paleoanthropology.
　　Having answered to my satisfaction *why* males are so
different from females and *how* this difference came to be,
I went on to survey the *effects* of our very different psychobiology today. Violent crime, ecological havoc, war,

famine, social injustice, cultural and spiritual bankruptcy
...just a few of the problems we face which are inextricably linked with male psychobiology.

In the three years I've worked on this question I have
come to understand, empathize with, and not fear so much
the male of the species. At first, every new tidbit I
found about males' inborn proclivity for aggressive behavior, every newspaper article detailing their atrocities
against each other, women, and the planet, would bring
me to hate and fear them more. There was a point when
I knew too much about masculine psychobiology to be com-
fortable in the same room with one of "them."

Then I came to know, if for no other reason than my
own physical discomfort arising from such paranoia, that
I (and this book) must transcend the determinism of the
position that since men's brains, bodies, hormones, genes
and conditioning are such as they are, men must continue
to act accordingly. I knew that I must thoroughly docu-
ment those factors which predispose men to be the aggressive, insensitive creatures that many of them are, that I
must also show *how this came to be* , and, most importantly, that I must show *how they can change* . There are
enough unread doomsday books smoldering on library
shelves. For my own peace of mind I had to get beyond
the prophesies of rising violent crime, nuclear war, famine, etc. that male greed seemed certain to bring upon
us all. The chapter entitled "Home Remedies" contains
practical steps we as individuals can take to reduce the
harmful effects of masculine psychobiological programming.
Not the least of these, of course, is to have fewer male
children (complete directions for this in appendix one).

ABOUT JUDGMENT, BLAME, AND PARANOIA

It was all too easy, as I wrote this book, to slip on
my feminist-politico cap and slide into rhetoric, judgment,
and blame. I have avoided that as much as I can, since
I have come to know that positing evil outside ourselves
(i.e. men are macho pigs, or all men are insensitive,
ruthless brutes) can only lead us into a debilitating paranoia. I want to emphasize that although men are responsible for the pain and suffering they cause, they are *not*
to blame. I believe there is no *conscious* evil, only ignorance. Though I am not clean of anger and fear, which

12

shows through, no doubt, in my very choice of male violence as a topic for this book, I am making an effort to
understand what makes men violent and how they can go
about changing, rather than merely listing their atrocities
and angrily telling them to clean up their act. I *had* to
understand men this way to ever come to love them...
which I have found I must for my own growth and wellbeing.

I want to thank my partner Gina for love, forbearance
and the faith which sustained my writing this book. And
very special thanks to Abbie Freedman, Dorothy Saxe and
Grendl Winkler for their help in the preparation of the
text, and to all the scientists and librarians who made
this book possible.

Chapter One

PSYCHOBIOLOGICAL SEX DIFFERENCES AND AGGRESSION

Of all the animals, the boy is the most unmanageable.
--Aristotle

All personality traits are subject to the influence of both genetics and the environment, but as the case for the latter has been amply stressed in recent years, we will begin with the newly discovered contribution of biology to human psychological sex differences. We will learn why "boys will be boys," and why, *universally*, males are the violent sex.

THE SEXUAL BALANCE SHEET

From conception on, there are physiological differences between the two sexes which shape their psychological development. A male fetus is, from the beginning, less capable of surviving than a female fetus; approximately four times more males than females are spontaneously aborted or miscarried. Most of these male fetuses have gross malformations which have resulted from genetic error. All diseases and physical aberrations common to newborns and infants are more prevalent in males than females, with the single exception of whooping cough. During the first year of life 33% more boys than girls die from these congenital malformations and diseases. So, in

15

fact, even though about 150 males are conceived for every 100 females, girls outnumber boys in most cultures because so many males die during gestation and early infancy. The boys who survive infancy are much more likely to suffer the psychologically adverse effects of illness and deformity than are girls. One-third more boys than girls are born blind, for example, and boys, in general, are more susceptible to hearing defects, speech defects, mental retardation, autism, epilepsy, cerebral palsy, heart defect, and more. This difference in medical problems is life-long. In the U.S. women live an average of eight years longer than men.

At birth, the average girl is more mature than the average boy, as indicated by the development of various physiological systems, including bone ossification. According to two experts in this field, J.E. Garai and A. Scheinfeld, a girl is:

> ...actually a much better developed organism.
> Surveys of studies of maturation show that the
> female neonate is approximately one month to
> six weeks ahead of the male neonate in develop-
> mental acceleration. The gap in maturation
> widens in scope with the progressive increase
> in age, with women reaching the terminal matu-
> rational stage around age twenty-one and men
> at about age twenty-four, on the average. [1]

Girls get their teeth before boys and are quicker to learn physical coordination. They sit up, crawl and walk earlier than boys. They talk earlier too, since intellectual development is also influenced by physical maturation. In a study of 30,000 elementary school children it was determined that girls are:

> ...more mature at every age level, surpassing
> boys in mental age by four months in the sec-
> ond and by eight months in the eighth grade...[2]

Though males are born less physiologically mature, they are definitely born stronger than females. Garai and Scheinfeld say of this:

> Males exhibit consistently greater strength
> than females at all ages. From early infancy
> on, males display greater muscular reactivity

16

which expresses itself in a stronger tendency
toward restlessness and vigorous overt activity.
This excess of motor activity in the male appears to be related to the greater oxygen consumption required to fulfill his need for increased energy production. [3]

To keep up their greater strength, males begin to eat
more than females shortly after birth. They have significantly different needs for various vitamins, minerals and
nutrients than females throughout life. The U. S. Department of Agriculture, for example, suggests that adult females need only 83% of the protein that the average male
needs. A male five-year-old is known to need about 15%
more calcium than a girl of the same age. The differences in nutritional needs are related to the differences in
physical activity:

In general, the male organism seems to be
comparable to an engine which operates at higher levels of speed and intensity and which therefore needs a greater amount of "fuel" than the
less energetic female organism. [4]

Physiologically, then, we can see that girls and boys
differ in far more than their sex organs. Boys' greater
vulnerability to all manner of gestational, birth, and early
infancy stress is undisputed and can not help but have an
impact on their psychological development. Their greater
strength, too, as we shall see, has a direct bearing on
their behavior.

PSYCHOLOGICAL SEX DIFFERENCES IN EARLY INFANCY

The time when we can best ascertain that some sex
differences are biologically determined is immediately after birth, when the mother has yet to influence her child
by differential handling. During the newborn period we
can safely assume that whatever sex differences we find
are genetically and/or hormonally controlled.
One difference which has been found by several researchers is that the female newborn is more sensitive to
stimulation and pain than the male. Girls react more in-
tensely when their blanket is removed suddenly, or when
a jet of air is released onto their abdomen, [5] and when

their lips are touched.[6] Even from day one of life, the female has a higher galvanic skin response. In a way, the old cliche about females being "thin-skinned" applies here. Girls are more sensitive to the external environment from birth.* Girl infants smile more often than boys, while boys startle more often when surprised by noises or other stimuli.[7, 8] Boys display greater physical strength from day one of life--they can lift their heads higher than girls.[9]

These sex differences in "response tendencies and behaviors," according to Dr. June Reinisch,

> ...are evidence for the existence of sexually dimorphic patterns which would be difficult to attribute to the influence of social or cultural learning. [10]

A male baby is generally more trouble to his parents even in the first few weeks than is a girl. He is more apt to develop colic and to stay awake crying more hours of the day. He will take, on the average, several months longer to toilet train and he will be more finicky and rejecting of his first solid foods. [11]

A study done by Kagan and Lewis shows that girl infants are more interested in a varied environment than boys are.[12] For music, boys prefer one tone steadily

*Psychologist Judith Bardwick says: "The idea that this early sensitivity is a necessary precondition for empathy and imagination is supported by studies of older girls and women. Obviously a lot of learning occurs in the years after infancy, but older females are more prone to fantasy than older males (L'Abate, 1960), are more emotional (Castaneda and McCandless, 1956; Goldstein, 1959), have a swifter perception of details and subtle cues (Anastasie, 1958; Bakan and Manley, 1963; Pishkin and Shurley, 1965), have a better memory for names and faces, and have a greater sensitivity to other persons' preferences (Exline, 1957, 1962; Witryol and Kaess, 1957), as well as a greater freedom of emotional and intuitive experiences. Female infants seem to be perceptually precocious when compared with males (McCall and Kagan, 1967) and, at a minimum, this may allow them to establish more detailed and accurate perceptions of the stimulus-world earlier than boys, especially that stimulus-world composed of people." (*The Psychology of Women*. New York: Harper and Row, 1971)

repeated in an unvarying tempo. Girls prefer complex
jazz patterns. Girls are interested in a pattern of flash-
ing colored lights while boys' attention is more easily
sustained by a single light blinking on and off. Girls show
more interest in a movie than boys. These differences
persist through early infancy and are even further accen-
tuated when the children are one year of age. At this
point girls are more interested in all more-complex stimuli than boys are, including oral readings.

In another study, Lewis found that infant girls have a
marked preference for faces when given a number of stimuli to respond to.[13] This suggests that girls have a
greater sensitivity to social stimuli than boys from the
beginning. In fact, girl infants who are only three days
old are more responsive to the cry of another infant than
are boys the same age.[14]

Howard A. Moss has found that, in general,

> ...male infants tend to function at a less well
> organized and less efficient level than do female
> infants. The males were more irritable and
> seemed less facile than females in responding
> to learning contingencies, particularly in regard
> to social stimuli. This difference in the rate
> of learning between the sexes may be partly at-
> tributable to the males being more prone to
> physical distress at this stage of development
> and thus less frequently at an optimal state for
> monitoring and assimilating environmental events
> than are females.[15]

Anneliese Korner reports that male infants are less
"behaviorally stable" than females, which means that from
day to day they are less consistent in their behavior than
females.[16] Boys are less predictable in all their needs
which the mother must attend to, such as hunger, sleepi-
ness, bowel movements, etc. Korner points out that such
unpredictability puts a strain on the mother-infant interaction; several studies indicate that it has "a very disorgan-
izing effect on the mother, her care-giving efforts, and
her self-confidence." Korner goes on to discuss the long-
range implications for the child:

> Behavioral unpredictability in infancy is also
> associated with developmental deviations in later
> life; for example, Thomas, Chess and Birch

19

found in a longitudinal study that children who developed behavior disorders were infants who, among other early deviations, were highly unpredictable and irregular in their functioning. [17]

There are, then, significant sex differences in newborns' physiological and psychological functioning which it would be most difficult to attribute to differential conditioning. But as a further check on this possibility, we should look at the findings about another species which, we can safely assume, would be quite unlikely to share our sex-role stereotypes.

In his study of infant sex differences in rhesus monkeys, Goy concluded that:

> Within a month after birth, male rhesus monkeys are wrestling, pushing, biting and tugging, while the female monkeys are beginning to act shy, turning their heads away when challenged to a fight by young males. [18]

Even if one is not convinced that this behavior is free of conditioning, the question arises as to why the rhesus parents would want to inculcate such strongly stereotyped behaviors in their young. If this is just an arbitrary arrangement, "just a matter of cultural conditioning," then why, in the majority of mammalian species and in every human culture that has ever been studied, is the male conditioned to be aggressive and the female to be passive? The answer is that mammalian parents and human parents as well (cross-culturally) are responding to an innate difference in the behavior of their young, perhaps accentuating it then with their own responses, but certainly not creating it a priori.

H. F. Harlow, the famous primatologist, concludes from his studies:

> These secondary sex-behavior differences probably exist throughout the primate order, and moreover, they are innately determined biological differences regardless of any cultural overlap.... We believe that our data offer convincing evidence that sex behaviors differ in large part because of genetic factors. [19]

CHILDHOOD SEX DIFFERENCES

Of course, the further we follow the child in development the less it is possible to know what behavior is genetically engendered and what is due to environment. Acknowledging the interaction, it is still interesting to note the developmental differences in girls and boys and to ponder why and how parents would condition them so differently.

During the second year, children begin to string words into phrases, but girls attain a much more comprehensible patter earlier than boys do. Mothers have been found to understand less than 50% of what their sons say at 24 months of age while they understand 78% of what their daughters say.[20] This may have an important environmental bearing on male aggressiveness--if a little boy can not make his needs understood in words he will have to physically act out his demands.

Sex differences in activity level have not been firmly established, but those studies that do find a difference show boys to be more active than girls.[21] When boys are in the presence of other boys they are stimulated to a much higher activity level than when girls play with other girls or with boys.[22] Eleanor Maccoby, probably the foremost authority on sex differences, says of this one:

> It is clearly possible that there may be a
> constitutional contribution to the male's tendency
> to put out more energy, or respond with more
> movement, to certain stimulating conditions. [23]

There are clear sex differences in the kinds of emotion that boys and girls display. Girls, for example, tend to cry because they have been physically hurt, while boys cry more out of frustration at not being able to manipulate an object or another person.[24] They are more susceptible to sudden outbursts of temper; one long-term carefully-documented study found that between the ages of two and a half and five, boys became angry at least twice as frequently as girls.[25]

Females in most studies have proven to be more anxious than males, but this could be because females are also more honest in reporting their emotions. The sex difference in anxiety, then, might be at least partially a product of males' greater defensiveness. Nevertheless, there is some evidence to indicate that females are more fearful than males.

Females, in general, tend to be more nurturant than males.[26] Little girls are more attentive to their younger brothers and sisters and, according to one cross-cultural study, "during the ages 7 - 11...girls emerge strongly as the more helpful sex."[27]

Of course, playing with dolls and caring for younger brothers and sisters seem very much a product of the girls' conditioning to fit adult sex-role stereotypes. That this may not be the whole picture is indicated by researcher Richard Green:

> Maternalism (and its play-equivalent doll play) has also recently come under the scrutiny of neuroendocrinologists. Previously thought to be a purely sex-typed social-learning phenomenon, recent data suggest that it is, in part, neurally programmed. Nonhuman male and female primates show a clear difference in the extent and type of attention they pay to newborns of their species. Female rhesus monkeys do not even require exposure to adult maternal models for their greater interest in infants to emerge.[28]

In addition to their greater interest in nurturance of their siblings, girls typically choose smaller social structures than boys so that they are involved in one-to-one interaction and thus achieve a greater degree of closeness to others than boys, who typically choose to run in packs. The average female group consists of two or three girls, while boys usually congregate in groups of four or more. This may be highly significant, according to Eleanor Maccoby and Carol Jacklin:

> We suspect that the size of social groups has a great deal to do with dominance patterns. Large groups can not so easily function without a dominance hierarchy as can small groups; is the size of girls' social groups in part a reflection of their reluctance to enter into dominance hierarchies and compete for positions in such hierarchies?[29]

Two of the best-known and extensively-documented sex differences involve perceptual and intellectual abilities. Females *at all ages* are superior to males in verbal

22

skills. On the other hand, males at most ages are superior to girls in visuo-spatial skills. This means that they
are more capable of determining their position or an object's position in space, and that they tend to be better at
intellectual activities that involve spatial reasoning, like
geometry.

These two abilities do not balance out as far as their
usefulness in learning situations goes. Verbal abilities
are generally called upon far more often than spatial
abilities in schools as we know them today. Hence,
throughout the elementary grades and, according to some
studies, well into high school, girls do better than boys
in school. At the age of six, when most children enter
school, girls are twelve months ahead of boys in their
ability to learn.[30] By age nine the difference increases
to eighteen months. Boys the same age as girls have
three to ten times more learning and behavior disorders
and two-thirds of the children who have to repeat grades
are boys. Not until after grade school do boys excel on
learning tasks, and then the tasks are mechanical and
mathematical. Psychologist Judith Bardwick says of boys'
superiority in these skills:

> I suspect that there is a general and consis-
> tent selectivity in cognitive skills where boys
> have some tendencies toward the objective and
> "thing-related" and girls toward the intuitive,
> verbal, and "people-related." [31]

A clear picture of this distinction emerges from studies by Eric Erickson on the kinds of things children build
and how these relate to sexual difference.[32] He worked
with 150 boys and 150 girls who were ten, eleven and
twelve over a two-year period. They were all "normal"
children recruited through the Berkeley California Guidance
Study at the University of California. Erickson gave them
the "task" of constructing a scene on a table which they
would find exciting as a set for an imaginary motion picture. The children were given as much time as they
needed and hundreds of props from which to choose. After
they had constructed the setting they were asked to tell
the plot of the movie they were imagining. Erickson's
conclusion:

> The differences themselves were so simple
> that at first they seemed a matter of course.

23

History in the meantime has offered a slogan for it: the girls emphasized the inner and the boys the outer space....

This then is typical: the girl's scene is an *interior* one, represented either as a configuration of furniture without any surrounding walls or by a *simple enclosure* built with blocks. In the girl's scene people and animals are mostly *within* such an interior or enclosure, and they are primarily people or animals in a *static* (sitting, standing) position. Girls' enclosures consist of *low walls*, i.e. only one block high, except for an occasional elaborate *doorway*. These interiors of houses with or without walls were, for the most part, expressly *peaceful*. Often a little girl was playing the piano....

Boys' scenes are either houses with *elaborate walls* or *facades with protrusions* such as cones or cylinders representing ornaments or cannons. In boys' constructions more people and animals are *outside* enclosures or buildings, and there are more *automotive* objects and animals moving along streets and intersections. There are elaborate *accidents*, but also traffic channelled or arrested by the *policeman*. While high structures are prevalent in the configurations of boys, there is much play with the danger of collapse or *downfall*: *ruins* were exclusively boys' constructions. 33

Ten to twelve-year-old boys are already confirmed in their interest in violence. Judith Bardwick offers one possible explanation of the clear difference in how boys relate to the inner and outer spaces in the environment and the ways that they can feel separate from (and thus do violence to) other people, animals and things:

The body concept of the male, perhaps related to the demanding insistence of penile erections, is likely to be more differentiated than the global body concept characteristic of women. How well one discriminates between separate elements or how global one's perceptions are seems to be related to the articulation and differentiation of the self from the environment. 34

24

The male child, in accordance with his body concept, is less integrated with his environment and less sensitive to external cues like other people's faces. He acts *upon*, rather than acting *in relation to* and so begins a lifelong pattern of establishing separateness and one-up-manship rather than affiliation and cooperation with others. The female child, as is clear from Erickson's work, is interested in including others in her world and acting *in relation to* them--not in competition. The goal of one-up-manship essential to aggression is clearly less strong in female children.

Body concept may be one source of male behavior, but we will see in the next sections that more important contributors to male separateness and aggression are hormonal and ultimately genetic in origin.

THE AGGRESSIVE SEX

Nearly everyone in sex difference research agrees that males are universally the more aggressive sex:

> ...it is clear that it is a virtually universal feature of mammalian (and, indeed, of the vertebrate) species that the male is more aggressive than the female. [35]

> The evidence for greater male aggression is unequivocal... [36]

> Human aggression is a problem for men, not women. It is men who wage wars, engage in bitter competition, fight each other individually, and maintain vendettas lasting for years or even decades.... Status as a male is to be achieved by being aggressive, and masculinity is perhaps the most basic aspect of a man's identity. [37]

In a survey of studies done in over 600 different cultures, D'Andrade reports that males are invariably more aggressive than females. [38] The famous Harvard University "six cultures study" carried out by teams of researchers around the world found that males are the aggressive sex. [39] In fact, all cross-cultural research to date, according to Maccoby and Jacklin, has shown that males are

25

more aggressive than females. Of the sixty-six *clinical* studies which they choose to review in their definitive *Psychology of Sex Differences*, only five find females more aggressive than males.

From toddler age, boys engage in angry outbursts roughly twice as often as girls and are much more likely to attempt physical injury of their target. They grab toys, attack other children and ignore requests from parents and peers. They quarrel with more children more often, and generally are more aggressive in all areas of behavior than girls, with, possibly, the single exception of verbal aggression.

Some researchers have been struck by the obvious difference in energy expenditure. It is as though boys are constantly under pressure; the slightest frustration can trigger an explosion:

> Parents' comments about aggression or activity in their children seem to imply in boys a force barely held under control, "dynamic," "a bomb shell," "bold," "belligerent." These mothers felt that the cup was running over: "A great deal of unnecessary energy," "so much energy he doesn't know what to do," "so much energy he can't use it all up."... Parents of girls seem more likely to equate aggressiveness with the personal reaction of anxiety and confusion, rather than with a release of uncontrollable gross motor energy. [40]

> Corinne Hutt, in her excellent book, *Males and Females*, details her experiments with male/female aggressiveness. She concludes:

> Our studies of the social behavior of preschool children...illustrate a noteworthy interaction between innate predisposition and environmental opportunity....Boys are twice as aggressive as girls (aggression here including verbal aggression), but even more interesting is the fact that it is predominantly boys toward whom this aggression is directed. [41]

Simply put, the boys manage to irritate each other enough so that aggression is the outcome twice as often as it is with girls.

An earlier study had shown that this peculiar ability of males not only to be 'vindictive' but also to elicit 'vindictiveness' was true of adults as well (Taylor and Epstein, 1967). When a similar task was carried out with undergraduates and with shock as punishment, males were found to be much more aggressive than the females. Once again male 'opponents' were treated more harshly than females, and increasingly so. [42]

The sex difference in aggression is in evidence in all age groups which have been studied. Thomas Detre has found that there are approximately twice as many behavior problem aggressive boys throughout the school grades as girls and three times as many aggressive boys in kindergarten as girls. [43] Nearly all studies of high school age people and young adults have shown men to be more aggressive than women. I am not aware of studies done with the elderly, but there is no reason to suppose that the sex difference would reverse in old age, except as a factor of males' earlier senility.

The clear-cut case for the sex difference in aggression led psychologists to begin to suspect that this, and possibly other sex differences in behavior, are under biological influences. It is nearly inconceivable, otherwise, that 1) 600 cultures would have chosen arbitrarily to have men do battle while women keep house, 2) that "boys will be boys" even when they are too young to have been "socialized" to any great extent, and 3) that not only humans have adopted this pattern, but nearly all mammalian species as well. A *congenital* difference in the emotional proclivities of males and females is clearly indicated.

ANDROGENS, AGGRESSION AND DOMINANCE

The relation between the male sex organs and aggression has been obvious to animal breeders for centuries; castration has been used to tame aggressive bulls for at least 5,000 years. Only in the last two or three decades, however, have scientists technologically corroborated folk knowledge and shown that throughout phylogeny, androgens, the male sex hormones, are prime facilitators of aggression.

Recently, aggression research has increasingly become

the province of biology rather than psychology, the social
sciences, or anthropology. We are only beginning to understand the very complicated interplay of hormones and
their neural mechanisms, but this much is clear: male
aggressiveness (whether in mice, monkeys or humans) is
connected with the level of androgen circulating in the
bloodstream and the particular organism's sensitivity to
it, which has been determined by heredity. There is no
doubt that environment and conditioning influence an individual's propensity for aggression (we will take a careful
look at these factors in chapter two), but the fact remains
that the male of the species does not begin life with a
propensity for peacefulness anywhere near that of the female, and equalization, in most cases, requires social
inhibition of the male's inborn biological proclivities.

Throughout the mammalian species, with a few notable
exceptions like the golden hamster, androgen is the sine
qua non for male aggression. Even before the contemporary sophisticated techniques for hormone assay were
available, it was clear that androgen was inextricably connected with aggression because 1) fighting does not begin
in most animals until puberty when the androgen level
skyrockets, 2) this fighting can be brought on prematurely
by injecting the animal with androgen, 3) animals who have
specific sexual periods each year when their androgen
level increases also fight most often at this time (as in
the rutting season of deer), and 4) castration of the male
usually reduces aggressive behavior and subsequent injections of androgen restore it. [44]

Many species throughout the animal kingdom form
dominance hierarchies or chains of command; nearly always males have authority over females, but they also
must work out which males will be subservient to which
other males. Altering the androgen levels of males in a
dominance hierarchy by castrating them or by injecting
them with testosterone, the major androgen in most species, can topple the king of the mountain and transform
him into a snivelling sycophant, or cause the least as-
sertive of animals to become a tyrant. Most of the literature on animal dominance hierarchies stresses that although they are usually established by tests of strength
(fighting), they serve, in the end, to decrease intermale
aggression by insuring that each male knows the unlikeli-
hood of his being able to win fights with males who have
already proven to be tougher. Dominance hierarchies
then are seen to be benign inhibitors of otherwise limitless

aggression in animals.

This may be a tolerable counterbalance for male aggression in monkeys and chickens, but it is hardly an acceptable solution for human male aggression. Undoubtedly the chain of command in the military, governmental and industrial establishment is a dominance hierarchy which does serve to reduce direct intermale combat within the system, but unlike their monkey cousins, male humans do not limit their aggression to power tests with their peers and the simple protection of territory and property. Since the invention of weapons, the preventive force of dominance hierarchies has been insufficient to stop human male aggression. A gun in the hand of a one-hundred pound army private could immediately destroy any physical inhibition he may have felt about attacking a hated general. Dominance, even if it were not ideologically and politically repugnant, is not a possible deterrent of violence for contemporary men.

An animal's position in the dominance hierarchy, as well as the amount of aggression it displays, are reflections of one-up-manship which are inextricably connected with the level of circulating androgen and the sensitivity of the individual organism to it as genetically preprogrammed. In an early study by Allee, Collias and Lutherman (1939) it was found that injecting female sex hormones into a rooster or castrating him caused him to become timid and to lose status in the pecking order.[45] Bennet (1940) found that male ring doves increased the area of the territory they fought to defend when injected with testosterone.[46] In the last decade, when easier and more precise hormone measurement has become possible, the covariance between androgen and social dominance/aggression has become even more firmly established. Rose, Holaday and Bernstein reported in 1971 that their experiments with male rhesus monkeys showed that those with higher plasma androgen levels displayed more aggressive behavior and elicited more submissive behavior from their subordinates and occupied higher positions in the dominance hierarchy than their compatriots who had lower male hormone levels.[47] W. D. Joslyn reported in 1973 that injections of androgen even into *female* rhesus monkeys could totally upset the dominance fruitbasket.[48] He gave three young females androgen and they increased their aggressive behavior to the point that they replaced the most aggressive males at the top of the hierarchy. When Joslyn withdrew the androgen injections, the aggres-

sive behavior persisted for about a year and then the females returned to their expected place at the bottom of
the hierarchy.

Another research team has discovered that a stable
male rat hierarchy can be disrupted by injecting estrogen,
which is thought to inhibit the action of testosterone. The
rats at the top can be made to fall to the bottom of the
hierarchy by a single injection of the female hormone.[49]
Numerous other experiments throughout the mammalian
class have confirmed, with very few exceptions, that androgen level is a key to aggression and dominance.

Because of ethical questions few experiments have
been done with human males. Persky et al. broke ground
in 1971 with their finding that there is a direct relationship
between normal young adult males' production of testosterone and their scoring on psychological measures of aggression and hostility.[50] Plasma testosterone was moni-
tored over a period of time in healthy men eighteen years
of age and over, and compared with their scores on standardized tests of aggressiveness administered throughout
the testing period. The chart below shows a dramatic
correlation between the amount of testosterone and the
amount of aggressive feeling the men expressed.

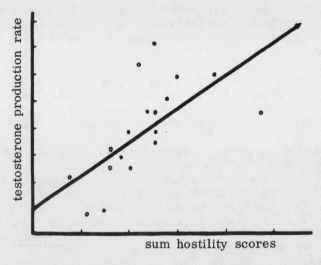

(Adapted from Harold Persky, *et al.*, "Relation of Psychologic Measures of Aggression and Hostility to Testosterone Production in Man," *Psychosomatic Medicine*, 1971,
33: 265.)

(A secondary and as yet unexplained result of the experiment is that even though androgen production declines in men over thirty, these researchers' tests with older men show little or no reduction in aggression and hostility.)

There have been four subsequent studies exploring the correlation of androgen and aggression in normal men. One team of experimenters who used a research design very similar to Persky et al.'s report a failure to replicate his findings.[51] However, Kling et al. report a definite correlation between androgen levels and aggression in psychotic patients.[52] Kreuz and Rose, though they found no correlation between androgen levels and amount of fighting over a two-week period in prisoners, did find that those prisoners with a history of more aggression had higher testosterone levels than the prisoners without aggressive histories.[53] A research team headed by J. Ehrenkranz found that *both* those prisoners who are highly aggressive and those who are socially dominant have higher plasma testosterone levels than those men who are not aggressive and who are not strongly dominant.[54] Those men with the highest aggression scores had the highest androgen levels, men who were socially dominant but not as aggressive as some others had the next highest androgen levels, and those who were neither aggressive nor socially dominant had the lowest scores, as shown on the diagram below.

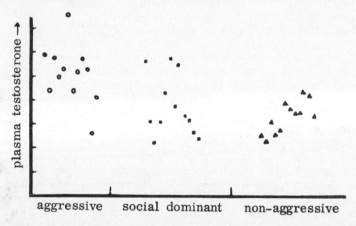

(Adapted from Joel Ehrenkranz, *et al.*, "Plasma Testosterone: Correlation with Aggressive Behavior and Social Dominance in Man," *Psychosomatic Medicine*, 1974, 36: 469.)

An interesting side note to this study was the finding that the most aggressive men scored higher than any of the others on paranoia when given a battery of psychological tests. Ehrenkranz et al. ruled out the possibility that those men who secreted more androgens were more aggressive because they were of greater stature or a different age than others. Though androgen is known to increase physical development, in this study the men with high androgen were not larger than the men with lower levels and age was controlled for as well.

Many clinical cases have been reported where an alteration in men's level of androgens correlates with variations in aggressiveness. It has been known for some time that castration decreases asocial acts.[55, 56] "A number of clinical reports have shown," according to Meyer-Bahlburg, that "testosterone treatment of juvenile patients may stimulate increased aggression in both aggressive and passive children..."[57] D. E. Sands, for example, gave adolescent boys suffering from feelings of inferiority and low confidence injections of the androgen Diandrone to alleviate their problems. But he found that when Diandrone is given to "normally aggressive" or overly aggressive boys it is likely to produce outbursts of rage.[58] E. B. Strauss et al. report similar findings using the androgen dehydroisoandrosterone.[59]

It is important to emphasize at this point that the correlation between aggression and androgens is just that-- a correlation, not a causal link. Although the evidence strongly indicates that high aggression is a factor of high testosterone, the direction of causation has yet to be established. High aggression or high social dominance could, in some as yet unknown way, increase androgen levels. A study by Rose et al. would seem to indicate that this is sometimes the case.[60] This research team found that when male rhesus monkeys who are low on the dominance hierarchy are placed with females whom they can dominate and with whom they can have as much sex as they like, their testosterone levels rise spectacularly and remain high. When the monkeys are defeated in a fight, however, their androgen levels fall and stay down for some time. The point is that although most of the evidence would seem to indicate that high androgen *causes* high aggression, sometimes the social influences on the animal can cause the change in androgen levels. Maccoby and Jacklin summarize this:

...hormone levels constitute an open system.
At the present state of our knowledge, it would
appear that a high testosterone level can be both
a cause and a result of aggressive behavior.[61]

Another complicating factor which we must consider
is that measuring a male's level of circulating androgen
provides, at best, only part of the picture about his proclivity for aggression. A man's *sensitivity* to androgen is not so easily measured as the quantity of it in his
bloodstream. This sensitivity is determined in human
males during the earliest months of fetal life. More precisely, it is determined at the moment of conception when
the particular genetic contributions of each of his parents
combine to form the hormonal blueprint for the future
child.

FETAL ANDROGENIZATION AND AGGRESSION

For thousands of years, animal breeders have known
that a female twin calf often is more masculine in her
behavior than her non-twin sisters. Since the female fetus was linked in utero to her brother via their blood supply, it was thought that something passed from brother to
sister during fetal development which caused the female
later in life to mount other females, to display male aggressive patterns, and to resist male attempts at mating
more often than non-twin females.

The substance which masculinizes the behavior of the
freemartin, as such a twin female calf is called, was
found to be androgen, the hormone produced by the newly-
developing testes of the male twin. Though the male hormone from the twin brother does not alter the female's
genitalia, it induces a distinctly male pattern of behavior,
in addition to making her sterile. How? By creating
male levels of androgen sensitivity in the neural substrates
for sexual and aggressive behavior in the female calf's
brain. To understand this more thoroughly we must learn
how sexual differentiation of the brain occurs in the developing fetus.

First it should be stressed that without the interference of androgen all mammals would be born with female
external genitalia. Until the eighth week of gestation the
human fetus is sexually bipotential; it has the primitive
antecedents of both female and male reproductive systems.

If no hormonal information reaches the developing structures, then the antecedent of the male internal sexual organs will atrophy and the female will proceed into maturity. Estrogen, the female hormone, is not necessary to
the development of femaleness. Only the *absense* of
androgen is necessary for the development of a girl. In
order for male genitalia to develop from the bipotential
fetus something extra must be added--*androgen*.

Similarly, all *brains* would be female if androgen
did not begin to circulate through the fetal bloodstream at
exactly the point in fetal development it does, the point
when it is possible to create androgen sensitivity in the
structures of the immature brain which will later be responsible for hormonal uptake and regulation. In the beginning all brains are female. Dr. Seymour Levine of
Stanford University describes it this way:

> It is an additive process. The proper male
> hormones must act upon the brain at the proper
> time for the brain to send patterns of maleness
> throughout the system. If the brain is not trig-
> gered in time, the fetus remains female. It is
> a struggle to become a male. [62]

The exact timing of the critical period when the mammalian brain is receptive to programming by circulating
androgen varies from species to species. Mice are born
relatively immature and their critical period is shortly
after birth. In guinea pigs and rabbits it appears to be
about midway in the pregnancy. For humans, however,
the time when the fetal brain can be masculinized (made
androgen-sensitive) is around the eighth week of gestation.

At this time, the degree of *masculinization* of both
the external sex organs and subsequent social/sexual proclivities are directly proportionate to the amount and
strength of the androgen circulating through the fetal system and the fetus's sensitivity to it. Both the amount of
androgen to be secreted and the fetus's sensitivity to it
are hereditarily predetermined by the genetic makeup of
the father and possibly to some unknown extent by that of
the mother. When the tiny testes of the eight-week-old
human fetus secrete androgen which then flows through the
bloodstream and reaches the brain, the nervous system of
the individual is permanently altered. The amount of androgen circulating through the fetus at this time will determine the proclivity for rough-and-tumble play and

34

threat behavior during childhood and the effects of sex hormones on behavior during puberty and adulthood. [63]

It is not known exactly how long the critical period is in human males when their otherwise female brain can be masculinized, but in some species it is as short as six hours. After that time, circulating androgen can not differentiate the sexual apparatus of a male from the inherent female genitalia, and can not sensitize the neural substrates* to androgens which would, in post-pubertal life, lead to "normal" male sexual behavior and aggressiveness.

Androgen during the critical period of gestation, then, is absolutely essential to the development of a male child. When the testes fail to produce the required amount of testosterone during the critical period, the child, even though genetically a male, will appear to be more or less like a girl, depending on the degree of the testicular malfunction. If the testes' failure is complete, the child would appear to be a normal female.

The more usual case, clinically, is that a male (XY genotype) fetus inherits a rare insensitivity to testosterone so that, even when his testes secrete it, every cell in his body which should be sensitive to it is not. This is known as the androgen-insensitivity syndrome. It is a matter of degree; in some cases there is a partial sensitivity so that the resulting child is a pseudo-hermaphrodite. Usually, though, the insensitivity is complete and the child is thought to be a girl at birth. Such cases come to medical attention because at puberty it becomes apparent that the young "girl" does not menstruate and that she has, in fact, only a shallow cavity where her vagina should be. **
Usually reconstructive surgery is performed to create a vagina and the teenager is given estrogen to stimulate normal female breast and body development.

There is a substantial amount known about such "male-

*Only in the last decade or so has science begun to really understand what these "neural substrates" are. In a later section we will be taking a careful look at all that is known about the physiological differences in the brains of males and females and how these differences affect many aspects of human behavior.

** There is no vagina or uterus because a hormone in the male fetus called the mullerian duct inhibitor causes these female organs to atrophy.

35

females" primarily because of the clinical studies of Dr. John Money and Dr. Anke Ehrhart.[64] For years they have been keeping records on the physical and psychological differences which result from insufficient prenatal androgenization. The following composite picture of the patients they have studied for some time should clearly indicate that, without androgen sensitization, a genetic male can be a very "feminine" female. It is difficult to even keep in mind that the patients being described are *all genetic males:*

> With respect to marriage and maternalism, the girls and women with the androgen-insensitivity syndrome showed a high incidence of preference for being a wife with no outside job (80%); of enjoying homecraft (70%); ...of having dreams and fantasies of raising a family (100%); of having played primarily with dolls and other girls' toys (80%).... The group incidence of exclusive heterosexual relations among the ten androgen-insensitive patients was 80%.... Six of the women rated themselves as above average in libido, having orgasm most of the time, and being reserved and passive in coitus; two rated themselves as above average in libido, always having orgasm, and initiating sex. The remaining two had not begun their sex lives.... The majority (90%) of androgen-insensitive women rated themselves as fully content with the female role, with only one being ambivalent.[65]

Of course, all of this could be seen as striking testimony for the power of sex-role conditioning. The only way to separate the feminity displayed because of female role-modelling and socialization from that caused by fetal androgen insensitivity would be to see how feminine a male child whose sex organs were removed at birth would be if he were raised as a girl.* Since no one would consider such an experiment with a human child, we must be content with the evidence from a penile ablation which occurred accidentally when a male infant was being cir-

*In addition, to create a fair test, the child would have to be injected with the amounts of androgen a boy of his age would normally produce.

cumcised at seven months of age. *66

The parents made the decision to surgically remove what was left of the male sex organs and to raise the child as a girl. At this time the case came to the attention of Dr. Money and Dr. Ehrhart at Johns Hopkins, who initiated a long-range counseling and testing program with the parents. This case was particularly unusual and important to science because the baby had an identical twin brother with whom his behavior could be compared.

The mother went to great lengths to "feminize" the child, dressing her in frilly dresses, letting her hair grow long, bedecking her in ribbons and lace. She was careful not to let her play with her brother's toys and to reward any "feminine" behavior she spontaneously came up with. From the mother's report, the child was successfully "feminized." Nevertheless, the doctors report that

> The girl had many tomboyish traits, such as abundant physical energy, a high level of activity, stubbornness, and being often the dominant one in a girls' group. [67]

Even though this mother stressed female role-playing much more than the average mother, she could not eradicate the aggressive tendencies which resulted from the early androgenization of the child's brain. The baby was born a male and would continue to evince male patterns of aggressiveness despite the loss of the penis, the addition of female hormones into the system, and intensive counter-conditioning.

The hormonal environment during the critical period of gestation exerts an incontrovertible force which can not be overruled by subsequent conditioning. Another accidental by-product of medical practice has shown that boys whose mothers were given estrogen during the critical period of gestation are programmed to be less aggressive and less dominant than males who have had no hormonal interference in utero. Dr. Richard Green and Dr. Yalom studied the behavioral effects produced by their having given pregnant diabetic women estrogen in an attempt to reduce fetal mortality. They assessed the male offspring

*In this case, the child was given estrogen, so the early androgenization should have had an even harder time influencing behavior.

of these women at age six and age sixteen and found that
at both ages they showed less assertiveness, aggressiveness, and rough-and-tumble play when compared to normal
controls and to sons of diabetic mothers who were not exposed to high levels of estrogen. [68] Estrogen, in addition
to having some possible influence of its own, is known to
decrease the effectiveness of testosterone on the male
nervous system. In this case, the evidence is strong that
it interfered with the process of fetal androgenization and
had a dramatic effect on the boys' subsequent behavior.

The next question which naturally arises is what
would happen if a female fetus were accidentally androgenized in her mother's womb. This is not an infrequent
occurrence. It is referred to clinically as the adrenogenital syndrome.

In this case, a genetic anomaly causes the adrenal
glands of the developing female fetus to begin secreting
androgen instead of the normal hormone, the androgen's
biochemical precursor, cortisol. Usually the timing of
the androgen release and the amount of it are insufficient
to cause a complete masculinization of the sexual organs.
Rather, a girl will be born with an abnormally large clitoris and perhaps a slight or no vaginal opening. The
decision is almost always to raise the child as a girl and
to perform corrective surgery on the enlarged clitoris
and the vagina.

From birth, however, cortisone must be administered
to the child or she will become ill. The cortisone re-
places the cortisol which the adrenals can not secrete
and, additionally, it has the effect of causing a decrease
in the androgen which would otherwise prematurely viri-
lize the child and cause male secondary sex characteristics to develop. So, in effect, the only hormonal difference between an adrenogenital female and a normal female is that the fetus has developed under the influence
of androgen.

The point here is to discover if even a female can be
made more aggressive by androgen when exposed to it
only in the womb. (There would be little or no subsequent androgen because no testes are present and the
cortisone controls that excreted from the adrenals.)

Dr. Money and colleagues set up a matched-pair experiment in which they enlisted the cooperation of school
officials and parents. [69] Each of twenty-five adrenogenital
girls was matched with a normal girl on the basis of age,
IQ, socioeconomic background and race. All fifty children

and their mothers were extensively interviewed with the
not unexpected result that the adrenogenital girls, even
though they had no knowledge of being different from any
normal girl, proved to be significantly more tomboyish
than their matched pairs. Twenty of the twenty-five adrenogenital girls classified themselves as tomboys and declared they were proud of it. Several of the matched
girls said they had been tomboyish at some point, but none
saw herself as a tomboy.

The adrenogenital girls' physical activity far out-
stripped that of the other girls. They enjoyed rough-and-
tumble sports as much as average boys do. Though none
of the adrenogenital girls was noted for physical fighting,
all were involved in some degree of competition for dominance in their peer groups. They preferred plain un-
adorned clothing and eschewed perfume and hair-styling
slightly more than did the controls. The adrenogenital
girls were indifferent to dolls and much preferred to play
with cars, trucks and guns. At adolescence they refused
to care for infants even when offered payment as a baby-
sitter. One-third of the girls said they did not want children when they grew up and nearly all preferred a career
to marriage.

In a subsequent study, Anke Ehrhart and S. W. Baker
studied seventeen adrenogenital girls and compared them
with their normal sisters.[70] Even though the adrenogenital girls had all undergone surgery and were maintained
on cortisone therapy so that they were physically indistinguishable from normal girls, their behavior proved to
be more masculine than that of their sisters, who were
presumably raised under very similar conditions. The
adrenogenital girls much more often preferred to play with
boys, they didn't like dolls or babies or traditionally female activities, and they engaged in outdoor sports and
fighting more than their sisters.

Given the new questioning of sex-role stereotypes attributable to the rise of feminism, we might say that these
girls' behavior might be preferable to that of their nicey-
nice matches, but sex-role conditioning was not at issue
here; the girls chose atypical female behavior *despite*
conditioning to the contrary.

HOW MALE IS A MALE?

In answer to the childhood ditty about sugar and spice

and everything nice and what are little boys made of?, we would have to arhythmically reply: androgen at eight weeks of life. Of course, a normal male requires subsequent androgen to masculinize the secondary sex characteristics and to function sexually in adulthood. The amount and strength of the subsequent androgen taken together with the individual's sensitivity to it as determined in fetal life is an indicator of how prone a male will be to aggressiveness and how sexually driven he will be.

It is impossible to determine how "androgenized" a male was during his gestation. We can measure current androgen levels, but science is not yet equipped to measure the *sensitivity* of body tissues to the hormone, which would have been established in utero. Variance in sensitivity accounts, perhaps, for some of the discrepancies which have been found between androgen levels and reported levels of aggression. Some men with a normal testosterone level could be extra-sensitive to it, and conversely, some men with high testosterone levels could be less sensitive than normal men and display less aggressive behavior. However, we can say that current androgen levels (which are in part determined by the degree of fetal androgenization) are to some degree predictive of current levels of aggression.

Men differ significantly from one another in their range of testosterone production. Congenital as well as environmental factors like nutrition, psychological state, physical exercise, climate and drug intake all influence a man's testosterone level. Alcoholic men, for example, have been found to have male hormone levels five to ten times higher than those of normal males.[71] This may partially explain why drunken brawls are nightly occurrences at many bars where men congregate. Any police officer can tell you that alcohol and male violence go hand in hand. Marijuana, however, decreases a male's androgen production if he smokes regularly. The recent report of the government's commission on marijuana smoking warned that the most deleterious result of repeated smoking was a loss of masculine drive and potency.

A male's testosterone production rate increases if he eats red meat regularly, and decreases if he becomes a vegetarian. The amount of sunshine a man gets and his general physical health all influence the rate of testosterone production. And the amount of sexual activity a man engages in influences it! A scientist, who for understandable reasons chose to remain anonymous, published

an account of an auto-experiment with testosterone level
in *Nature*, the British scientific journal.[72] In a most
unusual procedure he determined that his own *expectation*
of sexual activity increased the testosterone he produced.
He took a boat to a deserted island where he stayed for
three weeks. Knowing that his rate of beard growth,
since it is exclusively under testicular control, would directly reflect his testosterone production rate, he weighed
the hair which he shaved off his face each day and kept a
very careful record.

When he first went to the island he had just had a
farewell sexual meeting with his wife. Each day after his
arrival on the island, where he was careful to eat, sleep,
etc., in a pattern as close to normal as possible, his beard
growth decreased. It leveled off during the third week.
Unexpectedly, however, it suddenly increased a few days
before his planned return to his wife, which he explained
by saying that he was anticipating sleeping with his wife.

So psychological factors as well as many physical
factors can determine a male's androgen level. Some
men are less under the sway of the male hormones and
this difference is, in some cases, readily observable. A
man's range of testosterone levels can be estimated by
casual observations of his size, his body build, hairiness
and development of sexual organs, according to psychologists who have tested the validity of such measures.[73, 74, 75]
All men, then, are not alike--some men are more male
than others. One logical question which has arisen from
these findings is what bearing, if any, hormone levels
might have on male homosexuality.

Male homosexuals who are described as "obligative,"
which indicates that they are not just experimenting with
a sexual orientation but were ineluctably drawn to it and
probably could not change if they wanted to, have been
reported by some researchers as having notably different
male hormone levels. In addition, these same men have
been found to share one unusual personality trait: as boys
they rarely fought with others and they remained as low
in the boys' dominance hierarchy as girls do.[76, 77]

Although there have been many conflicting reports,
the consensus of the researchers at present is that all
exclusive male homosexuals (those who do not ever participate in heterosexual sex), and possibly a majority of
all homosexuals, have lower male hormone levels than
average heterosexual men.[78, 79, 80, 81, 82] One research team has found male homosexuals to have signifi-

cantly higher female hormone (estrogen) levels than average heterosexual men. There is some evidence to support the idea that male homosexuals were less androgenized in utero and are therefore less sensitive to androgens in adulthood, as well as producing less male hormone. [83, 84, 85]* Two quite early studies have made a strong case that male homosexuality is at least in part genetically determined. [86, 87] It was found that between 95-100% of identical twins are concordant for homosexuality while around 5% of fraternal twins are. Later studies have claimed that genetic causation is at least 30% of the total cause of homosexuality. [88] The indications are, then, that genetic programming may alter both the amount of a male's aggressive behavior and the kind of sexual activity he will participate in.

So far we have seen that males develop with different psychosocial potentials than females and that this difference is initiated very early in the life of the fetus. In the next section we'll go on to see *how* the message for male behavior is genetically programmed from the moment of conception.

THE X AND THE Y OF IT

Each cell in the human body has twenty-three pairs of chromosomes which contain genes, ultraminute segments of DNA that determine everything from eye color to our fingerprints to the shape of our nose. Usually, the only cells which do not contain twenty-three pairs of chromosomes are the mature egg cell in the female and the mature sperm cell in the male. By a process called meiosis, the egg cell casts off half its normal number of chromosomes in order to receive twenty-three chromosomes from the fertilizing sperm. Similarly, the sperm undergoes meiosis so that it will not have too many chromosomes.

Normally, when a male ejaculates during coitus, over four hundred million sperm, all bearing twenty-three chromosomes, begin the race up the female's vagina

*Most of the studies comparing lesbians with heterosexual women have not found any significant hormonal differences. There are only a handful of studies, however, so nothing definite can be said about this.

which may culminate in fertilization. If we examined some of these sperm under a powerful microscope we would find that twenty-two of the chromosomes, the autosomes or "body-forming" chromosomes, looked identical in every sperm, but that in approximately half of the sperm the remaining twenty-third chromosome, the sex-determining chromosome, would appear to be broken and roughly one-fifth the size of the largest chromosomes in the cell.

Rather than resembling an X which the rest of the chromosomes do, this chromosome more closely resembles a Y, or an X with one of its "arms" missing. If one of the sperm which contains this Y sex-determining chromosome wins the race up the vagina and is accepted into the egg cell, a male child will be conceived. If one of the other kind of sperm containing twenty-three X-shaped chromosomes wins, then a female will be conceived.

The twenty-three chromosomes of the mother's egg cell and the twenty-three chromosomes of the father's sperm cell will fuse and begin the process of replication called mitosis, whereby the original cell divides into two identical carbon copies of itself, and then these two divide to make four, and then sixteen, etc. If nothing goes wrong, each cell in the developing fetus will contain twenty-three chromosomes from the mother and twenty-three from the father. If it is a girl her two sex chromosomes in every cell will be X-shaped; if it is a boy there will be one large X-shaped sex chromosome from the mother and a very small Y-shaped one from the father in each of the cells in his body.

THE WORK OF THE Y CHROMOSOME

There has been much discussion among geneticists about what the "message" is that the Y-shaped chromosome carries. It determines the most basic of human differences, our sex. But how does it do this? The consensus of the scientists is that the Y chromosome carries very little information in its genes.[89] Its function is thought to be one of activating or deactivating specific parts of the codes contained in the genes of all the other chromosomes, the autosomes or body-forming chromosomes. So, the Y chromosome does not carry "male genetic information"; rather it activates patterns of "maleness" which are contained in all of the other X-shaped chromosomes. Or perhaps it would be equally correct to say that it cancels the intrinsic patterns of femaleness which would result without its interference. Its most important job is to insure that the fetus's gonads take a turn toward maleness before the eighth week of fetal life so that they will begin to secrete androgen. If androgen is not secreted by the fetus (even if it does bear a Y chromosome), then it will develop into a female. Nature's basic pattern is female. The Y-shaped chromosome causes the alteration which produces a male.*

The degree of the alteration depends on the particular activator genes on the Y chromosome. Just how this works is not fully understood, but many geneticists favor a hypothesis put forward by David C. Taylor and Christopher Ounsted:

1) The differential ontogenesis of the two sexes depends wholly on the Y chromosome.

2) The Y chromosome transmits no signifi-cant information specific to itself.

3) Transcription of expressed genomic information in males occurs at a slower ontogenetic pace.

4) The operation of the Y chromosome is to allow more genomic information to be transcribed.[90]

*There is a theory abroad that males are really mutant females. For a full discussion of this shocking proposition, turn to Appendix II.

In other words, all the information necessary to create a male is contained in the genes of the female, but, since the female fetus develops at a much faster pace than a male fetus there isn't time for all the information to be processed. The retarded development of the male allows more of the information on the genes to be expressed. Ounsted and Taylor give a simple analogy to help us understand this:

> The task of development is like a child mounting a spiral staircase. As males climb the staircase they tread on every stair and find on each step some instructions which they must follow.... Each instruction, basic to their development, takes time to fulfill. Females enter a directly comparable staircase, the equivalent information is potentially available, but the instructions include advice to proceed at a faster pace. To achieve this she will miss out certain steps and ignore their information.[91]

One of these steps is obviously the one that causes androgen to be secreted from the fetus's gonads at the eighth week after conception. And, to further the analogy, we will see that *how long* a male fetus lingers on this step may make a difference in the degree of maleness the child will evince.

We have seen that there is substantial variation in adult males' testosterone production and their frequency and degree of aggressive behavior. Although there are many environmental influences which alter the plasma testosterone level (temperature, physical and psychological stress, amount of sexual activity, alcohol, diet, etc.), still, there is a basic difference in testosterone levels between aggressive and unaggressive men. What could predispose one male to produce twice as much testosterone as another? The degree of androgenization of the fetal brain might be one factor. The particular coded instructions on the Y chromosome could control the androgen secreted at eight weeks of life, thereby creating potential differences in the degree of maleness which would show up in maturity.

Of course, it must not be forgotten that the *mother's* genetic makeup and her environment during pregnancy may influence the outcome since her hormones may interact differentially with her developing child's. Her progesterone, for example, may filter through the placenta to decrease the effectiveness of the fetus's androgens.[92] Or, conceivably, her hormone level might act to augment the effect of fetal androgen or cause a greater amount to be produced. All male children are subject to their mothers' hormonal balance in utero, but since aggression and high testosterone production can be transmitted from father to son through many generations of laboratory animals, the primary determiner of the fetus's testosterone production would seem certain to be in the *male baby's* genetic makeup, particularly that part which he has inherited from his father.

GENETIC MISTAKES

We now know, basically, what happens in the normal course of human sexual differentiation. But we have not considered what happens when Nature makes mistakes, as happens in one out of every two hundred births. What if the mother's egg cell failed to throw off half its chromosomes to make room for those of the sperm? Or what if the sperm didn't cast out twenty-three chromosomes so that it would carry only twenty-three to join with the egg cell's twenty-three? The improper separation of the chromosomal pairs during meiosis in egg or sperm is called nondisjunction. When such an abnormal egg or sperm joins with a normal egg or sperm, the fetus will have one or more chromosomes in addition to the usual forty-six. If the extra chromosome(s) are autosomes (body-forming), the mistake can be very serious or lethal. If, for example, there is an extra autosomal chromosome in the twenty-first group of the twenty-three pairs, a mongoloid child will result. This happens in about one of every seven hundred live births. The more usual outcome of extra chromosomes is the death of the fetus. A dearth of chromosomes is even more certainly lethal than too many.

Nondisjunction involving the *sex* chromosomes is what interests us here. The female's egg cell can carry two or more X sex chromosomes, and the male's sperm cell can carry two or more X or two or more Y chromosomes. Additionally, sperm which have no sex chromosomes at all can fertilize an egg, but there is no case in history where a live birth has resulted when a mother's egg cell did not contain at least one X chromosome. Non-

46

disjunction, then, can result in the following sexual anomalies:

45 chromosomes -- sex chromosomes XO

Here the mother contributes one X sex chromosome and the sperm contributes none. (The O means zero.) This is called Turner's syndrome; the females born with this defect have a dysfunctional reproductive system, a male body, and are shorter than the average girl.

47 chromosomes -- sex chromosomes XXY

Here the mother contributes two X chromosomes and the father the normal Y chromosome. This is called Klinefelter's syndrome; children with this particular anomaly are less male than the average boy. The testes are small and possibly undescended, breasts may develop, and male secondary sex characteristics may be late in maturing or nonexistent. Also, XXY children have a higher risk of being mentally retarded than the normal child.

47 chromosomes -- sex chromosomes XYY

The father's sex cell fails to cast off the extra Y chromosome and so two join with the mother's normal X chromosome. The resulting child will grow to an abnormal height, usually over six feet two, he will be very likely to develop an extremely bad case of acne, and he runs a high risk of becoming pathologically aggressive.

There are even more bizarre mistakes involving the sex chromosomes, but these are the more usual cases and are sufficient for our purposes here.

THE XYY "SUPERMALES"

Of the above sex chromosome anomalies, the most germane to our study is that of the XYY males. One out of every 550 men have the XYY genotype, but the real significance is not so much in their numbers as in the contribution the discovery of the XYY syndrome has made to our understanding of the impact of genetics on the normal male's behavior.

In the decade since this gender anomaly was discovered by P. A. Jacobs and her colleagues,[93] its behavioral consequences have been exhaustively documented in scientific journals throughout the world. Dr. Jacobs found, in a chromosome survey of a maximum security state hospital in Scotland, that men with the XYY genotype were disproportionately represented in the prison hospital when compared with the incidence of the mutation in the general population.[94] Now, ten years later, over forty major studies have been done in institutions throughout the world and over 14,000 men have been examined. There have been some conflicting reports, but by averaging the results of all the studies it has been found that the percentage of men in prison with the XYY genotype is approximately fifteen times higher than the percentage of XYY newborn babies, and that the percentage in mental hospitals is approximately three times higher than would be expected from their number in the general population.[95] Goldstein, in a recent review of the literature, summarized the evidence:

> These data indicate that individuals with an extra Y chromosome are at considerably higher than average risk for institutionalization.[96]

Psychological testing on institutionalized as well as non-institutionalized XYY men has revealed that they are, as a whole, more impulsive, more given to violent behavior, and that they are less capable of experiencing warmth and empathy with other people than XY men. Lissy Jarvik et al. relate a typical case history of a patient in an institution for the criminally insane who at age twenty-six was discovered to be an XYY:

> He had a history of antisocial behavior dating back to early childhood when, according to his mother's recollection, he was so uncontrollable that she finally tied him to a tree when doing her outdoor chores in order to prevent him from harming himself and others. Admitted to school at the age of 6, he created so much trouble that his parents were asked to remove him. Readmitted at the age of 7, he again beat up the other children and remained a disciplinary problem despite placement in a special ungraded

class, until at the age of 10, he was transferred
to a boarding school for disturbed children.
Ever since then he has been in institutions of
one sort or another. He would escape whenever
possible and invariably get into trouble on the
outside. Among his favorite pastimes was that
of killing chickens from neighboring farmhouses
by cutting off their heads. [97]

The extra Y chromosome has been found in some of
the most infamous murderers. Jarvik reviews their
cases:

> One of the first such cases was that of
> Robert Peter Tait, an Australian who was con-
> victed in 1962 of bludgeoning to death an 81-
> year-old woman in a vicarage where he had
> gone seeking a handout. In 1965, Daniel Hugon,
> a 31-year-old French stablehand brutally stran-
> gled a Paris prostitute, with no apparent motiv-
> ation. During the course of his trial in 1968,
> he was found to have an extra Y chromosome.
> In April 1969, six-foot, eight-inch, 240-pound
> John Farley, nicknamed "Jolly Green Giant"
> because he was usually good-natured and "Big
> Bad John" because he was subject to fits of
> violent temper, confessed to having beaten,
> strangled, raped, and mutilated a Queens, New
> York, woman. He was defended on the grounds
> that due to the presence in his cells of an extra
> Y chromosome, he had no control over his ac-
> tions or his judgment, and should therefore be
> found not guilty by reason of insanity resulting
> from a chromosome imbalance.' [98]

The news of the connection between chromosomes and
murder splashed across the tabloids. The public was
particularly roused when this information about chromosomes was being used to gain leniency for criminals who
had committed such heinous crimes. In some cases the
XYY defense has satisfied the legal requirements and convictions have been set aside; in others not, but the pub-
licity which ensued in either event firmly marked the connection between chromosomes and aggression in the public
mind. What more important scientific contribution could
there be than information on what causes a man to fight

49

and kill amongst his own species?

The discovery of the XYY syndrome in 1965 by P. A. Jacobs was a andmark because it was the first time that a specific behavioral abnormality other than retardation could be undeniably linked to a chromosomal aberration, and it constituted a pioneering breaththrough in the centuries-long nature-nurture debate. Environmentalists, who will not allow that some part of human behavior may be genetically predetermined, have made the usual protests and attempted to dismantle the evidence piece by piece, but now, a dozen years after Jacobs published her report, the sensationalism has settled and the sheer volume of the documentation has begun to silence the reaction. On the whole, the only fur still flying is between social scientists, not the psychobiologists and geneticists who actually study the interaction of genes and behavior.

One rather lame attempt to discredit the idea that an extra Y chromosome contributes to aggressive behavior was based on the idea that the "tallness" of XYY males might have elicited unfair treatment from their peer groups when they were children. This and the fact that they might appear to be more threatening than they really mean to be because of their height were taken to explain their high arrest rates. But subsequent studies of the behavior of giants and their rate of incarceration showed that tallness was not a factor.[99] Also, it was found that "there is no increase in height in boys with XY chromosome patterns who are institutionalized for antisocial behavior."[100] This is not to say that their extraordinary size could not have contributed to their ability to perpetrate violence, but that it is not the *cause* of aggressive behavior.

The extra Y chromosome predisposes these men to be more aggressive, but how does it do this? Physiologically, how are XYY men different from XY men? Since the extra Y has been called from the beginning "an extra dose of maleness" the first logical thing to check would be the XYY's level of testosterone. Goldstein summarizes the findings of the few studies which have been done:

> The excretion of testosterone in the urine of criminals with the XYY chromosome pattern tends to be higher than normal values in ambulant men. However, when prisoners with this chromosomal abnormality are compared with

appropriate controls of the same age and size
who have a XY chromosomal pattern and are
institutionalized for the same type of crimes,
there is no significant difference between the
urinary testosterone values of normal XY prisoners and the XYY prisoners.[101]

In an early study of the testosterone level of institutionalized XYY males J. P. Welch found that:

Plasma of XYY males is significantly higher
in testosterone which can explain their 'criminal' aggressiveness. It also suggests the interesting possibility that there may be a dosage
effect of genes governing the production of testosterone and located on the Y chromosome.[102]

Three studies have shown that XYY patients who were
in maximum security hospitals had a higher testosterone
level than patients in regular psychiatric hospitals and
the general population.[103, 104, 105]
So far, the data is too sketchy to really come to any
hard and fast conclusions. It has been established that
prisoners, on the whole, have a higher level of testosterone in their plasma than uninstitutionalized men. Whether
or not XYY prisoners have a still higher level is unclear.
There may be other factors which influence the findings
on XYY's besides their chromosomal makeup. For example, there may be environmental factors like social class
which we need to consider:

The role of social class must also be considered in the high risk of incarceration for XYY
males: a genetic survey by Robinson and Puck
indicated that sex-chromosome abnormalities
came almost exclusively from low social classes, whereas autosomal disorders were distributed evenly across social classes.[106]

Additionally, it has recently been found that part of the
information for how a male XYY's body will develop includes instructions for delayed maturation of the cartilage
that joins bone structures. It is quite likely that the clo-
sure of the fontanelle, the soft spot on the top of a young
child's head, is delayed in the XYY leaving him more
vulnerable to brain damage.

We need to remember, too, that there is great individual variety in the "message" of the Y chromosome.
The doubling of a "weak" Y chromosome might not cause a man to be any more male than a normal XY male.
This may account for some of the discrepancies in the prison studies and may also explain why there are XYY males leading a normal, relatively nonviolent life outside prisons and mental institutions. *

The number of chromosomes, though significant, may not be so important, it turns out, as the strength of their message and this, oddly enough, may be dependent on the *size* of the chromosome itself. Christopher Ounsted and David C. Taylor say of this:

> The Y chromosome can vary considerably in size and this remains constant over generations. In several families a large Y chromosome has been associated with a syndrome not unlike that associated with the XYY syndrome.[107]

The anatomy of the Y chromosome is just beginning to be understood. So far it has only been examined under a light microscope; in time new techniques will undoubtedly allow us to understand the quantity and quality of its message and the way the message affects the body's aggression systems.

A neurologist, Richard F. Daly, has found that an extra Y chromosome predisposes men to have an extraordinary number of neurological abnormalities.[108] He found that ten of the twelve XYY men he studied who were hospitalized in maximum security hospitals had "abnormal neurological" patterns. He disqualified the findings of abnormality in one patient since his may have been due to excessive alcohol; thus, there was only one XYY patient, in reality, who was free of neurological disorder. The problems included distortions in body symmetry like one side of the face being visibly larger than the other, tics,

---

*Also, even if we find that XYY males have no higher levels of androgen than normal males, we must not forget that they may have been more sensitized to it by higher levels of testosterone during fetal androgenization so that a little androgen in adulthood might go a long way. The *sensitivity* of the neural substrates for aggressive behavior will be a much more difficult study--perhaps impossible with human subjects.

speech defects, epileptic seizures, and numbness in
various bodily parts. From his findings on the neurological disorders Dr. Daly concludes:

> This objective evidence of brain dysfunction
> in these individuals lends support to the notion
> that the emotional disturbances to which XYY
> males seem predisposed are the direct result
> of their aneuploid state rather than, for exam-
> ple, the result of emotional conflicts rising from
> problems of being tall....
> It is possible that future microscopic exam-
> ination of the brains of XYY males may reveal
> the sites of pathology suspected on the basis of
> the clinical findings.[109]

Further evidence of XYY abnormality in brain function
has been provided by comparing the electroencephalograms
(brain wave charts) of XYY's to normal men's. G. W.
Fenton and colleagues found that XYY males in a high
security hospital for criminals had significantly more EEG
abnormalities than other patients in the hospital which:

> ...almost invariably involved the EEG back-
> ground activity and consisted of an increased
> frequency of unduly slow alpha rhythm, and a
> generalized excess of theta activity.[110]

Such a brain wave pattern is characteristic of young
children, but is considered pathological in an adult.
Johannes Nielsen has discovered that this EEG pattern is
typical of XYY's not only in institutions, but that it is
found in the same percentage of XYY's who are currently
not institutionalized. Roughly 32% of XYY males show
this abnormal EEG pattern.[111]
Fenton et al. compared XYY's EEG patterns with
those of another chromosomal anomaly, the XXY's.[112]
Approximately 19% of the XXY males showed abnormal
EEG activity of the same order of seriousness as the
XYY's. XXY males are often mentally retarded, sometimes aggressive according to some reports, but have
been found not to be involved in as serious crimes as
XYY's. Could their extra X "tone down" some of the
problem? Murray Goldstein points out that XXY men have
lower androgen levels than normal men and that they also,
in his estimation, evince less aggressive behavior:

The effects of decreased testosterone levels can be partially evaluated in patients with Klinefelter's syndrome, who have an extra X chromosome and so have a sex chromosome composition of XXY. These individuals have a male appearance, subnormal testosterone values after puberty, and characteristically are apathetic, timid, passive and have little energy or initiative.[113]

Despite our rather lengthy look at the XYY syndrome, it should be remembered that the real importance of such studies is not so much in assessing the danger of the XYY male to society since, numerically, it is a relatively rare aberration, but rather in understanding the problem of maleness and aggression and how it is connected with the Y chromosome in the *normal* male. Lissy Jarvik and colleagues sum up the significance of the XYY studies to the study of aggression and how they may contribute to the possibility of saving the planet from male destruction:

> The future of research into the nature and causes of aggression and hostility is of more than academic interest. The problem has been with us for countless generations, but as our population continues to spiral upward at an alarming rate and our planet becomes crowded to its very limits, the importance of working with, rather than against, each other, also increases. Disaster will follow if we do not make a concerted effort to understand ourselves now. Hopefully, the XYY genotype can contribute to such an understanding. Hopefully, the condition of 'war of every one against every one' will cease.[114]

In 1969 Pearson et al. pioneered a new technique for staining the Y chromosome; now it is possible to quickly test large numbers of males to determine the number and size of their Y chromosomes.[115] It is to be hoped that with this new technique a better understanding of the contribution of "an extra dose of maleness" will soon be reached and that the consequent understanding of "normal male aggression" will follow. We can only hope that less of the problem is genetic in origin than seems certain to be the case in XYY's, but whatever the outcome, the survival of all of us depends on our finding a way to decrease the male propensity for violence.

We will be discussing some possibilities for this in chapter five, but first it will be well to understand as much as is known about the way maleness affects the aggression circuitry in the brain; we need to get an idea of the odds we are up against. We will go on, then, to explore sex differences in the brain and their effect on behavior.

SEX DIFFERENCES IN THE STRUCTURE AND FUNCTION OF THE BRAIN

Strange as it may seem, science is in the dark ages about sex differences in the micro-structure of the brain. Only in the last decade have a few reports been made about cellular level sex differences. Basically what has been found is that, in certain areas of the female brain, the nerve cells are larger and shaped differently from males',[116] and that certain cells in the female brain absorb estrogen more readily than the corresponding cells in the male brain.[117] The latter is probably responsible for determining that females will ovulate and that males will not, but the behavioral implications of all of these microscopic differences have not really been explored.

There are, then, some sex differences in brain cells which are genetically determined. Environment can influence the brain too. Humans are particularly susceptible to the exigencies of the environment since we are born with less mature brains than any other animal; i. e., we are born with less than a quarter of the number of brain cells that the average two-year-old has, so that three-quarters of our brain development takes place after birth and is subject to environmental molding. But it is important to remember that *environment* includes the child's prenatal conditions and its birth as well as subsequent physiological and psychological experiences.

BRAIN DAMAGE

Interactions between the developing fetus and its uterine environment can be dramatically different for males and females. Just how genetic sex causes these differences is not yet known, but this much is clear: many more male fetuses than females suffer the effects of problem pregnancies and traumatic births, and, as a consequence, more male children incur brain damage.

Statistics in nearly a dozen different countries show that there are more boys than girls with all forms of brain damage.[118] On the average, there are 150 boys afflicted with cerebral palsy for every 100 girls, 140 boys for every 100 girls with epileptic seizure disorders, 400 boys for every 100 girls who are autistic, and 500 boys for every 100 girls who are organic hyperkinetics.[119] Also, a baby boy is almost twice as likely as a girl to have syphylis, which almost inevitably causes neural damage. Possibly related to these statistics is the fact that first admission rates to mental hospitals in the U.S. are 20% higher for men than for women.[120]

Most people would think that brain damage occurs too infrequently to have much bearing on male behavior in the population as a whole. In an article summarizing the problems with medically assisted birth, Kay Weiss points out that this may not be the case:

> Some scientists state that 50% of Americans sustain subclinical, undetected 'minimal brain damage' at birth which manifests itself in learning difficulties, emotional impairment and violent, non-rational behavior.[121]

The yearly increase in the detected brain-damaged population is phenomenal. There are now six million people in the U.S. who are retarded, and this is only a small portion of the total number of brain-damaged which would include those afflicted with cerebral palsy, epilepsy, dyslexia, hyperkinesia, autism, etc. *All* of the known forms of behavioral impairment resulting from brain damage are more prevalent in males than females. If half of all Americans are victims of brain damage, there are a disproportionate number of males among them. To understand why this is so we must look at the differences sex causes in the male infant's vulnerability during pregnancy, birth, and early development.

FETAL ENVIRONMENT AND SEX DIFFERENCES IN BRAIN STRUCTURE

The male fetus develops more slowly than the female

fetus from the time of brain androgenization on, as we have seen. Because the Y chromosome is dictating that more genetic information be evoked in order to masculinize the fetus, its development as a whole is retarded compared to that of females. At each stage of gestation the male fetus is less able to cope with the risks because it is less well developed. By the time of birth, the male fetus is almost one month behind the female and so, even though it is significantly larger than the female, it is much more vulnerable to the stress of delivery. It is as though all boys are born at least one month premature.

As we have seen, male fetuses are less able to survive in the uterine environment. Various reports have shown that approximately two to three times more males than females abort during the first four months of pregnancy. Christopher Ounsted and David C. Taylor report:

> Throughout pregnancy the losses due to abortion, miscarriage and stillbirth all show an excess of males. Many of these losses are abnormal fetuses and in these males are especially over represented.[122]

Those who do not abort may be exposed to a less satisfactory uterine environment than girls since the majority of mothers who experience complications during pregnancy give birth to boys.

Toxemia is a problem for mothers carrying male fetuses much more often than for mothers carrying females. The more severe the mother's poisoning the more likely she is to be carrying a male child.[123] The chemicals which the stress of poisoning give rise to, as well as the poisons themselves, cross the placenta to affect the fetus. Numerous studies have found that children born to mothers who suffered toxemia in pregnancy are at a significantly higher than average risk for brain damage. (A further discussion of toxemia and brain damage will follow in chapter five.)

That the male fetus *causes* toxemic pregnancy is a likelihood which is just beginning to be understood. Several researchers have proposed that the problem lies with a "histoincompatibility between mother and fetus, due to Y-chromosome-dependent antigens."[124] The Y chromosome directs that certain proteins be synthesized by the male fetus which cross the placenta into the mother's bloodstream. These are so foreign to the mother's system that her body declares war on the invading chemicals and toxemia of both mother and fetus is the result. It is almost as though women are not made to bear male children. Female physiology insures that the average pregnancy will be more difficult when a woman is carrying a male fetus, and that more male fetuses will die during gestation.

Not only is the gestation period more difficult and hazardous for male fetuses, but the birth process itself claims more male lives than female. The histoincompatibility between the mother and the male fetus may have some bearing on this also. Margaret Ounsted has done a number of studies which suggest that:

> ...antigenic dissimilarity between the human
> mother and her conceptus may contribute to the
> enhancement of fetal growth rate.[125]

Boys are an average 5% heavier than girls at birth in the U.S. This sex difference in birth weight cuts across all cultures, races, ethnic groups and classes under all conditions of nutrition. It is widely known that the majority of fetuses who are too large for unassisted birth are male. The amount of time a woman spends in labor is greater and the fetus is at risk for a longer time if she is bearing a male child. The dilation of the cervix may not be sufficient for the larger head circumference of the male infant and brain injury can result from the consequent compression or as a result of forceps delivery, which is more common with boys than with girls.

The larger the infant, beyond the optimal size for survival, the greater the risk of brain damage during labor and birth. This is particularly true of medically assisted deliveries as opposed to births without chemicals or obstetrical intervention. In the U.S. 54% more boys than girls die of injury at birth.[126]

The longer labor time for the birth of male infants increases the already more vulnerable male's risk of death or brain damage. During each contraction, the oxygen supply to the baby's brain is severely reduced. In the absense of oxygen, the fetus's brain cells die rapidly. The longer the labor, the greater the number of contractions and the more brain cells the baby stands to lose. Brain cells, unlike most other cells in the body, cannot regenerate, so the loss incurred during labor and delivery will be permanent.

This is bad enough, but medical science has made matters worse. According to a recent study, more than 50% of women admitted to U.S. maternity hospitals are given labor-inducing drugs, which can bring on labor whenever a doctor chooses to administer them.[128] A number of brain cells are destroyed during each thirty to forty second contraction in the normal course of events; the labor-inducing drugs, such as oxytocin, lengthen the contraction period thereby depriving the fetus of oxygen for a longer time and destroying even more brain cells. Kay Weiss concludes that labor-inducing drugs:

> ...probably contribute more than any single obstetrics procedure to the brain damage suffered by U.S. infants. They are unsafe because it is not possible to determine proper dosage for each individual woman. The woman herself is producing oxytocin in labor.[129]

A physician cannot know what would constitute an over-dose. Some women are hypersensitive to the labor-inducing drugs so that, even with a minimal dose, the drugs cause their uteruses to contract for eight to ten minutes at a time. Needless to say the babies are asphyxiated and born severely brain-damaged.[130]

The point to remember here is that male infants are always at higher risk--the greater the number of insults to infants during the birth process the higher the percentage of male casualties there will be. Labor induction is just one of many interferences with birth that cause an increase in brain injury, thereby increasing the proportion of affected males.

Another contributor to brain damage is the sedation of the mother during labor and delivery. The medications rapidly cross the placenta with the effect of depressing the baby's respiratory center. The resulting delay in the baby's breathing causes brain damage. This is not to say that women should not be given help with their pain, but that other methods less risky for the baby should be found.

Why do women need all these artificial aids to birth? In most cases we don't. One of the major problems is that women, by being made to life flat on their backs during delivery, do not receive the natural assistance of gravity. Kay Weiss describes the difficulty:

The woman cannot make use of the force of
gravity to help push the baby out; proper functioning of abdominal muscles and intra-abdominal
pressure on her uterus are prevented by her
position; and her uterine muscles have been ren-
dered slack by the anesthetic.... Lying with the
weight of the uterus on the aorta, the flow of
blood to the uterus is slowed...when the uterus
is not bathed in oxygen-carrying blood, pain reg-
isters there as it would in any muscle contract-
ing in the absence of oxygen.[131]

Another delivery room technique which is a major
contributor to brain damage is the early clamping of the
umbilical cord after delivery. As soon as the baby's feet
are out, most doctors put a clamp on the cord and sever
it. Dr. William F. Windle, a noted expert on obstetrical
procedures, says that this one is particularly detrimental
to the newborn:

...in any delivery it is important to keep the
umbilical cord intact until the placenta has been
delivered. To clamp the cord immediately is
equivalent to subjecting the infant to a massive
hemorrhage, because almost a fourth of the fetal
blood is in the placental circuit at birth. Depriving the infant of that much blood can be a factor in exacerbating an incipient hypoxemia and
can thus contribute to the danger of asphyxial
brain damage.[132]

The U.S. Public Health Service reached the following
conclusions about brain damage in a study completed in
1972, which has yet to be made public:

The horizontal birth position, early clamping
of the cord and 'elective' induction are always
unnecessary in obstetrical practice, and they
are the main contributors to infant oxygen
stress and brain damage, from its serious form
of cerebral palsy to minimal damage which is
never detected. Research on monkeys suggests
that all children born from the horizontal position may suffer some degree of asphyxiation
and death of brain cells because this position
cuts off proper flow of placental blood to the

infant.[133]

In other cultures, mothers use natural sitting positions for childbirth which make labor induction and general anesthesia unnecessary. Forceps are rarely used in most of the "underdeveloped" countries. In the U.S. they are used in 35% of all births.[134] The U.S., where more birth intervention is practiced than anywhere else in the world, ranks fifteenth among the nations of the world for the percentage of live births. The infant death rate reflects the problems of contemporary obstetrical care; far too many babies suffer respiratory distress and asphyxiation because *too* much is done rather than too little. Who can say how many surviving brain-damaged people would have been born normal without medical intervention? Contemporary midwives, who are often practicing outside the law in the U.S., have a higher percentage of live births to their credit than the average American hospital;[135] it is quite likely that the children they deliver are also freer of brain damage.

It is important to understand that a loss of brain cells does not just decrease intelligence, but that it can also increase the likelihood of impulsive aggressive behavior:

> Under normal conditions, the limbic brain*
> is dominated by and synchronized with the func-
> tions of the neocortex. A series of checks and
> balances exists in both of these parts of the
> brain, so that the violence associated with the
> fight or flight reactions and governed by the
> limbic system is kept under control. Damage
> to the brain structure--the head--upsets the
> balances between limbic system and neocortex.
> The perfect synchronization between them that
> is so necessary for an adequate and reasonable
> response to environmental stimuli is lost, and
> so is control over violent inclinations.... The
> link between structural brain disease and ag-
> gressive, assaultive behavior is unquestionably
> plain.[136]

*The limbic brain is that part of our brains which is most concerned with emotional behavior. See page 65.

It is impossible to say how much of the male propensity for aggression is caused by brain damage, but it is definitely a factor we should study, since it will be easier to correct this part of the problem than it will be to correct the factors which are entirely under genetic control.

SEX DIFFERENCES IN PSYCHOPHYSIOLOGICAL DEVELOPMENT

Although the *structural* differences between normal male and female brains have been little explored, the *developmental* differences are well known. Girls are born with a more highly developed brain.[137] Dr. Beatrice Hamburg estimates that boys do not catch up with girls in cerebral maturation until they are eight years old.[138]

Psychologists have been reluctant to admit the very real difference brain immaturity makes in the developing child. Although the sex difference in learning ability which is evident throughout the elementary school years is widely acknowledged, few people are willing to accept that some part of boys' learning problems are genetically influenced.

Here we are more concerned with behavior problems than learning disabilities, although the two problems overlap. It has recently been found that the male slower cerebral maturation may contribute to the problem of sensory deprivation in infancy and the typical antisocial behavior which results from it. If the environment is limited, as in an orphanage or a home where too many children compete for the parents' attention, male children may develop more serious behavioral defects as a result of social deprivation than females. Whereas all children's intelligence and behavioral adjustment is adversely influenced by a lack of stimulation and love in infancy, male children may be more seriously damaged because, given their slower brain maturation, they are less able to perceive what little stimulation is available to them.

Experiments with primates have shown that males are less able to overcome the negative results of partial or total isolation in infancy.[139, 140] The repertoire that is developed to compensate for lack of stimulation--beating their heads against the walls, perpetual masturbation, maiming themselves with their own teeth, and *hyperaggressiveness*--is more likely to be permanent with a male monkey than a female, even if they are both introduced to a rich environment after the initial period of isolation. If the monkeys who have been raised for their first six months in total or partial isolation are released into the wild, female monkeys are able to adapt more successfully than males are, and therefore they are more capable of surviving. Preliminary studies have shown that more than twice as many females are able to adjust to their new environment and to extinguish parts or all of their old compulsive behavior while males, according to one of the leading researchers, Dr. Gene Sackett, "rigidly repeat old behaviors that might have been useful in a deprived setting but are inappropriate in a more enriched environment." [141]

Mark Rozenzweig et al. made one of the most remarkable discoveries in modern biology when they found that sensory deprivation actually changes the physical characteristics of animals' brains. [142] Brain weight, the size and number of the cells, the number of connections that the neural cells have with one another, and the chemical interactions of the brain--all these are subject to *environmental* influence. Animals who have been provided with an enriched environment during their infancy actually have heavier more neurally developed brains. Those who have been raised in a deprived setting are limited in their behavior because of their reduced brain development.

Male animals, then, have been found to be less resistant to the negative effects of sensory deprivation. Given equal deprivation, males' brains are more vulnerable to ill effects and their behavior is more severely affected than females'. Dr. Sackett, who has been working with sensory deprivation in primates for some time, suggests that prenatal androgenization is responsible for the male monkey's being less resistant to the permanent ill effects of deprivation. He has yet to fully test this theory, but considers it probable that males are less able to adjust because of the sex difference in cerebral functioning which is a factor of the male's prenatal androgenization.

Since the male primate and the male human infant can perceive less of what is available in the environment, special care must be given to afford them stimulation which they can perceive. Male infants depend almost entirely on skin contact for their information about the world, whereas females see earlier and perceive differences in sound earlier, and therefore experience more of their surroundings from the start.

In order to assure "equal handling," a mother would have to coddle her infant sons more than her daughters. Since male infants cry more than girls, are more subject to colic, and generally are awake more than girls in the first six months of life, it would seem that they would get the extra handling they need. But studies on how mothers handle girls and boys have shown that even though at first the mother accedes to the greater demands of a boy, she wears out in time when she discovers, if only subconsciously, that the greater handling does not decrease the infant's fussiness, but only serves to positively reinforce it. She begins to understand that by rewarding fussy behavior she creates more, and she withdraws some of her physical attention from the male infant. The behavioral impact of this can not be measured, but primate studies do suggest that at least part of male antisocial behavior is a result of social deprivation in infancy.

ACCIDENTAL BRAIN INJURY & AGGRESSIVE BEHAVIOR

So far we have seen that males are more susceptible to brain damage inflicted by the prenatal and birth environment and perhaps to psychic damage in infancy. Unfortunately, their higher susceptibility to physical brain damage does not end at birth. The infant's fontanelle, the soft spot on the top of the head, does not close to fully protect the brain until a child is nearly two years old. In keeping with girls' greater overall skeletal maturity, we find that the girl's brain receives the protection of a fully closed skull sooner than does a boy's. In addition, boys are more exploratory in the creeping, crawling and toddler stages and more likely to sustain head injury from falls.

The very fact that boys are in general more impulsive and aggressive from infancy to adulthood creates the circular effect of predisposing them to more injury which can cause increased aggressiveness. And, to make matters worse, the most aggressive males are the ones who most often sustain head injury. Whether it be on the playground, the football field, or the battlefield, the male propensity for violence increases their susceptibility to environmental augmenters of violence.

In this country, we have institutionalized the knowledge of male aggressivity with higher insurance rates for male drivers. It isn't that they are any less alert or intelligent

The Brain (front view)

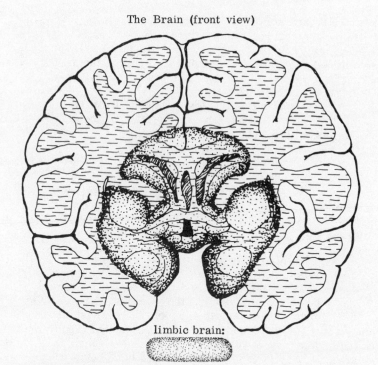

limbic brain:

(sagittal view: a side view sliced through the middle)

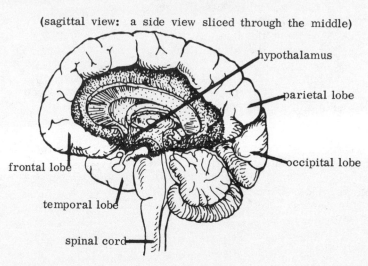

hypothalamus

parietal lobe

occipital lobe

frontal lobe

temporal lobe

spinal cord

(Drawings adapted from *Violence and the Brain* by Vernon Mark and Frank Ervin; Harper and Row, 1970.)

or well-trained for driving than females--it is that they are more aggressive behind the wheel and more often inflict and incur injury. Approximately three million people are injured in automobile accidents every year in the U.S. in which, according to Mark and Ervin:

> Head injury is the most frequent lethal injury. ...In 33% of head injuries, internal tissue and organs of the head are injured. [143]

This is not to say, of course, that all brain injury increases violent behavior. But the fact is that the area of the brain which is most concerned with the regulation of aggressive behavior is most vulnerable to head injury. Mark and Ervin discuss the danger to the brain of accidental injury:

> Head injuries in growing children, adolescents, and adults are very likely to damage the undersurface of the frontal lobe and the tips of the temporal lobe--in other words, those parts of the limbic brain that lie closest to the bones of the skull. Normally, brain and bones are separated from each other by a cushion of fluid and a tough membrane. But if the head is struck hard enough, or if the body suddenly hits the ground with some force, the frontal and temporal lobes may be jarred against the base of the skull. The resulting damage to the brain stem is indicated by the loss of consciousness. It often happens, however, that when the brain stem recovers and consciousness returns, the injured person undergoes a period of uninhibited, aggressive and combative behavior. [144]

Whether the result of heredity or accidental injury, structural brain abnormalities are definitely a part of the problem of male aggressiveness. It will be well to understand as much about this component of violence as we can, both for the sake of the men who are afflicted and for their victims.

RIGHT BRAINS AND LEFT BRAINS: STRUCTURAL AND FUNCTIONAL SEX DIFFERENCES IN NORMAL BRAINS

The most obvious structural feature of all our brains, whether male or female, damaged or whole, is that there are two of them, a right brain and a left brain. The two halves, which appear to be identical mirror images of each other, are partly joined in the middle by a bundle of nerve fibers called the corpus callosum. So far we have only the vaguest hint that there are size and structure differences between these two hemispheres which are sex related.*

*Buffery and Gray have reviewed what little is known about sex differences in brain structure:

In his study of variations in cerebral drainage, Matsubara (1960) found that the right-sided vein of Trolard was larger than the left-sided vein in girls but not in boys. Since this vein is usually the major vein in the cerebral hemisphere *opposite* to that subserving speech (Di Chiro, 1962), this finding has been related to sex differences in cerebral dominance and in verbal skills (Lansdell, 1964).

...given the correspondence between language function and the structural asymmetry of the adult human brain, together with the indications of a sex difference in *structural* asymmetry *after* the emergence of speech, one might expect that the 'pre-language', neonatal and even fetal human brain would show *structural* asymmetry *before* the development of speech and that such asymmetry would be greater in female than in male brains of the same age. Some support for the former expectancy has been reported by Wada (1969) and cited by Geschwind (1970) and by Bever (1971). It is to be hoped that investigations relevant to the issue of sex differences in the structural asymmetry of the neonatal human brain will soon be carried out.

Anthony W. H. Buffery and Jeffrey A. Gray, "Sex Differences in the Development of Spatial and Linguistic Skills," in *Gender Differences: Their Ontogeny and Significance*, ed. by Christopher Ounsted and David C. Taylor. London: Churchill Livingstone, 1972.

More is known about sex-related *functional* differences; even so, there is wide disagreement among the experts. It is clear, though, that 1) there are definite differences in the side of the brain that males and females tend to use for solving particular problems and the resulting degree of problem-solving success, and 2) that men and women differ in their ability to use both brains simultaneously and the opposite ability, that of excluding the activity of one side of the brain in order to "listen" more clearly to the other. After a general review of sex-related hemispheric differences in brain structure and function, we will go on to see how those hemispheric functions at which the male excels are related to aggressive behavior.

In keeping with the female's overall faster pace of development, at birth there are more functional neurons in the girl's brain than in the boy's. Specialization of the left side for certain tasks and the right side for other tasks is not complete until age eleven in either sex, but girls are thought to establish earlier division of labor between the hemispheres. Some studies have shown that girls at age two are already using primarily the left hemisphere for verbal tasks as would an adult of either sex. Boys do not show this mature lateralization pattern until age five. [145, 146, 147]

Early lateralization is thought to facilitate left-brain learning. [148] The reasoning here is that by genetic prearrangement each side of the brain has its job to do and that confusion ensues when both of them try to work on a problem at once. The speed of learning would be increased, then, by learning to silence the side of the brain not involved with the particular skill to be learned or problem to be solved. The girl, who develops an earlier use of the left brain for left brain tasks, to the exclusion of the right brain, would be expected to learn and use language earlier and better than boys.

As we have seen, one of the most extensively documented sex differences is that of girls' superiority in verbal learning. At every age, from early childhood to adulthood, females are more proficient in understanding and speaking language. This clear-cut superiority is due, we are told by some researchers, to girls' earlier and more complete lateralization. The girl's left brain is free of the right brain's interference earlier, so learning of language can begin earlier. [149] The early start, plus the clearer division of labor which develops, are both taken to

The Brain (top view, with optic nerves exposed)

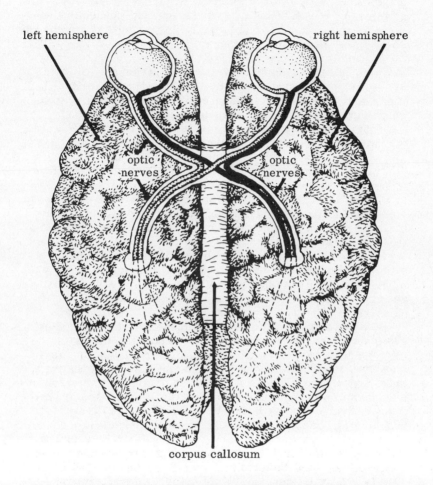

left hemisphere

right hemisphere

optic nerves

optic nerves

corpus callosum

   In at least 99% of the human population, the left side of the brain is responsible for language and analytical abilities, and the right side of the brain is in charge of spatial ability, musical and artistic ability, parts of mathematical ability, etc.--essentially those functions which are nonverbal.

(Drawing adapted from Maya Pines, "We Are Left-Brained or Right-Brained," *New York Times Magazine*, September 9, 1973.)

explain females' greater verbal ability.

In general, as you'll remember, males score higher on tests of right brain spatial ability than females do. In addition to orienting the body in space and connecting accurately with objects in the environment, spatial ability encompasses mechanical ability:

> There is a high correlation between mechanical aptitude and spatial ability and it is therefore relevant to note that from pre-school age onwards boys surpass girls in the mechanical ability of assembling objects, toys, etc. and in mechanical reasoning, the boys being an average 35% better than girls on the mechanical reasoning subtest of the Differential Aptitude Test. [150]

One logical reason for superior spatial ability would be superior vision, but this does not explain the sex difference since males' vision has been shown to be less acute than females'.

Perhaps incomplete lateralization facilitates spatial ability, or perhaps the male is born with a right brain with more potential than the female's. Another possibility suggested by psychologists who are reluctant to posit an *inborn* sex difference in spatial ability is that little boys, whose language development is somewhat retarded, of necessity begin to move in space and relate to objects and people physically in order to make their wishes and feelings known. Whereas a girl might be able to verbally make her mother understand that she wants a toy on an inaccessible shelf, a boy, rather than undergo the frustration of trying to make himself understood, might try to reach for it. With enough positive reinforcement, the male child would choose this mode of getting what he wants more of the time, thereby "training" his right brain more than a girl would. That this is not a total explanation is indicated by lower animal studies. Male mice, rats and other wild rodents, equal in intelligence to female age mates, are more exploratory than the females are and better able to perform the spatial task of running a maze. Since language is, of course, out of the question for either male or female rodents, the explanation that spatial ability is increased because of a lack of verbal ability is not sufficient. [151]

One extensive study has shown that even two-week-old boys are more accurate and directed in reaching and grasping behavior than their female age mates. [152] Spatial ability has, in fact, been shown to be transmitted hereditarily. Gray and Buffery say of this:

...there is good reason to believe that the human sex difference in visuo-spatial abilities is under the control of the sex chromosomes. [153]

Their idea is that early androgenization is responsible for masculinizing the basically female brain so as to cause male somatic sexual characteristics, the male propensity for aggressive behavior, and the male superior spatial ability. The degree of androgenization during the critical period would affect all three of these measures of maleness. In fact, it has been found that males with an excess of estrogen (female hormone) in their systems have lower spatial abilities than normal males, [154] and that males with high androgen levels (especially XYY's) have a high spatial ability relative to their general intelligence. [155] Research has revealed the male superior spatial ability in widely divergent cultures. Male Australian aborigines and American and European school boys all show a spatial ability superior to their female age mates. [156]

Though there have been no studies of sex differences in lateralization in higher animals, Jane Goodall has reported definite primate male superiority in one spatial skill, the aimed throwing of objects. [157] In fact, this skill, which is only used in the context of aggressive encounters by free-living chimpanzees, is never displayed by females at all. The point here is that spatial skill may be inextricably connected with aggressive behavior. Beatrice Hamburg, a noted expert in evolutionary biology, says of this:

It would appear that male superiority in spatial ability has probably conferred selective advantage in three major areas critical to human survival: expansion of territorial range, enhancement of hunting skills, and heightening of aggressive potential in agonistic encounters. [158]

It may be very much to the female's credit that she performs less well in the skills which, according to evolutionary biologists, evolved because of the male desire to increase territory and to do battle with fellow creatures.

Superiority at spatial ability may not be a feather in

the contemporary male cap either. There is evidence that inordinate right brain skills correlate with psychopathic aggressive behavior. P. Flor-Henry reviews the evidence in the article excerpted below which appeared in its entirety in *The British Journal of Psychiatry*:

Psychopathy, notably aggressive, criminal, homicidal psychopathy, is very highly associated with the male sex (and also with temporal lobe abnormalities). Wechsler states: 'The most outstanding single feature of the sociopath's test profile is his systematic high score on the performance,* as opposed to the verbal part of the scale...' Again Camp (1966), comparing acting out and delinquent children, both with and without EEG abnormalities, notes that, irrespective of the presence or absence of EEG abnormalities, boys have significantly higher performance IQ than verbal IQ both when matched against a standard population and when compared with acting out girls.

...the relative inferiority of dominant (left) hemispheric organization in the male is apparent. The relationship between reading retardation and delinquency is well known, and although the latter is often regarded as a psychological consequence of the former a much more fundamental association between the two may exist: both being parallel manifestations of dominant hemispheric dysfunction.

...Biologically determined gender related lateralized differential hemispheric vulnerability distinguishes the male brain from the female brain. In the female the dominant hemisphere is functionally more efficient than the non-dominant hemisphere. In the male the converse is true: the organization of the non-dominant hemisphere is relatively superior to that of the dominant hemisphere. The superiority of girls in language acquisition and skills, the superiority of boys in visuo-spatial abilities, in exploratory drive and aggressivity derive immediately from this differential cerebral organization. The excess of males exhibiting infantile autism (a cardinal feature of which is complete absence of language, or language retardation), developmental

*The part of the IQ test which tests right brain abilities.

72

dyslexia (fundamentally a defect in linguistic organization), and childhood epilepsies...can all be understood as varying manifestations of this dominant hemispheric vulnerability characteristic of the male gender. [159]

What Flor-Henry is suggesting here is that there is something wrong with males' left brains and that those males who are more severely affected are more likely to be psychopathically aggressive. We should remember that the degree of right brain functioning may be genetically linked and dependent on the *degree* of fetal androgenization. Flor-Henry suggests that males may be left brain deficient to the extent of their right brain superiority. If this is so, it could be the result of over-androgenization at the eighth week of fetal life. This would be in keeping with the male's overall greater vulnerability, from conception to death, to the exigencies of his environment.

Males are more susceptible to all manner of brain dysfunction than females and, partially as a consequence of this, they are more likely to develop aggressive behavior disorders. Even normal males are predisposed to aggressive behavior by a brain which functions differently from a female's. In the next section we will look at some specific biochemical differences between the two sexes which are directly responsible for differences in behavior.

FIGHT OR FLIGHT:
THE ROLE OF THE ADRENAL GLANDS

Recent biochemical studies of aggression have focused on the catecholamines: norepinephrine and epinephrine. Norepinephrine is the precursor of epinephrine in biosynthesis. The role of these two catecholamines will be immediately clearer if we demystify their names. "Epinephrine" is the name most scientists use for what is more commonly called adrenaline. And, of course, norepinephrine is equivalent to noradrenaline.

We have all felt the incredible surge of energy which epinephrine produces when we are confronted by danger. Sometimes our reaction is so swift that we only begin to "feel the fear" after the danger passes. What we feel are the continuing bodily reactions to epinephrine coursing rapidly through our bloodstream--shaky knees, speeding heart and rapid breathing, to name a few. Epinephrine pours into the bloodstream from the adrenal glands, creating a host of physiological changes which assist us in overcoming danger. Tired muscles are, in a split second, revitalized with nurturing sugars which epinephrine causes to be released from reserves in the liver. Circulation to the parts of the body irrelevant to dealing with danger, like the stomach, is attenuated, and blood, therefore, becomes more readily available to the heart, the brain and the limbs. The blood pressure increases, and that, along with increased respiration, enables a faster clearance of wastes from the system and a greater intake of oxygen. Through all of these means, epinephrine creates a huge burst of energy which, if we escape the danger rapidly, we may feel for some time after the threat has passed.

Epinephrine helps us to survive danger by enabling more successful *flight*, but what if the choice is to stand and *fight* rather than to flee danger? Subjectively most of us can tell the difference between how our bodies feel when we are angry and when we are afraid. The different body states are, at least in part, dependent on the balance of epinephrine and norepinephrine secreted by the adrenal gland. So then, where and what is the adrenal gland, and how does it "decide" to release the chemicals which enable us to flee danger, or to secrete the mixture which best prepares us to fight.

The Endocrine Organs

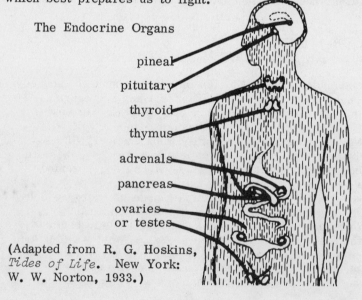

pineal
pituitary
thyroid
thymus
adrenals
pancreas
ovaries
or testes

(Adapted from R. G. Hoskins, *Tides of Life*. New York: W. W. Norton, 1933.)

There are two adrenal glands, one over each of our two kidneys. (*Adrenal* is derived from the Latin word meaning "near the kidneys.") Small yellowish organs, they are only about one to two inches long, and usually weigh less than one-third of an ounce apiece. The insides and the outsides of the adrenals produce wholly different hormones. The outside, the adrenal cortex (*cortex* comes from the Latin "bark" and is descriptive of the way the bark encloses the tree) comprises 90% of the organ. The inside, the adrenal medulla (Latin for "marrow" is descriptive of the medulla's position within the cortex, as marrow is within the bones) is, then, only 10% of the total mass of the adrenal gland, but it is this portion which makes epinephrine and norepinephrine available to the body.

Here we are concerned only with the inner portion of the adrenal gland, the adrenal medulla. Now that we know what and where it is, we still must ask how it can "know" the external situation and prepare us to flee or to fight. At this point, suffice it to say that the brain, via a channel of command involving the secretion of certain neurotransmitters, instructs the adrenal gland to secrete a particular amount of epinephrine or norepinephrine. The message from the brain, carried by the sympathetic nervous system, tells the adrenal glands when to secrete what, how much to secrete, and when to shut down secretion.

Brains, like the responses they engender, are different; there is no one formula for epinephrine/norepinephrine secretion that every brain would command the adrenal glands to produce at the sight of a tarantula, for example. Obviously, hundreds of environmental variables could change the human response to a spider. How the spider is perceived is of primary importance. A two-year-old might have absolutely no chemical or emotional reaction, the spider just appearing to be one of the many things in the environment which he/she can not figure out. A banana stevedore, who sees such creatures every day, may be so accustomed to them that he automatically stomps them with his boot and goes on unaffected with his work. On the other hand, any spider, even the most harmless and whimsical daddy longlegs, could provoke a profound chemical reaction and concommitant fear response in a person who believes that all spiders are harmful.

People's physiological response to danger, then, is very much affected by how significant they perceive the threat to be. But, *some* of how we perceive threat is influenced by our genetic makeup—that is, some brains are physiologically more likely to respond dramatically to low level threat than are others, given the same conditioning and the same dangerous stimuli.

In addition to having individual thresholds for what will cause our body to prepare for danger, we also have individual thresholds for what will provoke us to anger. These too are decided both by conditioning and by the chemical balances of the brain. A genetically influenced consequence of maleness--*androgen secretion*--has a profound effect on the chemical balance of the brain involved in "deciding" when a stimulus will provoke anger and how intense the anger will be.

The genetic contribution to this threshold effect for fear and anger will become clearer if we leave the human species for a moment and consider some other animals. The study of lower animals is what first led science to an understanding of the epinephrine/norepinephrine response and how it relates to differences in emotional reaction to threat. Numerous researchers have found that aggressive animals like the lion have a high norepinephrine/epinephrine ratio in the adrenal medulla. 160, 161, 162 Fearful animals, like the rabbit, whose survival depends on their ability to flee danger, have a higher concentration of epinephrine than norepinephrine. As a rule, the higher the proportion of norepinephrine in the animal's adrenal medulla, the more aggressive the animal will be. According to B. T. Donovan, "noradrenaline makes up only 2% of the amine content of the rabbit medulla, 9% of that of the rat, 12% in the hare, and some 17% in man." 163 Fifty-five percent of the total amine in the lion's adrenal medulla is norepinephrine. Of course, all of these figures are averages, and there is great variety between members of a species. For example, it has been found that some strains of rats have high adrenal medullary NE/E ratios, and, not surprisingly, these turn out to be the most aggressive strains, specifically those who compulsively kill mice. 164

The animals in whom it has been possible to assay the exact percentages of adrenal NE and E have all been "sacrificed" and had their adrenal glands removed for chemical analysis. The procedure is different with less expendable animals like monkeys and chimps, but the results have paralleled those of the studies mentioned earlier. Catheters have been implanted into the hearts of monkeys which draw continuous blood samples while the animal engages in its normal activity or is exposed to a variety of stressful stimuli. Mason et al. found that those procedures which elicited a strong NE response were unpleasant, and those which were familiar to the animal. Stimuli which promoted epinephrine secretion "contained an element of uncertainty, unpredictability and threat."[165]

Joseph Brady clarified this in his research which he summarizes by saying that when a relevant behavior is available, and one that the animal already knows, NE is the dominant response; i.e., when a situation is familiar and an animal knows how to overcome the threat (by *fighting*), NE is prominent. [166] When the animal is helpless, as when approached by a larger or stronger unknown animal or object, the epinephrine response occurs.

J. J. Schildkraut supports this conclusion:

> Increased epinephrine excretion seems to occur in states of anxiety or in threatening situations of uncertain or unpredictable nature in which active coping behavior may be required but has not been achieved. In contrast, norepinephrine excretion may occur in states of anger or aggression or in situations which are challenging but predictable and which allow active and appropriate behavioral responses to the challenge. [167]

In addition to its role in facilitating aggressive reaction to a provoking stimulus, NE is also thought to act as a stimulating agent in carnivores which causes them to attack and kill their prey when no threat to them is present. M. C. Goodall suggests that the high proportion of NE in feline animals supports this view. [168]

Such clear-cut correlations between body chemistry and behavior were important early indications of the wisdom of pursuing psychobiology as a branch of medicine. Experience can alter body chemistry and body chemistry can alter the perceived experience and the nature of the behavioral response. An animal with a high medullary norepinephrine/epinephrine ratio simply will not, can not, respond with the same degree of "cool" to a provoking situation as an animal with a higher epinephrine to norepinephrine concentration. But, as suggested in the tarantula example, experience can definitely influence the catecholamine balance. We can see the synergy of genetics and environment most clearly at this level. The simplistic insistence that *only* genetics or *only* environment determine human behavior has been forever laid to rest by this understanding of the interplay of chemistry and emotion.

Naturally, scientists are most interested in interindividual *human* differences in adrenomedullary secretion and how they might relate to emotional behavior. Since "sacrificing" the subject or putting a catheter into a person's heart are out of the question, urine analysis is used to determine catecholamine concentrations. The proportion of NE/E excreted in the urine is thought to be an accurate reflection of the proportion secreted by the adrenal gland.

Many rather whimsical experiments have been devised to determine the correlations between the ratio of NE to E secretion and behavior. F. Elmadjian compared the ratio of ice hockey players who had been involved in aggressive encounters with the ratio of the goalkeeper who had been waiting anxiously, but who had not actually played any role in the aggressive interaction of the game. [169] He found that the men who had just been involved in aggressive encounters had a high NE/E ration, while a high secretion of E was found in the goalkeeper who had been passively anxious. Elmadjian also discovered that boxers secrete more E in the period while they are waiting for the fight to begin, and more NE just after the fight is over. Von Euler found that airplane passengers excreted more E, while pilots excreted more NE. [170]

Several studies have been done to determine if there is a difference in the NE/E ratio of mental patients who are displaying aggressive behavior from those who are anxious and passive. Elmadjian did a study using standard psychiatric rating scales to assess the behavioral mode of normal and psychotic subjects. [171] He found that aggressive hostile behavior was positively correlated with NE excretion, while self-effacing or fearful behavior correlated with a high E excretion.

Studies done by several research teams have conclusively shown that infants are born with a high NE/E ratio and that the ratio inverses as maturation proceeds. [172, 173, 174] This very nicely complements the psychoanalytic concept as Funkenstein has suggested:

> According to theory, anger directed outward is characteristic of an earlier stage of childhood than is anger directed toward the self or anxiety (conflicts over hostility). [175]

As the child matures, he/she internalizes the social proscriptions against violent behavior, and the NE/E ratio correlates with this change. Depression or anxiety, taken to be the turning of socially repressed anger toward the self, increases as the child matures, and the epinephrine/ norepinephrine ratio concomitantly increases. Of course, it is impossible to say how much of the chemical maturational change reflects conditioning and how much reflects the genetically determined chemical balance of the developing child.

Similarly high NE/E ratios have been found in infants of other species. Studies on the impact of varying degrees of conditioning against violent behavior have not been done with animals, but a most interesting study correlating the degree of counteraggressive conditioning with NE/E ratio in humans has. The implications of this study are of such consequence that a detailed examination of the work of Drs. B. J. Fine and D. R. Sweeney is warranted.

SOCIAL CLASS AND BIOCHEMISTRY

Dr. Fine and Dr. Sweeney took twenty-four hour urine samples from twenty-seven army enlisted men for three consecutive days. The samples were analyzed for NE/E ratio and these ratios were related to information about the subjects' socioeconomic background obtained from questionnaires. The doctors found that:

> ...individuals with low socio-economic backgrounds excreted significantly higher proportions of norepinephrine in relation to epinephrine than did individuals with middle-class backgrounds. 176

These data assume particular importance in the light of the fact that violent crime, particularly homicide, is strongly correlated with social class as well as gender. The question is, of course, *why* lower class persons should have a significantly different chemical balance and behavior pattern from other socioeconomic classes. Fine and Sweeney have proposed that the difference is the direct consequence of differential child-rearing practices between classes:

> With regard to aggression, considerable difference in child-rearing practices has been noted between the middle and lower classes since the beginning of the post-World War II period.... Middle-class

79

parents appear to be more permissive than lower-class parents with respect to the expression of aggression in their children. This permissiveness tends to be accompanied by rather strong control, primarily by means of deprivation of love or withholding of rewards. Lower-class parents, on the other hand, tend to be less permissive and to rely on physical punishment as a means of control. The middle-class techniques allow the child to express aggression but attempt to "socialize" it, i.e., to direct it into acceptable channels. The lower-class techniques do not allow the child to express aggression and, in punishing severely physically, i.e., in using aggression to punish aggression, justify the expression of aggression, further frustrating the child and increasing his aggressive tendencies.... 177

The relation of the NE/E ratio to the conditioning is less clear than the behavioral consequences of the child's being physically punished for aggressive behavior. Fine and Sweeney point out, however, that other studies have clearly shown that biochemical as well as behavioral responses can be conditioned, so that even when the child is not being physically punished, his/her chemical state may reflect the anticipation of being punished. As long as the agent of the punishment, the mother or father, are present, the chemical balance will be reflective of their mode of punishment. "In this sense," the doctors say, "the biochemical response can be viewed as 'learned' or 'conditioned'." 178

The social prognosis for such chemically/emotionally conditioned people is not good:

We expect that the "conditioning process" continues, and perhaps even intensifies, in adulthood. Here, the outwardly aggressive individual is exposed, to an extent, to threatening authority figures, e.g., bosses, police...who are themselves frequently outwardly aggressive, and who tend by their presence and actions to reinforce the already high aggression and biochemical levels. Simultaneously, rules and regulations, imposed by a "middle class" society, against the overt expression of aggression intensify the whole process.

Ultimately, in the more extreme cases, violent

aggression takes place with subsequent physical punishment, e.g., getting beaten up or put in jail, which in turn reinforces the whole dynamic process again. Speculatively, then, outward aggression appears to be a circular, self-perpetuating phenomenon. The seriousness of this spiral and the validity of the conceptualizations we have presented are attested to by the Henry and Short (1954) finding that both low socio-economic status and anger-out personality type are related to the incidence of homicide and severe physical violence. Viewed in this light, child-rearing practices assume even greater importance than they ever have heretofore.... [179]

At first, then, children of all social classes would be born with roughly equal catecholamine ratios, but those children who are physically punished for aggressive acts would, as the conditioning takes hold, gradually begin to evince different chemical/emotional behavior from those children who have been taught to redirect their aggression and who are not physically punished for it.

Fine and Sweeney stress the biochemical basis of aggressive behavior and question solely psychological methods of therapy:

...we wonder to what extent extreme outward aggression can be dealt with solely on the psychological level insofar as remedial action is concerned. Can a system which over many years has developed comparatively high levels of certain hormones, which themselves may perpetuate behavior, be modified by attempting to change the behavior? We pose this as only one of a multitude of questions which may be asked and which can form the basis of many years of challenging research. [180]

Obviously, the kind of "question" with which Fine and Sweeney conclude their article might be very upsetting to many people as it borders the terrain of psychosurgery. The class and racial implications are implicit. While we may not like what is indirectly being proposed here, it does seem that we must consider the evidence and find an acceptable way to help those persons who, because of adverse situations in their childhoods, are most likely to commit acts of violence against their fellow humans.

Needless to say, the educational process has a long way to go in convincing parents that by *not* sparing the rod they may indeed be spoiling the child--spoiling his/her chances of a normal emotional development and harmonious relationships with others.

SEX AND CATECHOLAMINES

The implications of this study of the effects of parenting on catecholamine excretion and violent behavior go beyond social class, and bring us back to the central concern of this book. *Female children* of all social classes are physically punished less often than *boys*. [181], [182] Murray Straus has found that boys are punished physically twice as much as girls. [183] Is it the case, then, either because of this or some other differential conditioning or because of genetic differences, that females generally have a lower NE/E ratio which is reflected by less aggressive behavior?

Though, of course, it is impossible to separate the effects of conditioning from those of genetics, it has been found that females generally have a lower resting level of catecholamine secretion than do males, and that the NE/E ratio is lower in females. Early studies on sex differences in catecholamine secretion acknowledged this clearcut difference, but proclaimed it invalid because of differences in body weight between males and females. After the researchers had made adjustments in their figures to compensate for variation in body weight, they found that the sex differences did not reach the .05 level of confidence and so they could not be called "significant." However, it has subsequently been determined that body weight does not influence catecholamine secretion or the effects of equal amounts of catecholamines on behavior. [184] All tests to date comparing the NE/E excretion of males and females in which "corrections" for body weight have not been made clearly show that females have a lower NE/E ratio. [185], [186] Indeed, given the universal statistics on female/male differences in aggressiveness, it would be most surprising if this were not the case. Some of these studies bear a more careful examination.

G. Johansson analyzed urine samples from nine sixth-grade classes in Sweden after two different experimental activities. [187], [188] The first was a "passive" situation in which the children watched an emotionally neutral film.

82

The second was a mentally demanding arithmetic test which lasted forty-two minutes. Urine was collected immediately after both of these activities and analyzed for catecholamine content.

Girls secreted less epinephrine and less norepinephrine in both situations. The sex difference was greatest during the active period, as can be seen from the graph below.

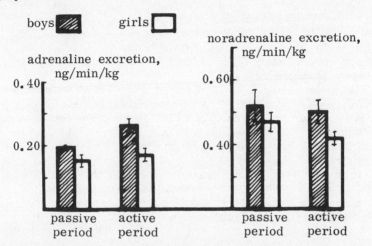

Mean excretion rate of adrenaline and noradrenaline by boys (n=99) and girls (n=78) in a passive situation (film exposure) and an active situation (test of arithmetic). Values corrected for body weight. (Adapted from G. Johansson, *et al.*, "Catecholamine Output in School Children as Related to Performance and Adjustment," *Report of the Psychology Laboratory University of Stockholm*, 1971, No. 326: 5.)

The researchers analyzed possible psychological and sociological factors that might have affected the data, but concluded that these factors had little influence on the results, which are more readily attributable to a clear-cut sex difference. As a side note, they report that the girls did significantly better on the arithmetic test, though they were not known to possess superior mathematical ability. Apparently, the boys' more extreme reaction to the challenge did not facilitate their intellectual performance. In fact, it would appear that extreme emotional/chemical responsiveness may interfere with intellectual performance.

Levi did a most interesting study of young adults' catecholamine levels. [189] He found that while the sex difference in catecholamine excretion was not significant in the forty-five females and forty-six males he tested after viewing both a comic film and a scary movie, that the differences were pronounced after a sexually exciting romantic film. The females in his study secreted significantly less NE during the sexually arousing film than did the males. Why would men secrete the "aggression chemical" when they are sexually aroused? We will be taking a closer look at the interconnectedness of sex and violence in the male psyche later on in this book. Suffice it to say that sex as men experience it has a chemical affinity, at least, to aggression.

Levi, in asking himself why the sex difference was so significant in this study, hypothesizes "that females are adrenomedullarily *less reactive*, at least in response to psychological stimulation." And he points out that similar studies have noted "such a female adrenomedullary 'hyporeactivity'." [190]

It is important to realize that in all of the studies mentioned it was *not* the case that male adrenal glands secreted more NE while females' secreted more E, but that while the sex difference is most notable in norepinephrine, males secreted more of *both* catecholamines. In other words, the chemical evidence does not support the notion of female anxiety and fearfulness as the counterpart of male aggressiveness. The stereotype of hyperemotionality usually assigned to women, may, indeed, have greater applicability to men, at least from the chemical standpoint.

BRAIN CHEMISTRY AND BEHAVIOR

The decision-maker as to which of the adrenomedullary hormones will be secreted when a person encounters a particular situation is the brain. Of course, there may be varying sensitivities in the secretory cells of particular individuals' adrenals which will respond at different thresholds to the messages which the brain sends via the sympathetic nervous system, but, on the whole, the commander-in-chief is to be found in the limbic (or emotional) brain, in particular, the hypothalamus.

A specific section of the hypothalamus serves as a control center for telling the adrenal medulla which catecholamines and how much of them to secrete at any one time. Of course, this still is not the "final cause"; detective work remains to be done to ascertain what clues in the hypothalamus as to whether a situation calls for flight or fight. Without a knowledge of the external environment, that is, without a connection to the five senses, the hypothalamus would have no way of knowing whether the adrenals should prepare to help us deal with a rattlesnake or an annoying fly.

The sensory areas of the brain must communicate the needs of the body to the hypothalamus. The "message" is sent chemically, via the neurotransmitters, some of which are dopamine, norepinephrine, and serotonin. We find, then, that norepinephrine, in addition to being secreted by the adrenal medulla to enable the fight response, also is one of the chemical transmitters which tells the central emotion control center which response to the environment is appropriate. But how does a neurotransmitter work?

Every nerve in our body, including those in the brain, is really a string of incredible numbers of tiny nerve cells, the neurons. In order for a message to move along the string of neurons, they have to make a connection with one another so that electricity will flow between them. Otherwise, the charge would not be able to leap the gaps between neurons which are called synapses. A chemical transmitter, like norepinephrine, is released from the presynaptic nerve ending; it changes the electrical potential of the cell membrane in the adjacent neuron, thereby generating a nerve impulse. Before each synapse, or gap between nerve cells, a little of the neurotransmitter must be released in order for the electrical impulse to move along the length of the nerve fiber. Our nerves, then, unlike electric wires or switchboard cables, need the the assistance of chemicals to transmit their messages electrically.

So, in order for the brain areas which perceive the environment to communicate with those areas of the brain which help the body adjust to that environment, neurotransmitters must help convey the electrical message. But how could a chemical possibly convey instructions for all the complicated adjustments the body must make in order to cope with the infinite possible variations in the environment? There is as yet no simple answer to this question from neuroendocrinologists, but evidence at this point suggests that specific neurotransmitters activate (and inactivate) specific cells in the brain. Particular proportions of the chemicals would activate certain behaviors by either activating the neural structures which facilitate them or by inhibiting those which which inhibit them.

Cells in certain areas of the brain are sensitive to norepinephrine, some more sensitive to dopamine or serotonin, some to all three. That is, the activation of certain cells in the brain can only be accomplished by norepinephrine and some require serotonin and some dopamine. The *behaviors* which these three chemicals enable are sometimes strikingly different. A person's reaction to a threatening situation may be mediated by a neurotransmitter which will enable him/her to make a speedy retreat. On the other hand, the same stimulus, mediated by another neurotransmitter, might provoke an angry attack.

The point here is that the adrenal glands secrete the enablers of fight or flight behavior *depending on the message they get from the brain*. This message is very much dependent on the chemical balances throughout the brain. And, in turn, the chemical balances are partially dependent on the nature of each individual's perception. Applying the tarantula example, we can see that the neurotransmitter formula secreted by a very fearful person may be very different from that secreted by a person conditioned to simply avoid the threat, or a person who has, in general, a different chemical balance in the brain.

Obviously it would be incredibly difficult to separate those chemical reactions which take place in a person's brain because he/she has been so genetically endowed from those that have become more likely because of the person's experience. The important thing is to recognize that both genetics and experience play a part. Lions are not born with the same balance of catecholamines as are rabbits, and no amount of experience will change that. On the other hand, dramatic interindividual differences develop within a species because of differential experience.

THE NATURE OF THE NEUROTRANSMITTERS: DOPAMINE, NOREPINEPHRINE, AND SEROTONIN

A sudden change in the level of the neurotransmitter norepinephrine in the brain can drastically alter human and animal behavior. It can cause a person to swing the entire length of the continuum between depressed passivity to aggressive hyperactivity within a very short time. Obviously a naturally occurring brain chemical that has such direct correlations with human psychological states has been the subject of much investigation. Many pharmacological studies have been done in an effort to learn how to control chronic depression and/or hyperaggression by altering the synthesis of norepinephrine in the brain with drugs. The data, so far, indicates a high degree of success. Countless persons today are able to function because of an artificial alteration of one of their neurotransmitters.

Basically, anything that increases the amount of norepinephrine available for use in the brain increases the level of excitation, general arousal, and aggressiveness in a variety of animals including humans. [191], [192], [193], [194] According to Joseph Schildkraut and Seymour Kety:

> All of the drugs that have significant effects on mood seem to have one or another effect upon brain norepinephrine--they either deplete it and produce depression, or favor its release or accumulation at appropriate receptor sites in the brain in association with antidepression, euphoria, or hyperactivity. [195]

Schildkraut and Kety say that "some, if not all, depressions are associated with an absolute or relative deficiency of catecholamines, particularly norepinephrine, at functionally important receptor sites in the brain." [196] And conversely, those psychiatric patients "who are agitated and/or psychopathic have elevated levels...of norepinephrine," according to Joseph Mendels and James Stinnett. [197] Not surprisingly, the dramatically fluctuating norepinephrine levels of those patients who fall into the manic-depressive category, that is, who are chronically depressed one day and euphorically hyperactive the next, have also been found to correlate almost exactly with their mood swings. [198]

Dopamine, another of the neurotransmitters, is the chemical precursor of norepinephrine in the brain. All of the norepinephrine synthesized in the brain is derived from dopamine. For this reason, it is difficult to know whether the effects of dopamine are due to its own interaction with the neurons of the brain or if the effects are really due to the increased availability of norepinephrine which increased dopamine levels facilitate.

At any rate, norepinephrine injected into the bloodstream will not pass the careful filtering system, "the blood-brain barrier," which protects the brain from harmful chemicals. Since dopamine, or L-Dopa will, it is used when alterations of norepinephrine in the brain are necessary. Whether because of its own properties or because of the enhancement of norepinephrine, increasing brain dopamine produces the same psychological effects as increasing brain norepinephrine would. William E. Bunney has described the sudden change in the behavior of chronically depressed patients which an injection of L-Dopa produces:

> Clinically, the hypomanic episodes observed in our studies were characterized by a sudden, clearly defined onset of increased speech, hyperactivity, increased social interaction, intrusiveness, sleeplessness, and some euphoria and grandiosity.
> Prior to the development of hypomania, the patients were characterized in the nurses' notes by descriptions such as "quiet..., depressed..., avoiding others..., speaks only when spoken to." In seven of the nine episodes there was a marked switch in behavior overnight from that of the previous day. [199]
> [One of Bunney's patients]...had been described as quiet and pleasant but avoiding staff on the evening before she awoke at 3:15 A.M. At this time, she was described as "talkative, very animated, and smoking with gusto." Throughout the day she energetically initiated and tried to involve others in a variety of ward activities, talked almost continuously and provocatively, and involved other patients and staff in discussion. She described herself as "full of energy" and as having "racing thoughts." ... She loudly dominated a group therapy session and ended an argument by slamming a book on the table. After another night with only two and one half hours of sleep and a second day of similar activity, during which the L-Dopa was discontinued, she slept six and one half hours and on the next day was described again as "quiet, pleasant...sometimes looking sad." [200]

Donald Reis in his studies of the connection of NE and aggressive behavior has found that "the release of NE in the brain is proportional to the intensity of the evoked behavior," [201] or, in other words, that there is a direct "dosage effect"--the higher the availability of NE in the brain, the greater the likelihood of aggressive behavior.

Serotonin is the final neurotransmitter we'll be considering. All evidence so far suggests that *lowering* the level of serotonin available for use in the brain *increases* the likelihood of aggressive behavior. 202, 203

The important relation to remember about the neurotransmitters in the brain, then, is that increased use of NE *increases* the likelihood of aggressive behavior while increased use of serotonin *decreases* the likelihood of aggressive behavior.

The neurons of the brain which are most affected by these two neurotransmitters are concentrated in the limbic or emotional brain, specifically in the hypothalamus, and NE and serotonin are found in very high concentrations in this part of the brain. Several researchers have located specific sites in the hypothalamus which, when electrically stimulated, cause the adrenal gland to step up its production of norepinephrine; other sites cause it to produce more epinephrine. These sites correspond exactly with those sites which are known to produce fighting behavior and fearful flight behavior respectively.

It is not known for certain how norepinephrine, acting as a neurotransmitter in the hypothalamus, *causes* the adrenal secretion of NE and E. There may be, in fact, other possible "aggression circuits." Male animals who have had their adrenal glands removed are still capable of fighting behavior if their testes are left intact, although the fighting is significantly delayed developmentally and is less violent. What is being proposed here is that the level of brain neurotransmitters is directly correlated with the degree of aggressiveness and also with the reactivity of the adrenal glands. The causal link has yet to be established, and there may, indeed, be more complicated and as yet unknown ways that the neurotransmitters mediate aggressive behavior, but for our purposes here the important thing is to understand the direct correlation of brain neurotransmitters with aggressive behavior. It is clear that anything which significantly alters the balance of neurotransmitters in the brain will have a corresponding and "dose-related" effect on behavior.

It will come as no surprise to the patient reader who has persisted this far in a difficult chapter, that female hormones and male hormones are capable of altering this very important chemical balance in the brain, and that the direction of the alteration will be opposite in the two sexes.

THE PRENATAL MASCULINIZATION OF
"THE NEURAL SUBSTRATE FOR AGGRESSION"

With this minimal knowledge of how neurotransmitters work, we will be able to understand more about "the neural substrate for aggression" which fetal androgen alters in early gestation. At long last, science is becoming clear on how androgen circulating through the bloodstream of the fetus can create a male type brain from the basic female pattern.

In lower animal studies it has been found that during the short period when the androgenization of the brain takes place in the neonatal male offspring, there is a drop in brain serotonin directly proportional to the amount of androgen circulating through the infant's bloodstream.[204] If females are castrated, so as to remove the influence of female hormones, and injected with androgen, a similar drop in brain serotonin occurs. From this point on, brain serotonin will be lower in the male (or artificially androgenized female) than in the normal female. Additionally, during this critical period when the brain is masculinized, norepinephrine levels rise. Again, the degree is dependent on the amount of circulating androgen. In all probability what is happening is that the androgen, by inhibiting the action of the enzyme monoamine oxidase, causes a sudden dramatic buildup in norepinephrine.

It is not clear why androgen should cause a depletion of serotonin, but the correlation is inversely proportional. By a mechanism which we are not yet clear on, then, testosterone acts on the immature brain to lower the serotonin available for use as a neurotransmitter at the same time that it serves to increase norepinephrine. It is thought that this chemical alteration "organizes" the organism's later responses to these two neurotransmitters so that neurons in the limbic brain become more or less sensitive to them in adult life, given the presence of circulating androgen.

The direction of the neurotransmitter alteration should not go without notice--serotonin is *lower* and norepine-

*In mice and rats androgenization occurs a few days *after birth*, rather than during prenatal life. Nevertheless, the process is comparable to that which takes place around the eighth week of human fetal life.

phrine *higher* during androgenization, as is the case with mature animals and humans displaying aggressive behavior.

Another biochemical change associated with the alteration in neurotransmitters which occurs during the androgenization process may be highly significant to an understanding of what makes a male a male. During androgenization, there is an impressive change in the DNA and RNA synthesis in the immature male brain.

DNA, as you'll remember from a preceding section, is the chemical of which genes are composed. RNA, a chemical replica of DNA, serves as the storehouse of memory and learning in the brain. It has been found that when an animal learns a new behavior RNA increases in volume in the areas of the brain concerned with that particular behavior.

Androgen circulating through the male brain during the organizing period "...causes the reduction of the rate of the synthesis of all RNA species common with normal female rats' forebrains, a selective reduction in some forebrain RNA species, at the same time it evokes the synthesis of some new RNA species which are not characteristic of the forebrain of normal females," according to one of the major researchers in this field, H. Shimada. [205] And not only is the genetic messenger, RNA, affected by androgenization, but DNA is too--the genes themselves. Androgen causes a definite drop in the amount of DNA in the brain. Another noted researcher, C. V. H. Clark, says of this:

> The higher DNA content found in the brains of female rats may be interpreted to reflect a greater density (number of cells per unit volume) of neurons or glial cells, as a result of either a higher number of cells (neurons and glial cells) or a smaller intercellular space.... [206]

Fetal androgenization, then, profoundly affects the synthesis of DNA and RNA in the brain, directly changes the genetic makeup of the organism, and even decreases the number of neurons in the brain. The male "message" to react differently to the environment than females do is delivered by chemicals which directly alter heredity. The connection of the RNA and DNA synthesis alteration and that of the neurotransmitters has not been explored, so our picture, of necessity, can not be complete. Nevertheless, we are much closer than ever before to an understanding of what "masculinizes" the brain.

ANDROGEN AND THE NEUROTRANSMITTERS IN THE ADULT MALE BRAIN

The primary neural structures concerned with emotional behavior are in the limbic brain. They are highly sensitive to norepinephrine and serotonin, and they also have a great number of cells which are especially sensitive to the sex hormones. The sex hormones are available in higher concentrations in the limbic brain than in any other area of the brain. Ample opportunity exists, then, for sex hormones to chemically influence the neurotransmitters in the areas of the brain most concerned with emotional behavior.

There are two ways that the sex hormones, male or female, could conceivably alter the availability of neurotransmitters in the brain: 1) they could step up or slow down their synthesis or, 2) they could change the speed at which the neurotransmitters are broken down or inactivated. The latter is the actual case. Some of the sex hormones slow down the inactivation of neurotransmitters, thereby increasing the amount available, and some augment the inactivation of neurotransmitters, thereby decreasing the amount available.

Each of the sex hormones has its own particular interaction with the neurotransmitters, but in all cases it is an indirect one. That is, testosterone does not chemically interact with norepinephrine to increase or lower its level, but rather testosterone interferes with the action of the enzyme monoamine oxidase (MAO) whose job it is to *inactivate* neurotransmitters.

Using 125 normal human males as subjects, E. L. Klaiber reached the following conclusion about androgen's effect on neurotransmitters:

An *in vitro* experiment indicated that testosterone directly inhibits MAO activity. Therefore, the overall results of the study seem to suggest that androgens inhibit brain MAO activity which, in turn, results in an elevation of brain norepinephrine levels. Increased levels of brain norepinephrine are then thought to induce a heightened state of behavioral reactivity.... [207]

B. L. Welch and A. S. Welch say of this "heightened behavioral reactivity":

There seems to be a remarkable parallelism between many kinds of aggressiveness and the general level of nervous reactivity. Most of the environmental, surgical and pharmacological treatments that have caused increases in aggressiveness have also caused a general increase in sensitivity to stimulation.... Many androgens act, in their own right, to increase the responsiveness of neurochemical receptors and to increase responsivity to painful stimulation. [208]

In other words, androgens cause an increase in brain norepinephrine and a related increase in aggressiveness. The more androgens coursing through a male's bloodstream, the greater degree of pain he perceives and the more likely he is to react against the source of it. If we can extend the concept of pain beyond the purely physical, it is possible that men may perceive greater psychological pain or threat than do females, given the same emotionally eliciting situation. Men, to put it bluntly, may generally be more paranoid. They might perceive others to be more angry, more threatening, more potentially harmful than they really are, and therefore their defense reactions might be sooner called into play than a female's would be. Men might feel called upon to fight given much less cause than it would take to so motivate a female, even if our conditioning were equal and females trained to fight as frequently as males. The interplay of chemistry and conditioning is, once again, called to attention.

In addition to adult androgen being associated with higher levels of norepinephrine in the male brain, there is a parallel reduction in serotonin. Men have less serotonin available for use in the brain than women at all times except during the late luteal phase of a woman's menstrual cycle. Restating the importance of these chemical measures, we should remember that high norepinephrine and low serotonin are both associated with increased aggressive behavior.

So, from the eighth week of fetal life, males are subject to a different neurochemical balance than are females.

The interplay of our bodily chemicals is enormously complex; we have only touched the surface here. The important thing is to realize that our biochemistry is an open system which is under the influence of both genetics and the environment. Lions are not rabbits, and males are

93

not females--there is a congenital and undeniable difference in their behavioral proclivities, particularly that of
aggression. But not all lions are alike. We have gone
some way now toward understanding why some males are
"more male" than others and why, as a consequence, some
have further to go in learning to interact peaceably with
their fellow creatures on this planet. But the picture is
not complete without a consideration of how the environment interacts with male biology. In the next chapter
we'll take a look at how the family, the media, and the
culture as a whole shape male behavior.

Chapter Two

VIOLENCE BEGETS VIOLENCE

Biology predisposes little boys to learn aggressive behavior more easily than little girls, but there is no law that says we must teach it to them. In this chapter we'll explore some of the ways we in our culture "make a man" out of a boy with time-worn child-rearing tactics and exposure to aggressive models of masculinity.

SOCIAL INTERACTION IN INFANCY AND AGGRESSIVE BEHAVIOR

We have seen in chapter one that boys may be more susceptible to sensory deprivation in infancy than girls, and that this environmental influence may actually change the structure of the brain, which will further modify behavior. Too little research has been done with human infants to warrant a firm pronouncement on this, but studies with animals suggest that males' behavioral symptomology will be more severely pathological if they are deprived of love and physical reassurance. [1,2] If it is the case that this male vulnerability to social-sensory deprivation extends to humans, and there is no real reason to think that it does not, then this has a bearing on male aggression, since one of the major symptoms of social-sensory deprivation is extremely aggressive behavior.

There are indications that human mothers spend more time cuddling male infants at birth, primarily because they are fussier and more demanding. But it should be remembered that male babies are less capable of perceiving sensory stimuli than girl babies because of their less mature nervous systems. Also, according to Dr. Howard Moss's study of human infant-mother interaction, in time mothers grow tired of male babies' insistent demands and they tend to withdraw their attention from males more than from females. [3] Primate studies have shown that monkey mothers push away their male infants earlier than they do their female infants, perhaps because the male bites its mother more, is more restless, and generally less pleasing to hold. [4] Essentially, monkey mothers show more hostile behavior to males than to females. It has been found that monkeys who experience hostility from their mothers in infancy are highly aggressive when tested at four years of age. [5]

We can not extrapolate from monkey to human infants, but until further studies have been done, we can say that there is at least a good possibility that human male infants experience some social-sensory deprivation in infancy which may contribute to aggressive behavior.

Howard Moss has found that the kind of stimulation that human parents afford their infants may be qualitatively different for boys and girls. Parents attempt to elicit smiles, laughs, and other such acknowledgments of interaction more from girls. He says:

> The mothers in our studies, and also the fathers where we have the information, seemed to show greater investment in the social behavior of their daughters than that of their sons. These differences in parental behaviors may have been influenced by the females being more often in an optimal state, where they were receptive to social stimulation. [6]

Moss points out that the female's more mature brain makes more mature responses possible, which may be responsible for eliciting these different behaviors from the parents. They quickly pick up that a girl is more capable of responding properly than a boy and therefore tend to expect more of her and provide her with a more challenging environment. The few studies on differential handling find that boy infants are more often subjected to rough horse-play almost from birth than are girl infants. [7], [8], [9] Fathers, in particular, have been found to interact more roughly with their male infants than with their female infants and this difference tends to increase as the child grows older. [10]

One of America's leading anthropologists, Jules Henry, moved in with a family in order to assess the father's and mother's interaction with their baby, Pete. He kept a journal in which he relates the following account of how the Portman family socialized their child toward violence when he was barely old enough to walk:

Stretched out in the big leather chair in the living room, with Pete on top of him, Mr. Portman "ate Pete up," opening his mouth wide and pressing it against the child's face. Pete loved it. Then Mr. Portman played a little ball with him. Next he swung him around like a dumbbell, like a barbell, and like a pendulum. Mr. Portman rolled Pete up on his own (Mr. Portman's) back and, on all fours, rode Pete around. Then he rolled Pete over on Pete's back, held him tight, and rubbed his face hard into the child's belly several times. He exercised Pete's legs; he crawled on all fours and growled fiercely at him....

Before Mr. Portman left this morning he was not so rushed that he did not have time to punch Pete twice in the belly. This was too much for Pete, who, though he smiled, went away from his father.

The difference between Pete's experiences with his father and mother could hardly be more dramatic: joyless (funless) acquiescence alternating in the mother with icy boredom and humiliation; intense, interested bodily collision in the relations between imp-of-fun father and son. Here roughness and toughness do the work of love: Mr. Portman expresses his love for his son through throwing him around, punching him in the belly, and imitating a devouring animal. Pete can not fail, therefore, to associate love with physical violence: to love a person is to throw him around, wallop him, and symbolically chew him up—in other words, to have fun. Pete tries a baby version of this on Elaine, his little playmate next door. Thus the toughness-love-

97

violence combination, so common in our movies, is here built into the child's flesh and bone through the basic mammalian function of play....

When Pete is a little bigger he will probably have toy pistols and cowboy chaps; his father will be proud, when Pete is about eight years old, to buy him his first real football togs. His toy box, mostly a collection of odds and ends now, will probably sprout soldiers, tanks, and artillery, and he may have a toy missile that actually goes off. As he matures he will enjoy guns, prize fights, football, hockey, Western movies, movies of gangsters and war, and stories of murder and robbery in the "funnies."... [11]

LIKE FATHER LIKE SON

Some of Mr. Portman's behavior may have been unconscious, but he was quite explicit in saying to Jules Henry that he wanted to toughen the kid up, to give him a workout. He wanted, as many fathers do, to make a man of his son. What Pete became, in fact, was a mental patient, but who is to say what factors really led to mental illness. The point here is that fathers, whether unconsciously or intentionally, attempt to mold their sons to be masculine--read aggressive. Eleanor Maccoby and Carol Jacklin have found in their analysis of the literature on this subject that:

> There is evidence that parents encourage their children to develop sex-typed interests, in part through providing sex-typed toys for them. Even more strongly they *discourage* their children-- particularly their sons--from engaging in activities they consider appropriate only for the opposite sex....
> Parents show considerably more concern over a boy's being a "sissy" than over a girl's being a tomboy. This is especially true of fathers, who seem to take the lead in actively discouraging any interest a son might have in feminine toys, activities, or attire. [12]

Maccoby and Jacklin suggest that one of the main reasons that fathers are so careful to discourage sissiness is their own fear of homosexuality. Presumably they do not consider lesbianism to be as likely an outcome for their daughters and are therefore not as concerned about their daughters being tomboys as they are about their sons being sissies.

To be masculine is practically synonymous in our society with being aggressive. A survey conducted for the National Commission on the Causes and Prevention of Violence revealed that 70% of over a thousand respondents agreed with the statement: "When a boy is growing up it is very important for him to have a few fistfights." [13] In general, it has been found that the more aggressive a father is, the more aggressive a son he will produce. J. N. Butcher, for example, reports that the fathers of juvenile delinquents who were notably aggressive had high aggression scores on a standardized personality test he administered. [14] Thomas Detre has found that an antisocial attitude on the part of a *father* is the best single predictor that a boy will become violent later in life. [15] L. M. Anderson assessed the personalities of parents of boys who were neurotic, aggressive and normal and found that:

> Mothers were not as important in influencing the development of characteristic pathology in their sons as were the fathers. [16]

HOW THE ROD SPOILS THE CHILD

Ninety-four per cent of Americans report being spanked as children. [17] In England approximately 97% of children have been spanked by the time they are four years old, and 62% of infants have been spanked before their first birthday. [18] With so much "correction" one would think that our offspring would learn that misbehavior does not pay. On the contrary, numerous researchers have found that the more severely a child is punished, the more likely he is to become an aggressive juvenile delinquent. The more violence a child experiences at the hands of his parents, the more violent he is likely to be to others as an adult.

What children learn from being whipped is that violence is a functional tool for getting what one wants and exercising power over others. [19, 20] The parents who beat a child provide a living example of how to use force to accomplish one's ends.

Extensive research has shown that physical punishment is one of the five major factors associated with the development of delinquency in young boys. [21] One researcher has found that men who have been convicted of murder were physically punished in childhood nearly twice as often as their brothers who have not committed murder. [22] Some were almost beaten to death. When they grew up many of these men did beat another person to death.

Ironically, parents have been found to beat their children most often in an attempt to halt aggressive behavior. [23, 24] What their punishment accomplishes is exactly the opposite of what they intend. It has been found that physical punishment tends to decrease a child's conscience, or his own internal moral standards, and to weaken his ability to make decisions for himself. [25, 26]

As mentioned in chapter four, boys are punished more often and more severely than girls. Murray Straus has found that boys are punished roughly twice as often as girls. [27] Maccoby and Jacklin have reviewed the literature on sex differential punishment and find that:

> ...with few exceptions boys receive more physical punishment than girls do. This finding is consistent over a wide range of ages, and is found both in interview and in observational studies. [28]

They also point out that fathers react more severely than mothers to their boys' aggressiveness and are more likely to physically punish a son for aggressive misbehavior than a daughter who does exactly the same thing.

Maccoby and Jacklin suggest that fathers are more punitive with boys because they perceive their sons as a threat to their masculine dominance:

> Perhaps a father, at least on some occasions, is reacting to a son simply as another male--reacting as though a threat to his dominance were involved when his son is angry toward him, whereas he feels no such threat when challenged by a girl. [29]

Whatever the reason, it is well established that boys are physically punished much more often than girls, that this is usually for aggressive behavior, and that they are more likely to be severely punished by their fathers than by their mothers. Additionally it has been found that boys are more likely to be verbally punished by their nursery school and elementary school teachers. [30] Boys are reprimanded more often and are especially subject to loud scoldings from their teachers.

Class, race, and ethnic background are strongly correlated with the amount of punishment meted out to children. Almost all studies have found that working class parents use physical punishment more often than middle class parents. A survey conducted for the National Commission on the Causes and Prevention of Violence showed that almost twice as many low-education parents reported frequent spanking as high-education respondents. [31] There is a predictable ratio between educational and income levels and violence towards children--as income goes up physical punishment goes down. [32]

Other factors related to class are also predictive of physical punishment and related juvenile delinquency. It has been found, for example, that physical punishment increases in direct proportion to the number of children in a family, [33] and that physical punishment is especially frequent and severe in female-headed families who are on welfare. [34] There is a direct relationship between the number of brothers and sisters a boy has and his likelihood of becoming criminally aggressive in his teens. And children of welfare mother-headed families are more likely to end up juvenile delinquents than others.

We have seen in the previous chapter that class-related frequencies of physical punishment may cause physiological changes which may later lead to highly aggressive personalities. Taken together with the fact that children are frequently brain-damaged by their parents' beatings, we can see that children are not just psychologically disposed to violence by parental punishment, but physiologically as well.

Class is not the only consideration, however, for certain ethnic groups, though poor, rarely punish children. Some American Indian tribes, for example, never use physical force on their children, while child abuse is high among American Blacks and Puerto Ricans. [35]

Suzanne Steinmetz has done a study which indicates that the type of work a father does may have as much to do with his tendency to use physical force as does class:

...Jobs which fell into the persuasive category like a salesman and business executives bring out individuals who identify with power and strength, and who utilize physical skills and control in interpersonal relationships. They have the highest scores.

Those individuals who are categorized as belonging to the *motoric* environment (e.g., dentists, truck drivers) prefer concrete methods of problem solving, using physical skills and strengths, but are not dominating; and they avoid personal relations. Thus, although they received the next highest physical punishment score, it is considerably lower than the mean score for parents in the persuasive category.

Individuals who are in the supportive (e.g., school teachers, social workers) and conforming (e.g., accountants, clerks) environments prefer concrete methods of problem solving, utilizing verbal skills rather than physical skills and strengths. Parents in both these environments have considerably lower punishment scores. [36]

Steinmetz and Straus, in their book *Violence in the Family*, offer the following "prescription" for the child-rearing techniques which will create a violent individual:

It would seem, then, that the prescription used by families to produce violent individuals contains one or more of the following ingredients: placing a high value on toughness and teaching children to fight; using physical punishment to increase frustration and to provide an appropriate role model in the use of violence; and--if an extremely violent individual is to be produced--using extremely violent methods of dealing with the child, especially severe and senseless beatings. [37]

In addition to the circular effect of punishing aggressiveness with aggression, studies have also shown that a physically punished child is more likely to be a harsh and violent parent and so to perpetuate violence down through the generations. [38]

In a particularly fascinating study, Drs. Leopold Bellak and Maxine Antell asked what it was in the German personality which had allowed the horrors of Nazism to

take hold and flourish. [39] They point out that nearly all
of the Nazi criminals had been seriously mistreated in
childhood. To test their hypothesis that Germans as children may be more subject to physical violence, they studied parent-child interaction on German playgrounds as
compared to Danish and Italian playgrounds:

> Results indicate that German adults are signif-
> icantly more aggressive toward German children,
> and German children toward other children, than
> are either the Italians or the Danes....
> The dramatically greater aggressiveness of the
> treatment of German children shown in this exper-
> iment fits the notion widely held by Germans them-
> selves that German culture is *kinderfeindlich*, or
> hostile to children. A West German poll showed
> recently that "up to 60 percent of parents believe
> in beating, not slapping or spanking, but beating
> their children." Munich psychologist Rolf Luckert
> has said, "We beat our children dumb in this
> nation." [40]

The researchers mention that the rate of homicide as well
as suicide and all accidental injuries is higher in Frankfurt
than in Florence or Copenhagen. Though they do not claim
that the parent abusiveness is *the* cause of German aggressiveness, their work strongly suggests that we take a long
look at how we in this country punish children.

MEDIA VIOLENCE AND THE SOCIALIZATION PROCESS

An incredible number of studies have shown that children act more aggressively after viewing a film or tv show
which has violent content than after viewing a neutral show.
More than fifty studies involving over 10,000 children have
shown that tv violence leads to real-life violence. Apparently in as many cultures as have been studied, the viewing of violence, whether real-life or on film, leads to aggressive reactions to low-level provocations. In addition
to this immediate effect, it has been found that children's
preferences for violent tv shows are predictive of how
aggressive or delinquent they will be ten years later. [41]
In fact, of all the situational factors which are known to
increase aggressiveness, it appears that the viewing of

television violence is one of the most potent. Most researchers are reluctant to say that one thing *causes* another and usually hedge their bets by saying "there is a strong correlation between...," but the case is so strong on television violence that prominent and highly respected researchers are now willing to stake their reputations on the connection between tv violence and aggressive behavior. In a 1974 report, Dr. Robert M. Liebert says:

> Social scientists are carefully trained to avoid statements of certainty. Even in the physical and biological sciences, professional and scientific reports are always couched in terms of probabilities rather than absolutes. Notwithstanding this tradition, it seems to me that it has been shown beyond the reasonable shadow of a doubt that watching television violence produces antisocial attitudes and behavior that would not otherwise occur among entirely normal children. [42]

Similarly, Leonard Eron concludes from his ten-year extensive study of tv and violence that:

> ...the most plausible interpretation of these data was that early viewing of violent television caused later aggression. [43]

But here comes the shocker. This was found to be true *only for boys*, not girls:

> It should be emphasized that this direct positive relation between violence of **preferred** programs and later aggression was true only for boys. For girls, while the suggestion is not as strong as for boys, there **are** indications that viewing television violence may lead to lessened aggression. [44]

There are several reasons that have been suggested: 1) girls are socialized away from aggression, and thus prefer less violent tv to begin with, 2) female characters are not as violent as male characters on tv and are therefore not as potent role models for aggression, and 3) females are often victims of male violence on tv and little girls identify with their pain. [45] But whatever the background, the point is that girls are not influenced by television violence, which has been found to be a major contributor to boys' aggressive behavior.

Much attention has been focused of late on the amount and degree of violence depicted in television. The National Commission on the Causes and Prevention of Violence has issued a monumental report on the results of a two-year analysis of media violence. [46] They found that television is the medium people use most for entertainment. (According to another major study, the average American child born today will by the age of eighteen have spent more time watching tv than any other activity except sleep.) [47] The statistics of the National Commission report, show that in 1967 and 1968, 81% of all television programs included violence. [48] About 400 people per week are injured or killed on tv--about five per program for prime time shows. The highest violence rate is found in crime/western/adventure stories, but this is closely followed by children's Saturday morning cartoons.

Most Americans feel that there is too much violence on tv, but predictably, those who do approve of the level of violence tend to be those who are most violent themselves: young, uneducated males who live in densely populated urban areas. [49]

Even though there have been many reports of the effects of television violence, the networks have increased rather than reduced violence on tv. There is a small difference between the networks; CBS comes out with slightly less violence per hour than NBC or ABC, but all are increasing their proportion of violence every year. [50] It is obvious that unless public pressure is brought to bear, an increasing diet of tv violence will continue to socialize American males toward aggressive behavior.

A few people, tv producers among them, have attempted to convince the public that violence is good on tv since it acts as Aristotle proposed violence in drama acts, as a catharsis for one's personal pent-up aggression. Plato, who argued that viewing violence increased one's aggressiveness, turned out to be right, according to numerous contemporary psychological studies. It is simply not true that you can "get violence out of your system" by viewing violence.

Relatedly, it has been found that participation in or observation of contact sports does not let off steam and decrease male aggression any more than violent tv does. Kenneth Moyer, who has probably written more than anyone

else about the physiological correlates of aggressive behavior, reports that the neural systems involved in violence are sensitized and aroused by competitive sports. [51]
Unless an individual has learned how to inhibit physical
release of the tension such arousal generates, violence can
result. Goldstein and Arms did a study to determine what
effect competitive sports have on aggressive behavior.
They found that hostility significantly increased in persons
who had just viewed a football game. [52] However, they
found no increase in hostility in people who had observed
a gymnastic exhibition. They point out that intense competition can lead to catastrophic consequences:

> In May, 1964, a riot, precipitated by a refer-
> ee's decision, erupted at a soccer match in Lima,
> Peru, killing a number of spectators; the war be-
> tween El Salvador and Honduras has been traced to
> a soccer match between those two countries, and
> additional outbreaks of violence have occurred at
> soccer matches in Great Britain and at boxing
> matches in New York's Madison Square Garden. [53]

The ridiculousness of the catharsis idea is made clear
in this humorous analogy from two noted psychologists in
aggression research, Alfred Bandura and Richard Walters:

> While therapists, educators, and parents are fre-
> quently heard to defend the exposure of children to
> violent television and movie material, as well as
> children's participation in highly aggressive body-
> contact sports, on the grounds that aggressive im-
> pulses will thereby be reduced, few adults in North
> American society are likely to argue that vicarious
> participation in sexual activities will bring about a
> decrease in the observer's sexual responses. In-
> deed, considerable care is taken to exclude adol-
> escents from "restricted admission" movies, pre-
> sumably on the grounds that such exposure may
> generate sexual excitation and premature imitative
> sexual behavior. [54]

How ironic it is that children are excluded from viewing love-making while they are allowed to watch a number
of murders every day. We can only hope that someday
we in this country will follow the lead of several Northern
European countries which x-rate their movies by the de-

gree of violence rather than sex.

There are more theories about the socialization of
aggression than we can go into here--for example, there's
the Freudian idea that failure to breast-feed children and
too early toilet training increases frustration levels and
therefore aggressive behavior. Some readily available
books on these theories are listed in the chapter notes. [55]
Many are derived from anthropological and sociological
observation, whereas we have been more concerned in this
chapter with data from controlled psychological experiments.

Whatever the slight variations in the various theories,
most agree on the basic ways that our culture socializes
males to be aggressive. Differential handling of males
and females in infancy, the rewarding of a boy's masculine
self-assertion and the denigration of "sissy" pursuits, physical punishment throughout childhood--these are the major
ways that parents create bullies. Then, in league with
the media, they provide a child with a daily diet of murder and mayhem so that he has a vivid model for every
violent act known to humankind.

But the socialization problem doesn't stop here; though
the influence of parents on boys' aggressiveness is certainly a major one, we can not forget that the schools,
the children a child associates with, what he sees on the
streets where he lives--the society at large--all have a
major impact on a boy's psychosocial development. Even
parents who are very clear in their values about aggression and who have provided a loving and gentle environment are often undermined by the other influences which
are brought to bear on children.

This was brought home to me when I went shopping
recently in Berkeley for a child's game which did not
involve and promote violence. I went to a specialty game
shop on Telegraph Avenue about three blocks from the
University of California, where I supposed the student
influence would strongly support a selection of good games.
Medieval times are remote enough that I can sometimes
forget that chess is a war game, so I was not overly
offended by the ten or twenty different styles of chess
sets which comprised one room of the shop. But when I
discovered that in the other room there was not one single game which did not involve war or capitalistic competition I was shocked enough to ask the store attendant
why everything focused on war and money-making.

"That's what sells," he assured me. I reminded him that he could hardly know whether anything else would sell or not since he had provided not one single alternative to cops and robbers, GI Joe, *Monopoly* and all its imitators, and *Intergalactic War*, etc. He shrugged his shoulders and returned to his account book, obviously despairing of a sale to such a squeamish female.

Parents can not raise a child in a vacuum. When our schools are training grounds for violence, kids' programming is among the most violent on television, comic books, toys and games are saturated with violence--how can we expect to produce non-violent citizens? What is clearly indicated is a total change in public attitudes and values. We must come to an understanding of why men are aggressive and what can be done to remedy the situation.

We have gone some way towards understanding the psychobiology of aggression and we've taken a brief look at how socialization compounds the problems of male biology. The question about which we all must be curious now is how in the world things got to this sorry state in the first place. How did males come to be the way they are? How did society, this one in particular, become so violent? Is it a freak accident that males are physiologically inclined to be aggressive and have, therefore, created a society focused on this trait?

In the next chapter we'll seek the evolutionary trail of the sex difference in aggression. We may have to go back some fifteen million years, but if we can gain some answers to our questions, if we can see where and how things went wrong and gather clues as to what we must do now to change them, it will be a worthwhile journey.

Chapter Three

THE EVOLUTION OF THE SEXES

We turn now to asking *why* men have evolved with the physiological propensity for aggression. In seeking the roots of a behavior which may have a fifteen million year history, we must speculate on events about which there is little concrete evidence. I am entirely dependent on the learned opinions of the paleoanthropologists who are respected in their field. Certainly neither I nor they would claim that the picture of human evolution which we now have is gospel truth. We simply haven't much to go on. In fact, all of the prehistoric human or near-human remains ever excavated would nicely fit into one casket. The experts disagree among themselves about nearly every question in human evolution; what I have tried to do is to come to a somewhat artificial consensus among them on the question of how men evolved to be a violent species while women did not.

Naturally there are exceptions--peaceful men, violent women--and it is important to realize that in the big picture of human evolution the details of individual differences become obscured. We are dealing with broad generalizations, sweeping pronouncements about men we never laid eyes on. Perhaps the information we have so far will turn out to be only a small part of the picture, but if we are to understand how to right the mess we have made of this world, it seems imperative to find out, as best we can, what went wrong and when. It is with that purpose firmly in mind that we explore our beginnings, and *not* to say that because things have always been a particular way they must remain so.

That there is a striking behavioral disparity between males and females should be clear. D'Andrade's analysis of sex-role differences in over six hundred cultures, mentioned in chapter one, certifies that there is a fundamental pattern across all human societies: males are more concerned with sexual needs, more interested in pursuing dominance, less responsible to others, less nurturant, and less able to express emotions other than anger, and are, of course, more aggressive. [1] Females are more nurturant and are almost universally given the child-caring role. (The sexual division of labor was functional in nearly all the societies which D'Andrade reported on: men were involved in the occupations which required periods of travel and the making of tools and weapons, while women were responsible for the home-based activities of gathering fuel, water and food, and making and repairing clothing.) How is it possible that so many cultures, some completely cut off from contact with any other people on earth, should have developed such similar ways of divvying up the duties of their life-support systems? And, of course, the ultimate question of this book--why is it that men are universally the violent sex?

HOW MEN LEARNED TO KILL

No one has ever attempted to estimate how many men have murdered each other since they "arose" from apes. Lewis Richardson in his book, *Statistics of Deadly Quarrels*, has calculated that between 1845 and 1945 alone, fifty-nine million men were killed in wars or were the victims of deadly quarrels. [2] And this is in "civilized" times when constraints of law and custom, reason tells us, should have limited aggression. What of earlier times, more primitive peoples? When, in fact, did the killing begin?

The usual assumption is that men learned to kill in order to survive the attacks of predators. When ape-men descended from the trees to begin a terrestrial life, it is thought that they had to protect themselves from hungry tigers, lions, panthers, and the like, and thus learned the

110

use of weapons in order to survive.

The noted paleoanthropologist, Louis B. Leakey, pointed out that this can not be true because pre-men had no natural enemies. [3] Accounts of "man-eating" animals are mythic "precisely because," he tells us, "they were so rare." Lions, leopards and tigers do not normally eat human flesh--only when the animal is sick or has been wounded, or when its normal food has been killed off by hunters. Leakey says that there is only one animal who would attack a human in 100,000 members of the carnivore population. The beasts to whom pre-men were supposedly prey simply do not like to eat human flesh and are repulsed by the smell of it. Leakey gives this account of his own unpalatability:

> I myself have slept on the Serengeti plains with an African when we could not get back to camp because of a car breakdown. Five lions came and sniffed at our heads and around our faces. We were both awake and kept very quiet, but they did not attempt to kill and eat us. They were not aggressive nor were we, and we were not considered food to eat.... The whole of the literature makes it clear that even when a normal lion or leopard or tiger has killed a man who had been aggressive to it or had interfered with its cubs, or had wounded it, unless it is a man-eater (as psychopathic as a madman today), the animal will kill the aggressor, then turn up its nose and walk away, and not eat the dead human....I seriously believe that one of the things which protected many early primates, including early man, in the defenseless days before he had weapons or tools, and when he was living on the ground, was that he was unpalatable to the carnivores. [4]

This was nature's way of endowing early men with a built-in defense so that they need never have developed the capacity for aggression in order to defend themselves. But, according to some of the most respected paleoanthropologists, ape-men had barely managed their descent from the trees before they began to kill, not in defense, but in pursuit of meat.

David Pillbeam estimates that hominids, who were only a step away from their apish ancestors at the time, may have begun to hunt and kill small animals fourteen million years ago. [5] In the 1960's Leakey produced evidence of ape-men's meat-eating when he found antelope skulls alongside the remains of a fifteen million year old hominid. [6] Not just a few antelope skulls, but twelve hundred fossils in addition to the ape-man himself. The skulls had been fractured in a way that no animal could have managed without tools. Leakey found a lump of lava with battered edges which may have been used to smash the bones. If so, this would be the first tool ever used. Of course, evidence of meat-eating does not necessarily prove that these ape-men did the killing themselves. But, short of a general antelope plague, there is little to explain why so many of them should have been found surrounding the bones of our earliest hominid ancestor. And since killing an antelope with one's bare hands would have been quite impossible, it is likely that even at this incredibly early date ape-men had developed weapons which enabled them to run down antelopes in great number.

The experts do not agree about when the first meat-eating and small-game hunting began. Estimates are millions of years apart. But they are generally in agreement about the likely sequence of events and their consequences, whether it was fifteen million years ago or five million years ago: pre-men must have witnessed the kills carnivorous animals made and, eventually, some animal who had eaten his fill must have left enough meat remaining on a carcass to tempt ape-man's or man-ape's palate. In time, pre-men lightened the task of removing the meat from the carcass by inventing a sharp-edged cutting tool for the purpose. Leakey recounts the sad eventuality:

> Once he reached the point where he was able to scavenge meat from carcasses killed by the lions, leopards and cheetahs, protohuman could ask himself, "Why shouldn't I *kill* for myself?" If he had the brains for it, he would start thinking of a way to do this. [7]

Our ancestors need not have become aggressive to defend themselves. They were not acceptable prey. The first competition, the first necessity to become one-up, was brought about when hominids decided not to wait for the remains of the lion's dinner, but, instead, to devise a way to drive the large carnivore away. This may also have been the beginning of male bonding—one man can not frighten a lion, but a troop of screaming men coming down on a solitary lion enjoying its dinner could have accomplished their purpose. At this point we can already see the possible beginnings of sex-role differences. Even before the invention of weapons, and consequently, hunting, it is clear that a female who was either pregnant or nursing a small child would have been less apt to play scarecrow to a dining lion.

The change from merely salvaging what otherwise would have been wasted in response to a possible shortage of vegetation, to the active competition for flesh and the aggression that this necessitated, marks the turning point where the notion of profiting by violence came to our ancestors. From this, early men went on to develop weapons which allowed them to kill animals from a distance, at this time large mammals. Later they turned, as few animals then or now ever do, to killing within their own species, the primates. Leakey says that there is clear evidence that early men regularly killed giant baboons. It was only one step from this to extending their aggression to each other. "Thus," Leakey says, "from being wholly unaggressive, with nothing but a built-in defense mechanism, man eventually came to arm himself with such things as bolas, bows and arrows, and then nuclear weapons." [8] A rather condensed statement on fifteen million years of hominid history, perhaps, but nonetheless accurate.

When they began to hunt for meat, men denied their primate heritage and took power over other animals. All of the primate family which we most closely resemble--monkeys, chimpanzees, gorillas, and apes--have remained predominately vegetarian. In captivity they can learn to eat meat, but in the wild state they rarely do. In some locales they are known to supplement their diet with insects, birds and small animals, but estimates are that animal food makes up at most one per cent of their food intake. Only primates who have been raised in total isolation in a laboratory setting and who grow up to be psychotics actually prefer a constant diet of meat.

When men began to kill to satisfy a hunger for meat they fundamentally changed their relation to their universe, as anthropologists Sherwood Washburn and C. L. Lancaster explain in their oft-quoted article, "The Evolution of Hunting":

> Hunting changed man's relations to other animals and his view of what is natural. The human notion

113

that it is normal for animals to flee, the whole
concept of animals being wild, is the result of
man's habit of hunting.... Prior to hunting, the relations of our ancestors to other animals must have
been very much like those of the other noncarni-
vores. They would have moved close among the
other species, fed beside them, and shared the
same waterholes. But with the origin of human
hunting, the peaceful relationship was destroyed,
and for at least half a million years man has been
the enemy of even the largest mammals. In this
way the whole human view of what is natural and
normal in the relation of man to animals is a product of hunting, and the world of flight and fear is
the result of the efficiency of the hunters. [9]

As we shall see, the decision to kill damaged all of
men's relationships--to themselves, to other animals, other men, women, children, and eventually to the cosmos.
Of course, the objection can be raised that men may have
needed to kill in order to survive. This was true particularly during the tremendous climatic upheavals of the Plio-
cene and Pleistocene Ages. There undoubtedly were times
when vegetation alone would not have provided a sufficient
diet. Men could have turned to eating eggs and small
birds as primates do in times of need, but need they
have decided to kill rhinoceroses to keep from starving?
And once the drought or the temperature emergency was
over, need they have kept on killing?
      We can't view every animal on earth that lives by kil-
ling as a murderer or "unnatural." Lions kill, cheetahs
kill, even our domesticated dogs will kill if they are hungry enough. Why should we expect men to do any differently? Leakey has answered this question by pointing out
the clear difference between killing as a means of obtain-
ing food when you are naturally a predator, and the kind
of predation men adopted:

      I would entirely agree that in dealing with ani-
      mals which are, by nature, predators, one must
      clearly distinguish between predation and aggression.
      But I would still be inclined to suggest that when a
      creature, namely a hominid, who is by nature not
      a predator, goes into the predatory field, he does
      so only by virtue of having become an aggressor...
      because what he is doing is abnormal to his nature. [10]

114

Humans, like all the primates, do not have a physical constitution compatible with a meat diet. As anthropologist Kenneth P. Oakley writes:

> From the endowment of nature we should be vegetarians. We lack the teeth evolved by true carnivores, and we have the long gut associated with a herbivorous diet. Furthermore, we are the only members of the Hominoidea accustomed to eating meat on any considerable scale. [11]

In addition to the digestive problems which meat-eating caused, meat greatly increased human disease. Parasites and bacteria abounded in the flesh men scavenged. When they killed a large animal and attempted to keep the meat for later use it rotted in the hot African sun before they ate it. Food poisoning must have been a common occurence.

If men wanted to make themselves sick, sobeit, but the consequences of hunting go far beyond a primordial belly ache. Hunting changed men in body, mind and spirit. The legacy of early men's decision to hunt and kill other animals is carried in the genes of men today. According to Washburn and Lancaster, human physical and psychobiological evolution was almost entirely the product of the hunting adaptation:

> [Hunting]...has dominated the course of human evolution for hundreds of thousands of years. In a very real sense our intellect, interests, emotions and basic social life--all are evolutionary products of the success of the hunting adaptation. ...The genus *Homo* has existed for some 600,000 years, and agriculture has been important only during the last few thousand years....Agricultural ways of life have dominated less than one per cent of human history, and there is no evidence of major biological changes during that time.... The entire evolution of man from the earliest populations of *Homo erectus* to the existing races took place during the period in which man was a hunter. [12]

Those traits which were adaptive for killing are those which modern men are heir to. Evidence of this is not hard to find as Washburn and Lancaster point out:

115

The extent to which the biological bases for killing have been incorporated into human psychology may be measured by the ease with which boys can be interested in hunting, fishing, fighting, and games of war. It is not that these behaviors are inevitable, but they are easily learned, satisfying, and have been socially rewarded in most cultures. The skills for killing and the pleasures of killing are normally developed in play, and the patterns of play prepare the children for their adult roles. [13]

Even though very few men on this planet need to hunt for a living now, the evolutionary trait persists in expressing itself. Without even the plausible excuse that killing is necessary for survival, men disguise their bloodlust as "sport" and frequently do not even eat the animals they kill. The truth, pure and simple, is that reenacting their progenitors' taking power over others is exciting and intrinsically pleasurable as Washburn and Lancaster say:

Men enjoy hunting and killing, and these activities are continued as sports even when they are no longer economically necessary....In former times royalty and nobility maintained parks where they could enjoy the sport of killing, and today the United States government spends many millions of dollars to supply game for hunters. Many people dislike the notion that man is naturally aggressive and that he naturally enjoys the destruction of other creatures. Yet we all know people who use the lightest fishing tackle to prolong the fish's futile struggle, in order to maximize the personal sense of mastery and skill. [14]

DOMINANCE, SUBMISSION AND MALE BONDING

The prehistoric decision to hunt *large* animals about a half million years ago meant that men, who previously had been able to scavenge on their own or in temporary groups just large enough to frighten away other scavengers, and who could kill small animals on their own, now needed to band together in order to overpower animals ten times their own size. At first glance it appears that the necessity to cooperate in the hunting of large animals would have had a beneficial effect on social interaction. This trait of cooperativeness could have become an asset in the human gene pool since those males who could work best with one another would have been those who would more often have survived long enough to produce offspring.

But was cooperation between males really what resulted from large game hunting? Did the prehistoric hunters become adept at collective decision-making--something we today find almost impossible? It is far more likely, based on the evidence of the relations between other hunting animals and the politics of the primates in general, that "cooperation" consisted mostly of the ability to form a tight chain of command, and, in fact, *dominance* and *submission* insured concerted group action rather than voluntary cooperation.

Certainly, if the organization of all-male groups today and during the approximately 3500 years of recorded history is any indication of the efficacy of male voluntary collective cooperation, we must ask why a chain of command with clear subordination of each rank to the one above it is the pattern universally chosen in the military, the church, government, boarding schools, fraternities, etc. The male bond, which large-game hunting in groups necessitated, increased the demand for a political organization with a clear chain of command. The word of the strongest and most adept killers was law--or the "grunt," as the case may be, since hunting and hierarchy may well have preceded language. Successful hunting among prehistoric males demanded a quick and ready response pattern when meat became available. There was no time for collective decision making when a rhino was coming over the ridge, or during the butchering and eating of the kill when scavengers were circling.

Robert Ardrey, probably the most widely-read of prehistory theorists, has pointed out that **meat-eating,** as infrequent as it is among non-human primates, instantly changes the degree of dominance which the male exhibits toward his troop members:

> The ape's relations are amiable, it is true, and
> if not egalitarian in the gorilla, certainly approx-
> imating the relationship in the chimp. But Goodall
> observed that when meat was at stake--when a
> chimp, for example, had caught and killed a mon-
> key or a bushbuck--the dominance of the killer
> was total. All others sat about with supplicating

117

hands, and while he dispensed a favor or two, he munched his meat in the alpha role, ignoring his inferiors. But the chimp kills infrequently. Our ancestors killed for a living. [15]

THE BEGINNINGS OF WAR

Competition *within* the male group was reduced by the strong dominance structure, tyrannical as it may have been, which facilitated the hunt. Competition *between* groups of prehistoric men, however, was greatly increased by meat-eating and hunting. Whereas herbivorous animals of different species can occupy the same territory relatively peacefully, carnivores can not. Predatory animals are not likely to trust others like themselves, full well knowing that they might be the victim of the same bloodlust which inspires their own actions. They lead wary and solitary existences, always on the lookout for enemies.

When prehistoric men became big game hunters they became possessive of the territories where their prey could be found. Washburn and DeVore describe how large game hunting brought about the delineation of territory and the necessity to "defend" it against strangers:

> The sources of vegetable food are normally so widespread that the overlapping of ranges does not appear serious, but with the hunting of large animals the matter is entirely different. If strangers hunt game, or even disturb it, scaring it from its normal routes, the plans of the local hunters are ruined. Hunting man requires a large area free from the interference of other hunters. When man became a hunter, his relation to the land changed from one in which a small range was adequate to one that demanded a large territory. [16]

With the birth of big game hunting over half a million years ago, then, we have the beginnings of the demand for private property and men's idea that they could "own" the earth. True, it was group ownership to begin with, based on the male-to-male bond which hunting necessitated, but ownership, nonetheless, which men would fight to retain. Territory based on men's blood rights over animals inevitably led to human bloodshed. Prehistoric war was the eventual consequence of the hunting adaptation.

The competition between hunting groups for large game territories increased as the human population increased. The hunters marked off their territories more precisely and began to defend them. Whereas we know that a certain type of pre-men called *Australopithecus robustus* who were vegetarians were able to live alongside other groups who were hunters, no records have ever been found which would indicate that two hunting bands could occupy the same territory for long. In fact, it has long been suspected that Cro-Magnon Man exterminated Neanderthal Man in humankind's first large-scale war. Both were large game hunters.

Washburn and Lancaster sum up the inevitable consequences of competition for territory and how men came to take pleasure in taking dominion over the earth and each other:

> Until recently war was viewed in much the same way as hunting. Other human beings were simply the most dangerous game. War has been far too important in human history for it to be other than pleasurable for the males involved. [17]

Men evolved from herbivores who did not need to kill and who had no means of killing; yet they became armed predators. They took the leap, as few primates do, to killing within their own species. It is postulated that men simply developed too fast for their own good. Their intelligence allowed them to invent weapons before their brains had evolved enough control mechanisms to keep their use of them within bounds.

All carnivores have instinctive mechanisms by which they control competitiveness within their own species. The clear signaling of submission by those who might have otherwise been attacked usually prevents a loss of life. Though male fights for access to females sometimes are vicious, they are rarely fatal. Each loser knows how to acknowledge defeat and each winner knows how to recognize and honor that acknowledgement. Fighting to the death is clearly not an advantage to a species; with the single exception of human males, animals have evolved with safeguards which protect against interspecific murder and warfare.

There has never been an animal war, but the earth has only rarely been free of human war. Lyall Watson says in *The Omnivorous Ape*:

119

We came from unarmed herbivory to armed
carnivory quickly, so we did not have enough time
to develop the proper safeguards. Instead of going
through the tens of millions of years necessary to
develop big teeth and sharp claws, we short-cir-
cuited the whole process and acquired spears and
daggers in a few hundred thousand years. We got
killing weapons without the usual instinctive inhibition against using them on ourselves. All we have
is a taboo enforced by moral and religious opinion.
This goes some way toward preventing us all from
eating one another; it works particularly well with
members of the same groups, tribe or race. But
it is not nearly strong enough to prevent man from
frequently killing other men--and occasionally eating
them. [18]

Almost every society on earth has regarded killing
members of certain other human societies as desirable,
and nearly as many have at some time practiced cannibalism. The taboo against cannibalism has, for the most
part, taken hold in modern civilization, but only in very
recent years has humankind begun to suspect that we should
institute a similar taboo on warfare:

It is only recently, with the entire change in the
nature and conditions of war, that this institution
has been challenged, that the wisdom of war as a
normal part of national policy or as an approved
road to personal social glory has been questioned. [19]

It is clear that human murder had its source in hunting and the selection of a meat-eating way of life. There
may have been a short time during a possible matriarchal
period between 6,000 to 10,000 years ago when women
were able to maintain a taboo on killing large animals and
other humans, but clearly their power was short-lived, for
recorded history begins with slaughter and warfare. The
half million-year-old evolutionary legacy of large game
hunting may have been too entrenched in masculine psycho-
physiology for a purely cultural prohibition against killing
to have worked for long.

Elizabeth Gould Davis in *The First Sex* describes how
men, naturally remorseful for taking life, in time came to
assuage their guilt by positing a male god to whom they
could do penance by killing:

120

The institution of sacrifice was a product of
man's shame and guilt at these drastic innovations.
Whereas the goddess had been satisfied with of-
ferings of fruits and vegetables and the foreskins
of circumcised males, the new male god demanded
sacrifices of blood. [20]

Out of guilt, then, the early patriarchy offered up animal
and even human blood in recompense for killing and eating
what humans were never intended to eat. The guilt was
even consciously recognized by some, and still the killing
went on once men had developed the taste for flesh. Lionel Tiger in *Men in Groups* points out that to this day
when Orthodox Jews eat meat, they must eat only animals
which have been slaughtered by a shochet, a ritual slaugh-
terer, who must sharpen his knife anew before each kill
and say a prayer indicating that he knows he is acting
against nature, but that his intentions are basically good
anyway. [21]

Male aggression as we know it today is not simply the
product of culture, the legacy of patriarchal religion, or
whatever doorstep that feminists have tended to lay the
evil at, but rather it is the result of the decision to hunt
large animals which men made at least a half million
years ago. If there was a "Fall," if Adam sinned, surely
it was then.

THE PREHISTORIC DEVELOPMENT OF SEX DIFFERENCES

What prevented early women from taking the male path
to violence? Our biology, simply put. That, and the dramatic change in the biological development of the human
infant concurrent with men's becoming large game hunters.
By half a million years ago, the adult human brain had
evolved to the point that it was at least three times as
large as our earliest hominid ancestors' and, in some cases, the adult brain was larger than ours average today.
If the human fetus's head had tripled in size it is easy to
see that a tremendous problem would have developed. It
would have been too large to pass through the mother's
pelvis if some adjustment had not been made. The com-
promise was that the female pelvis expanded some, and is
notably wider than the male's today, and most of the infant's brain maturation was delayed until after birth.

(Today babies are born with a brain only one-fourth the size of a two-year-old's.)

As a consequence of this delayed brain maturation, human prehistoric newborns became less capable of taking care of themselves than any other animal then alive. They were totally dependent on their mothers for all their needs and for a much longer period of time. At the same time that delayed brain maturation was beginning so that infants were being born more and more helpless, the prehensile grip which monkey infants are born with was leaving the human evolutionary scene. This meant that the young could no longer travel as readily as they had before. Mothers were less able to cavort around the countryside when they were obliged to cradle an infant in their arms. And obviously, with their arms full, they were certainly unfit candidates for participation in the hunting of large game. That their arms were frequently full is a reasonable assumption since certainly there was no birth control, and not even a glimmer about what caused babies in the first place.

Consequently, a great distinction developed between the roles of males and females. The men went off hunting with their all-male pack and the women stayed at home taking care of baby, waiting for the men to bring home the bacon. Even if a few early women had refused to stay at home and had joined the hunt, their likelihood of producing children, and thus of contributing their cantankerousness to the gene pool of the group, would have been greatly diminished because of their higher exposure to death, to miscarriage, and to the loss of their children, had they taken them along.

The majority of women stayed at home and gradually came to accept their dependence on the males for at least a part of their food and their infants'. They were still quite able to gather enough vegetation to feed themselves, and probably could have managed to obtain enough animal food to fill their quota of protein and B vitamins by robbing birds' nests and capturing small animals. But it is easy to see that such small animal harvesting would have begun to seem pointless when men were dragging home more rhinoceros than they could eat before it rotted.

The beginning of large game hunting marked the beginning of sexually dimorphous roles. Small-game hunting could have been done near the home base where women could have participated. According to William S. Laughlin, noted anthropologist, women have been found in contemporary primitive societies who participate equally with the men in small game hunting. [22] When prehistoric men began to hunt large animals the rigors of the hunt escalated beyond what women were capable of. First they had to find the elephants, rhinoceroses, etc. and then they often had to keep running for several days as the animal might take that long to finally drop from the minimal wounds which early hunters could inflict on such large beasts. Clearly, because of the demands of maternity, women were not cut out for the big kill. The female and male evolutionary paths diverged, as a result, and psychological differences developed which are still with us today.

In the half million years of organized male hunting for large game which encompassed nearly the entire span of human evolution, the male system adapted to the dangers of the hunt. It is not hard to understand why today they are more wary, more alert to threat, and more likely to react to that perceived threat with attack than are women. Their bodies evolved to meet the needs of the hunt. The brawniest and those most able to endure running after their prey, sometimes for the two or three days it took the large wounded beasts to finally drop dead, obviously would be those who would survive long enough to make a greater contribution to the gene pool. Since early men could probably not have outrun many of the animals on earth at the time, we can readily see why attack behavior would have been favored over flight behavior. Those men who fled an animal who decided to turn the tables on the hunters would have had a greatly reduced chance of producing offspring.

As mentioned in chapter one, males have a notably greater spatial ability than females. One skill that hunters would have had to develop was an ability to tell exactly where their prey was and to estimate how long it would take them or their weapons to reach it. Their very lives depended on the understanding of the relationship between time and distance, their bodies and the body of their prey. It is no accident that today, given approximately equal practice, men will nearly always outperform women on target games like darts and precision archery.

Men today are less capable of estimating the size of their body than women are; usually they give an exaggerated estimate of their girth in body perception tests. Perhaps this is accounted for by the possibility that thinking big might have had survival value in tight situations during the prehistoric hunt. Confidence, albeit false, might have saved the life of a hunter or a warrior.

It is not hard to figure out why men might have a higher threshold for pain than women do. A wounded hunter would best have ignored his pain if he wanted to keep up with the hunting band which protected him. Without the protection of the troop he was dead. Too, he who showed his pain would have indicated submission and defeat. He would have lost status in the dominance structure and been less likely to have had access to females, and hence, offspring.

Males did not develop one ability that was crucial for females to develop in order to preserve the species--the nurturance of the young. Hunting males would have found no survival value in learning to relate lovingly to their children or their female consorts. Playing with babies or romancing with women was not consistent with the activities of hunter man.

Because the preservation of the species directly depended on there being enough women who survived long enough to bear a number of children and raise them to an age where they were self-sufficient, women's physiology became basically sturdier than men's. Females, from the cradle to the grave, are today more resistant to genetic aberrations and disease. It was only necessary that a few prehistoric men be available to impregnate women; thus, men's physical stability and longevity were not as strenuously selected for as women's.

Females developed different social traits which were compatible with their role in early hunting groups. Women dealt with all the complexities of relationships at the home base, as well as providing for the physical well-being of the dependent young and the elderly. Without a dominance structure like hunter males developed, women had to become expert at arbitrating differences. For this, language was a necessity. Additionally, females in prehistoric groups had nearly total responsibility for providing a model of speech for children to learn from. As two noted researchers in the etiology of sex differences point out:

> ...among primate species, there is no doubt that, as in mammalian species generally, the growing primate infant spends most of its time in the company of its mother. Thus, for language to evolve among primates, it must have been necessary for *females* to be particularly adept at the newly developing linguistic skills so that they would be

likely to use them in the presence of their offspring. It seems probable that this is the selection pressure which resulted in the existing human
sex differences in verbal ability. [23]

Although purely speculative, it is tempting to think that
males' adaptation toward hunting and participation in the
male dominance structure may have decreased their ability
to make fine moral distinctions, and their willingness to
follow suggestions which are not backed up by threats.

Finally, we can see that male physiology adapted for
the strenuous life of hunting would, of necessity, be different than females'. Men today have an average of one-
third more muscle tissue than women. This is largely due
to a genetic inheritance from their hunting ancestors. In
addition to muscle, men are plainly built differently. Their
bodies are more suited to running long distances and their
metabolism is geared for strenuous exercise. Perhaps
this accounts for the high activity level of most male children, and the fact that 78% of all hyperkinetic children are
boys.

One simple somatic difference which is universally sex-
dependent is a direct result of the hunting adaptation. According to A. Kortlandt and M. Kooij, men developed the
throwing style which any girl knows must be cultivated if
she wants to throw like the boys on the baseball diamond. [24]
The gorillas "throw like girls" to this day. The overhand
throw is a motor pattern which men developed over thousands of years of armed hunting; the vegetarian primates
and all females evolved without it.

Lionel Tiger in *Men in Groups* proposes that:

> ...hunting widened the gap between the behavior of
> males and females. It favoured those 'genetic pac-
> kages' which arranged matters so that males hunted
> co-operatively in groups while females engaged in
> maternal and some gathering activity. Not only
> were there organic changes in perception, brain
> size, posture, hand formation, locomotion, etc.,
> but there were also social structural changes. [25]

THE MALE-FEMALE RELATIONSHIP

The primary "social structural change" was the sexual

division of economic activity which large-game hunting engendered. All other primates forage for their food, the
mother providing for the infant's needs for the short while
when it is dependent on her. According to Washburn and
DeVore:

> ... Once hunting became important to the groups,
> children had to depend on adults for many years.
> ... Hunting large animals made children and fe-
> males economically dependent. [26]

Ardrey tells us:

> From the beginning of meat-eating, the female
> found that her place was in the home. Our homi-
> nid social group suffered, in consequence, func-
> tional segregation. There was the band of adult
> and sub-adult males who went out on the hunt. And
> there was the home group at the cave or living-
> site, the women, infants, boys too young to hunt,
> girls too young to reproduce. These were the
> collectors who scoured the locality for scarce edible
> fruits and plants, snared a bird or a rabbit, even
> caught a fawn or two. And so there was the man's
> world, and there was the woman's world, and
> there was obligation. Of almost two hundred spe-
> cies of living primates, we are the only one in
> which beyond the time of weaning anyone feeds any-
> body else. With meat-eating came division of
> labor and the obligation of the hunter to feed those
> who could not hunt. [27]

It is ironic that even though large-game hunting made
such a drastic change in the course of human evolution,
females never really needed the large amounts of meat
that the males provided. They did need some animal food
in their diet, but they were capable of providing it for
themselves.

Perhaps this knowledge that the killing of large animals
was not really necessary underlay some primitive females'
instigation of taboos surrounding the hunting and eating of
large game. Or perhaps females, because of their mother-
ing roles and the nurturance they had come to provide their
young, were more empathetic with the helpless, and resis-
ted male efforts to take life. Evelyn Reed, in her book
Woman's Evolution, has extensively documented primitive

126

woman's efforts to place controls on the killing and eating of large animals. [28]   Ms. Reed feels that the primitive taboos sprang from woman's desire to protect her children and herself from the ultimate in male hunting--cannibalism.

That men didn't stop with killing other animals is clear since cannibalism has been practiced in at least a hundred different cultures stretching around the globe.   There is unmistakable evidence of cannibalism in Paleolithic sites from 250,000 years ago. [29]   In fact, cannibalism was practiced over five million years ago, according to Raymond Dart, by our ancient ancestor, *Australopithicus Africanus* :

> Australopithicus lived a grim life.   He ruthlessly killed fellow Australopithecines and fed upon them as he would upon any other beast, young or old. He was a flesh eater and as such had to seize his food where he could and protect it night and day from other carnivorous marauders.... Life was bought at the price of eternal vigilance. [30]

Dart tells us that all men, up until Neolithic times, practiced cannibalism.   The taboos which women were able to instill in the world's primitive cultures finally controlled most of the eating of human flesh.   Yet, to this day the Tierra del Fuegians are known to enjoy flesh of their own species.   Lyall Watson says "they seem to be particularly fond of their old women." [31]   And, there were many reports of Cambodian soldiers devouring the fallen enemy during the recent war.

Evelyn Reed emphasizes that it was prehistoric woman, not man, who was responsible for instigating and enforcing the taboos surrounding the hunting and killing of meat and the protections against cannibalism. [32]   She notes the possibility of endemic differences in male and female nutritional needs and that this may be reflected in the sexual "food division" which is still observed in some contemporary primitive societies.   In the Masai tribe in East Africa, for example, the male diet is almost entirely milk, blood, and meat, whereas the women are predominantly vegetarian.

Some primitive women's repulsion for meat-eating was so great that they insisted that meat-eating men not be allowed to dine with them.   In fact, meal-time separation of the sexes, according to Reed, is one of the most widely observed of primitive taboos. [33]   In numerous primitive cultures male children are breast-fed and then given vegetable foods until they are between six and ten years old, when they are sent to eat meat with the males. Elderly men, in some cases, are readmitted to the women's dining room and return to a vegetarian diet.

In many cultures, primitive women have considered the act of hunting to be defiling and refused to associate with the hunters until they are purified of their uncleanliness. For a period that begins some days before the hunt and extends sometimes even as long as a month afterward, the women will not have sexual intercourse with the men. At the end of every hunt, such women insist on decontamination rituals before they associate once again with the men. Reed says:

> ...After every expedition, before the men could return to any kind of association with women, they had to be decontaminated of the blood they had shed, the flesh they had eaten, and the blood they had drunk in the hunt or fight. [34]

She quotes two accounts which are so explicit and to the point as to warrant recounting them here in full:

> ...Naturally, therefore, the shedder of blood is regarded as taboo. Amongst the Yumas of Colorado the manslayer is taboo for a month, during which time he must fast, and the Kaffir is "unclean" after a battle. Animal blood produces the same effects. The Hottentot after a hunt must purify himself from the blood of the animals he has slain. [35]

> ...Among the Thonga the slaying of enemies in battle entails great glory for the slayers, but also great danger to them. "They have killed. So they are exposed to the mysterious and deadly influence of the *nuru* and must consequently undergo medical treatment. What is the *nuru*? *Nuru* is the spirit of the slain which drives them to take revenge on the slayer. It haunts him and may drive him to insanity; his eyes swell, protrude, and become inflamed." He will go out of his mind, be attacked by giddiness, and the thirst for blood may even lead him to fall upon members of his own family. To avoid such terrible consequences

the slayers are placed under many taboos. They
put on old clothes, eat with special spoons, and
from special plates and broken pots. They are
not allowed to drink water. Their food must be
cold; if it was hot it would make them swell in-
ternally, because, say the natives, "they are hot
themselves, they are defiled." Sexual relations
are absolutely forbidden them. After some days
a medicine man comes to purify them and remove
their "black." When this has been accomplished,
all the implements used by the slayers during their
seclusion and all their old garments are tied together, hung upon a tree and left there to decay. 36

At some point women lost the ability to impress upon
the men that they killed other animals and other men at the
peril of displeasing the gods (goddesses) and the women.
Until the tragedy of the Vietnam war began to make it
clear that the real heroes were those who remained at
home or went to jail for their convictions, the majority of
women in our culture have fallen at the feet of those returning victors whose hands were bloodiest and bodies most
decorated with the symbols of their murder. Somewhere
along the way, we forgot our knowledge of the sanctity of
all life and the risk of annihilation which attends its squan-
dering. Surely our sisters knew nothing of the danger we
now face because of the male propensity for violence, but
by making it more complicated for men to both enjoy the
social rewards of the group and to hunt, they prolonged at
least for a while the time when men would come to take
dominion over the earth and all of earth's inhabitants.
It is not that primitive woman was more moral, more
in tune with nature, closer to angel than ape--it was, you'll
remember, woman's reproductive equipment which inclined
her to feel differently about the wisdom of killing than men
did. She was physically less capable of large-game hunting and came to associate that kind of killing with the in-
vasions of strangers who considered even her offspring to
be prey. Her defense could not have been a physical one,
as men have evolved to have greater strength and endur-
ance. Only by invoking their fear of the unknown, through
the use of magic if you will, and by withdrawing one of
men's most necessary pleasures--sex--could women enforce
their taboo. But these sanctions proved too weak a deterrent. Male physiology precluded the efficacy of less than
biological interdictions, and, in the end, the taboo was not

enough to prevent the rivers of history from running red with human blood.

Prehistoric women may well have unwittingly abetted the genetic transmission of those unfortunate proclivities which the hunting life had inscribed on the genes of the male of the species. Oblivious to any harm, they may have helped to insure that males would become progressively more aggressive and that their bodies would become ever more specialized for the hunt. Elizabeth Gould Davis has suggested in *The First Sex* that since it is known that meat-eating noticeably increases the size of the genitals, early women were more attracted to the most carnivorous and aggressive of the troop and mated with them, thereby passing on those traits to their male children. [37] This assumes that women have always been impressed by phallic size--something I just can't bring myself to accept. Rather, it seems that women might have paid homage to the best bread-winners of the troop by sleeping with them-- and that's assuming it was a woman's prerogative to mate with whom she chose. Lionel Tiger points out that female primates in general tend to choose males high on the dominance hierarchy to mate with. [38] Nothing attracts like success, as the saying goes.

In cases where it was *not* up to primitive women to choose who they would sleep with, the dominant and most violent males laid claim to them and prevented less aggressive males from having sex with them. Consequently, sex-linked traits associated with dominance and aggression are the ones which were contributed to the gene pool.

Peter Matthiessen, a member of the Harvard-Peabody expedition to New Guinea, was concerned with the question of which primitive men are allowed to contribute to the gene pool. Robert Bigelow recounts Matthiessen's findings:

> ...all men were equally competitive warriors in the Kurelo tribe. Some of them go to war with the others, but remain well to the rear. During lulls in the battle they are allowed to associate with, or even to sit beside, the greatest warriors. They are nevertheless held in some contempt, and their rank in the dominance structure is low. They are called "kepu," which means "a-man-who-has-not-killed."...they are never jeered or driven into battle, but any wives or pigs they have might be taken from them. Few kepu men have more than one wife, and many have no wives at all....the wife of

130

a kepu man, if he has one, might be raped by
other men. This...is the law, and should the
kepu man resist it he might be killed or expelled
from the group. 39

Obviously, in this case a woman has no choice but to conceive the children of the most violently aggressive men of
the troop.

With the exception of rape, in technologically advanced
societies, however, women usually have total power to decide who will contribute genes to their offspring. Hopefully, as the insanity of war and the brutality of killing
nature's creatures becomes more apparent to us, women
will begin to choose their consorts more wisely. Not
every girl longs for a John Wayne. In time, perhaps,
such men will be as untempting a marriage prospect as
Cro-Magnon Man--an outmoded specimen of the male of
the species, and a poor candidate for fatherhood.

Probably, more often than not, early women did not
have a choice as to whom they would have sex with. The
male, physically adapted for the rigors of the hunt, was
larger, more powerful, and more practiced in dominance
skills than the female. It is hard to imagine that a man
would run two days straight for the opportunity to kill a
beast ten times his size and viciously kill a member of
his own troop, but wait patiently for a woman to offer
her favors.

Many feminists have found it demeaning to admit that
women have always been dominated by men. The evidence from primitive peoples and from our primitive relatives suggests that males have had power over females
from time immemorial, with the possible exception of the
short period of matriarchy. Females have been subject
to male power just as low status males have been subject
to dominant males in the social hierarchy. Primate females needn't fight to establish a higher position in society, however. They obtain rank by consorting with higher ranking males. Females fuck their way up the social
ladder, so to speak. But even if they become the general's "wife" they are still subject to the will of the general.

Just as dominance is established between primate
males by intermittent tests of physical prowess, so the
male establishes his power over females by occasional
reminders of his brute strength. Ardrey gives the fol-

131

lowing account of how the boss baboon keeps "the wife" in line:

> The big male hamadryas has a harem of four or
> five females who must follow him at a distance of
> no greater than three meters. Should one stray
> further, then he leaps at her and reinforces her
> following response by biting her neck. That follow-
> ing is not innate, but perhaps learned in adoles-
> cence, was demonstrated when a female raised in
> captivity was turned free in Ethiopia. A male
> promptly annexed her. But no matter how pain-
> fully he might bite her, she could not follow him.
> She did not know how. [40]

It is important to emphasize that submission is learned
--it is the result of conditioning which is successful because of the physical difference in size and strength between the sexes. A male's ability to dominate a female
says nothing of his intelligence, his creativity, his value
as one of nature's creatures--it only says that he sur-
passes the female in physical power. It is preposterous
to use the argument that because primate and primitive
males have always dominated females that it is natural
that they continue to do so. Such an argument could as
easily justify slavery and cannibalism to one with limited
reasoning powers. If it were possible to condone a man's
dominating a woman by physical force as only "natural,"
then by the same logic we should have boxing matches to
determine who will be mayor, governor and president.
The point is that brute strength may have been an efficient
way of organizing society among primates or primitives,
but the time has long since passed when human interaction
could be facilitated by such an arrangement.
Unfortunately, females are subject to more violence
than just the husbandly reminders of who will wear the
pants. As it happens, males who are experiencing competitive tension with other males often redirect their aggressive feelings and attack the female or her children.
The old "I couldn't kill the boss so I'm yelling at you" syndrome. For the moment we are considering *origins* of
male-female relations, and hence we focus on primate and
primitive societies. The contemporary human counterparts
are myriad and so much a part of our cultural stereotypes
that we hardly need dwell on them. D. Hamburg describes
a typical case where the tension of a dominance struggle

between near-equals causes a chimpanzee male to vent his anger on a female and her young:

> Bananas are made available from time to time as a very attractive dietary supplement for both chimpanzees and baboons in the area. These are tense occasions when a good deal of threatening goes on between males of similar rank. What happens typically is that one of them will break off prior to fighting (usually high-ranking males do not fight each other) and attack a smaller, weaker, or less mobile animal. We saw one of those adult males attacking a mother with a ten-month-old infant clinging to her, giving her a severe beating, mainly with his fists and forearm. He did this to the same mother-infant pair three times within a week in these situations of redirected aggression. On one occasion he actually knocked them out of a tree from a height of about 30 feet. Thus, the infant, though generally treated with great tolerance, is not always immune to these episodes of redirected aggression.
> After a dominant male has established his control of the bananas, other chimps may try to get him to share with them. An experienced female, for example, may back up to him in a lowered posture. This is called presenting, and it is common in a number of primates in agonistic situations. After she gets up to him, he may put his arm around her waist and give her a hug or a pat on the head. [41]

First the female must endure the random violence of disgruntled male competitors and suffer their attacks on her offspring as well, and then, in order to get a morsel of food, the female must *back* towards the male with her ass in the air, which is the primate signal that she is ready for sex. Could there be a clearer case of buying kitchen privileges with those of the boudoir? And please notice that what the female chimpanzee gets is a pat on the head, not the banana.

Is it any wonder that females have had to come up with cunning devices to deal with such ornery creatures? "She uses sex as a weapon," men say of a woman who has learned to get her way, despite male dominance, by appealing directly to the male weakness for sex. Even female chimpanzees are versed in this trade-off of violence for sex. Females in a chimpanzee troop sometimes are successful in calming violent males by gently touching and stroking their scrotums. [42]

Peace-making via sexual seduction has developed into a fine art among the female langurs in India. Anthropologist Sarah Blaffer Hardy observed these monkeys for five years; *The Harvard Gazette* reported her finding that only through sexual deception could the female langurs save their offspring from being murdered by males. [43] Male langurs expend much of their energy trying to assert dominance over as many females as possible. The males viciously defend their "possessions" from invaders who try to put the make on the females. Early in their evolution, female langurs developed an adaptation which causes them to automatically return to estrus whenever they lose an infant. Male langurs evolved in a way that exploits this adaptation. Invading langur males who are successful in conquering the prior male overlords, kill all of the infants of the troop. This has a dual effect: it lessens the genetic contribution of the weaker males, and by bringing the females into heat, it immediately allows the contribution of more aggressive genetic material to the gene pool of the group.

The *Harvard Gazette* article shows how females have tried to circumvent this eventuality:

> ...while infanticide is adaptive for males, it is obviously less so for females, who are forced to waste all the energy they have put into bearing and rearing the child to that point. As a consequence, females have developed a number of strategies that protect their children. When an alien male approaches the troop, he is attacked both by the resident male and by the females, who thereby reduce the number of takeovers. Even when the resident male decides for some reason to tolerate alien males, the females do not; they will either attack him and try to drive him away or will themselves leave the troop. When a new male has taken over, the females may form alliances among themselves to protect each other's infants; even childless females play a role in defending the infants of others.

> Mrs. Hardy reports that she often saw females successfully delaying infanticide by these techniques, but only rarely were they able to prevent it in the

long run. For this reason, the most effective counter-infanticide strategy is probably deception. Males appear to tell whether an infant is theirs by remembering whether they copulated with the female. One often sees pregnant females presenting them selves to new leaders and shaking their heads. Ordinarily these are the signs females give when they are ready for fertilization. When the females that are already pregnant give these signals, one might suppose that they hope that when the baby is born the new male will be "fooled" into thinking it is his. [44]

SEX AND VIOLENCE

Infanticide was widely practiced by primitive peoples. Archeology suggests that prehistoric peoples sacrificed females much more often than males and some anthropologists think that human males evolved to be hypersexual, when compared with monkeys and apes, because of the selective advantage it would have afforded them to be able to produce more children from whom they could select only the strongest and most adept for hunting--the aggressive male children. Dr. Gordon D. Jenson says of this:

> I would suggest that hypersexuality permits a greater reproductive rate, which in turn permits a society to deliberately select males to enhance its strength. Studies of some primitive tribes living today in South America...suggest that prehistoric man had a surplus of births and practiced infanticide favoring males. The skeletal remains of adult fossil man show a sex ratio of 125 males to 100 females.... For early man, as with primitive man today, the preponderance of males could have served the needs of warfare and hunting, thereby enhancing the strength of the group and promoting its survival. Early in human evolution hypersexuality may have facilitated hyperaggression. [45]

Sex and aggression would appear to be inextricably connected in our primate and primitive heritage. Kenneth Moyer has written extensively on the connection between sex and violence:

...Freud has suggested that aggression is an essential and integral part of sexual feelings in the male. However, because of normal biological variability, sex-related aggression sometimes exceeds optimal bounds and becomes sexual violence with severe injury and, frequently, death as a result. Evidence of sex-related aggression abounds in the daily newspaper.... Although this type of aggressive behavior assumes its more variable and bizarre forms in the human, it is also found in other species....

Mating behavior in many species involves motor components that are very similar to those found in intermale aggression or in prey catching....In some cases, it is difficult to distinguish mating behavior from an intense aggressive encounter....

...Sex related aggression in animals sometimes exceeds adaptive bounds, as it does in humans. Carpenter has made extensive field observations of the rhesus monkey and reports that males frequently frequently attack estrus females. Observations of 45 estrus periods revealed that 22 females were attacked, and six of them were severely wounded. one of them lost parts of both ears, received severe cuts on the arm, and a number of wounds on the face and muzzle. Another had a leg wound severe enough to make her limp for several days. Others had deep thigh cuts, bruised noses, deep gashes, and one received such a deep wound in the hip that the motor nerve was damaged and she became a permanent cripple....

...aggression may constitute a sadistic component of the normal mating behavior of rhesus monkeys. A necessary condition to serial copulation and the consort relations seemingly is that the female be driven to a state of submission, of "awe" and of complete "rapport" in relation to the male. [46]

Such "rapport" is sometimes euphemistically referred to as "love." Females mistake such aggression for ardor at their peril. Briffault, in his three-volume classic, *The Mothers*, clarifies the terms:

It would be more accurate to speak of the sexual impulse as pervading nature with a yell of cruelty than with a hymn of love.... The male animal cap-

tures, mauls and bites the female, who in turn uses her teeth and claws freely, and the lovers issue from the sexual combat bleeding and mangled....
All mammals without exception use their teeth on these occasions. [47]

Women, before "buying him Brut," should consider the consequences of invoking man's animal nature. It has been found, in a study of prisoners, that the more sexual fantasies a man has, the more aggressive fantasies he has, and vice versa. When his sexual arousal is increased so is his level of aggressiveness. [48]

Among our predatory relatives, sex violence can lead to murder and cannibalism:

All carnivorous animals...are cannibalistic. Lions and tigers, which furnish favorite examples of mating among carnivora, commonly kill and devour their mates....Half-grown tiger cubs, orphaned by their mother being killed, are attacked and eaten by their father....Wolves commonly kill and eat their mates. [49]

Not only is there a clear correlation of sex with violence throughout the animal kingdom, but sex also plays a part in *male to male* dominance struggles and aggression. Culturally advanced human males have discreetly disguised this aspect of masculine behavior, but a look at primates and primitive human societies will enable us to see the pattern through the contemporary camouflage.

The Gothic variety of the male squirrel monkey provides a most graphic example. [50] He signals 1) his aim to dominate another male, 2) his intention to assault him, *and* 3) his amorous ideas about a female--all three--by shoving his erect phallus into the face of the other monkey while grinding his teeth. The courtship display is identical to the aggressive display. Ethologists have found this crossed-wire phenomenon in numerous reptilian and lower forms. The threatening intent of the male monkey's shoving his penis in the other monkey's face is made clear by the fact that if the subordinate monkey does not remain quiet and perfectly still during the display it will be viciously attacked. The female must show her "awe" or be assaulted just as the subordinate male must. The use of the phallus as weapon is very much a part of our animal heritage, but perhaps it is difficult to imagine the human counterpart.

Carlton Gajdusek, who has extensively studied the primitive peoples of New Guinea, reports that there are numerous groups who practice penile display to express aggression and dominance as well as fearful, erotic and celebratory feeling. [51] The males of the group display their erect phalluses to each other or to a stranger who threatens, in a somewhat ritualized dance. Dissatisfied with a handgun, so to speak, many of these groups wear huge tubular gourds on their penises to enhance their effectiveness as threatening weapons. The phallocrypts, as these are called, are sometimes so long as to interfere with the vision of the wearer.

By now the alert reader must be wondering how this behavior could possibly relate to a contemporary setting. It should be easy to see the connection if we consider that much of "civilized" male aggressive behavior is verbal, and note the nature of most of the phrases men use: Fuck you!, up yours!, motherfucker!, bust your balls!, kiss my ass!, jerk off! Could the connection between sex and aggression be clearer? Beyond the verbal, think about the aggressive gestures used in cultures around the world. In America it's shooting a bird, which loosely translates as "up yours," as does the frequent Italian fist display. Anal-genital slang and gestures undoubtedly form a part of the aggressive repertoire of every culture. Gadjusek points out that a nearly universal gesture, sticking out the tongue, derives from the same source as the phallic display, the tongue simply being a polite substitute for the erect penis. [52]

Any time that we find such a clear cross-cultural pattern it is time to ask what the biological foundations of such a behavior might be. As with sex-linked variation in aggressive behavior, which has been found to be at least in part due to differences in the brains of males and females, we might very well suspect that there is a neurological basis for the frequent connection of sex and violence. And indeed there is. P.D. McClean has found that locations which elicit penile erection, anger and fear are all located within a millimeter of each other in the limbic lobe of the human brain. Frequently stimulation of one of these points will trigger a response in the others. There is a "spillover effect" where fear can be sexually arousing and sexual arousal can provoke anger. That the connection of anger with penile erection is not a learned behavior pattern, but innate in the male organism, is supported by McClean's observation that:

> One sees combative behavior even in the nursing
> babe which will angrily fight the breast if no milk
> is forthcoming, and at the same time develop penile
> erection. [53]

McClean is struck by how the neuroanatomical evidence
supports Freud's early theorizing about violence and sex.
Freud had noted how many people were "turned on" by
horror movies, the sight of a house burning to the ground,
etc. He pointed out how cruelty was a part of the sexual
response even in childhood and warned parents that children who were given to torturing animals and insects could
well become prematurely hypersexual. McClean quotes
Freud:

> A number of persons report that they experienced
> the first signs of excitement in their genitals during
> fighting or wrestling with playmates.... The infantile
> connection between fighting and sexual excitement
> acts in many persons as a determinant for the future
> preferred course of their sexual impulse. [54]

Once we understand that electrical stimulation can spill
over from one location to another in the brain, and the
incredible proximity of the sites which elicit violence, fear,
and sexual excitation, we begin to grasp the reasons behind
sexual sadomasochism. Male violence can be sexual and
male sexuality is often violent. Though no studies have
been done on it as yet, it would be most interesting to see
if there is a higher threshold for electrical spillover between the sex-fear-anger areas of the female brain than the
male. This would not be necessary to "explain" the difference in male and female behavior since, even without
the limbic connections, the male higher brain could learn
to make the connections symbolically.

That the connection of sex with pain is predominantly
a male phenomenon is so apparent as to obviate discussion.
In America sadomasochism has become accepted enough
that during 1975 leading magazines, including *Vogue*, and
several fashionable department stores in New York City
used it as a ploy to sell clothing. One fashion feature in
Vogue showed a young woman in a jumpsuit being beaten
by a man with an eery grin on his face. The caption
assured us that this outfit "can really take the heat."

Recently a popular movie advertised that it portrayed "the ultimate sexual act--the only one which can never be repeated"--sexual murder. Where, we might ask, did men come up with this one? Who could possibly think that murder could have anything to do with eroticism? Once again, returning to our origins, we find that murder and sex were connected in many primitive cultures. Headhunting was pervasive in primitive tribes around the world; the impetus to this behavior was, at least in part, sexual. A man proved his sexual prowess by bringing home a head, and indeed in some cultures he could not marry until he had produced evidence of having killed. [54]

Today what remains of the headhunting practice is largely confined to the islands of New Guinea. Some of the customs of the tribes occupying the southern portion of the islands are described by Gadjusek, who studied the interconnection of headhunting and sexuality:

> The...Asmat father dutifully headhunted to assure the puberty and genital maturation of his prepubertal and early-pubertal son, who then slept with the head between his legs.... The headhunting ritual was associated with dancing and feasting, periods of licensed sexual promiscuity, and the complex initiation and training period for young prospective headhunters by older mentors, which usually involved an adopted father-son, and eventually homosexual, relationship. The failure to headhunt was considered to interfere with a man's fertility and his power to procreate. [55]

We may note, with interest, that in this case it is the murder of a male that is called for. But in our culture the latest baroque twist in "sexual freedom" calls for the death of a female. The following excerpt from an article in the *San Francisco Examiner* dated October 2, 1975, shows the length to which "civilized" man will go to satisfy his two interconnected drives--sex and violence:

The Ultimate Low in Pornographic Movies

> New York--Police are investigating reports of a bizarre brand of pornographic movies that show the actual murder and dismemberment of an actress on screen.
>
> Viewers reportedly pay up to $200 to witness

the filmed killings, detective Joseph Horman of the organized crime control bureau said yesterday.

Horman said very reliable sources say eight movies--called "snuff" or "slasher" films--are in circulation.

They were said to have been screened here, in New Orleans, Miami and Los Angeles, although no law enforcement office apparently has seen the films.

The Los Angeles Police Department says it checked out the story six months ago and found no evidence that such a film exists.

Horman said the films began with an actress and several actors engaging in a variety of sex acts. Soon, a knife appears, and the actress--obviously unaware of the nature of the film--is stabbed to death and dismembered.

He said a number of films simulate death, but the eight he is after show real killings.

"What is really astonishing," Horman said, "is that there is such a market. That's almost as astonishing as the fact that somebody would actually commit a murder for the purpose of making a film."

DOMINION AND DESTINY

Evolutionary argument has been frequently used to justify males' domination of each other and of womankind. It is important to clearly state, then, that evolution is not necessarily the reflection of "what is natural to the species" and therefore that which inevitably came to be according to nature's grand design; at least in human evolution, we are experiencing the final throes of an *unnatural* development, a *maladaptive selection* which we must consciously come to recognize as such and vigorously try to overcome.

At the moment, our task is the basic one of all species--figuring out how to survive. Human males have made that very basic and simple problem, which we share with all living things, into the nightmare we are now faced with. In the next chapter we'll look closer at how men's hunting heritage is expressed today and how men have come to threaten the life of the planet. In the chapters following the next, (take courage!) we will explore the possibilities

141

for our *conscious evolution* away from the hunting mentality. The days of Hunter Man are numbered--either he
goes or we all do--the choice is ours.

Chapter Four

MAN'S DOMINION:
THE HUNTER TODAY

We remain Upper Paleolithic hunters, fine-honed machines designed for the efficient pursuit of game. Nothing worth noting has happened in our evolutionary history since we left off hunting and took to the fields and the towns.... "Man the hunter" is not an episode in our distant past: we are still man the hunter, incarcerated, domesticated, polluted, crowded and bemused.
> --Lionel Tiger and Robin Fox [1]

We can no longer excuse human violence on the basis of our biological ancestry.   --J. P. Scott [2]

The psychobiology that underlies male behavior today is an artifact of men's early decision to take dominion over other creatures, other humans, and the earth. The message to *take dominion* is "wired into" the brains of men today; it specifies behavior which has come to jeopardize human life--indeed, all life on this planet.

Human biology is not destiny, however, for unlike all other living creatures we have a degree of consciousness which permits us to overrule negative programming, whether it be genetic or the result of adverse conditioning. The human neocortex has afforded us the unique opportunity to anticipate the future and to adapt accordingly. We can see the pathology of old programs and consciously choose to implement new ones. Neither the pawns of our ancient history, nor the helpless victims of our upbringing, we can foresee the consequences of our behavior and change before natural selection is brought to bear on us. Our evolution is in our hands.

The power to anticipate the future and to consciously alter its course is ours, but like all power it can be a-bused. We have seen how the abuse of power began with Hunter Man. The earth's ecosystem was flexible enough to absorb the losses for a long time, but the day is rapid-ly approaching when it will have reached the limits of tol-erance. Either we recognize this and use our power to dig out the root of the problem or we concede our right to live on the planet.

The chronic social and ecological difficulties we face are universal. No one is safe or protected. In order to cope with this degree of threat, most people attempt to block out all but the most immediate problems. We for-feit part of our unique human birthright--the potential for prior adaptation based on a wide-range view of the future. Who can stand to think of famine, nuclear war, poisoned air and water, violent crime, economic chaos, the energy crisis, racism, imperialism, sexism, etc. all at once? We bracket these off from one another and concern our-selves, perhaps, with those which we think will have the most direct effect on us. We assure ourselves that no one could possibly have the time to work on all at once.

Either we accede to "the inevitable," throw up our hands and declare that there is nothing we can do, or we blinker ourselves like horses so that we can devote our-selves to one cause while avoiding all others. We decide if we are Black that the root of all evil is racism. If we are women, then surely it is sexism. If we are poor, then it is unequal opportunity and the class system which causes our misery. But what if we are Black, female and poor? Then it becomes quite obvious that all problems are interlocking, that one is not "our problem" to the exclusion of any of the rest. If Blacks attain their freedom, if wo-men do, if the poor do, and that freedom consists of the right to eat poisoned food, to breathe poison air, and to live only in monstrous cities or on land contaminated by radiation--then who is free? The possibility of total nucle-ar destruction should make it quite obvious that none of us can be safe or free until we all are. But where to start?

It is precisely our unique human ability to see the wide range of past and future and to deduce the common causes of all our problems which we are called upon to use use at this point in history. Nature's cosmic dictum has always been *adapt or die*. The complexities of our problems today require that we do much more than adapt to our local habitat, the immediate challenges to *our* survival. We are at the point where what we must understand and adapt to is the confluence of *all* the challenges to *worldwide* survival. Our hope lies in our potential to see the whole, to find the root causes of our problems and a wholistic solution. We can no longer treat the symptoms and hope to effect a cure. In this chapter we will take an overview of some of humankind's most pressing problems in a modest attempt to unblinker our horses.

To begin with the least metaphorical tableau of contemporary Hunter Man, we should envision the fifteen million men in the U. S. alone who regularly hunt and kill other animals. 3 We must begin to open our ears to the cries of billions of animals who struggle for hours, sometimes days, in cruel traps; we must not fail to see the lakes of blood spilled by the seal clubbers; and we can not avert our eyes from the sight of a freshly killed deer draped over the hood of some yokel's car, spewing a trail of blood down the highway.

The suffering that hunters inflict on millions of animals each year is beyond our imagining. But we would be wrong to think that the full consequence of the hunters' plunder is animal suffering and the reduction and extinction of certain mammalian and bird species. One of the most horrific consequences of their killing is the opportunity it affords all of us to *do nothing* about it and thus to become accessories to their acts of violence. Few of us, even at this most basic level, protest the unnecessary wielding of power over other creatures and the wasteful taking of life.

We have seen the psychobiology which prehistoric hunting has left men heir to, but even the most primitive man on earth never killed what he did not intend to eat. Many contemporary hunters kill with no idea of eating the flesh they have taken. The sport hunters today make it absolutely clear that what hunters love is to kill, *not* to kill in order to eat. The glories of the chase supersede any moral feeling they may have. By separating animals into

145

"them" and "us" they can kill a deer or a rabbit with the same dispassionate ease as a soldier who is killing a "gook" or a "commie." A "non-person" is fair game.

The denial that we too are animals, the pitting of "us" against "them," is a deep-rooted tradition which goes as far back as the creation, if we accept Hebrew accounts. After God had made himself a male and a female He immediately gave them to understand what they could take power over:

> And God blessed them, and God said unto them,
> Be fruitful, and multiply, and replenish the earth,
> and subdue it; and have dominion over the fish of
> the sea, and over the fowl of the air, and over
> every living thing that moveth upon the earth. 4

After God had "purged the earth of wickedness" in Noah's time, He reaffirmed his position on the treatment of other-than-human animals:

> And the fear of you and the dread of you shall
> be upon every beast of the earth, and upon every
> fowl of the air, upon all that moveth upon the
> earth, and upon all the fishes of the sea; into your
> hand are they delivered.
> Every moving thing that liveth shall be meat for
> you; even as the green herb have I given you all
> things. 5

Whether Hebrew or not, throughout antiquity men all too willingly carried out the injunction to *take dominion.* Consider, for example, this account of the Roman "games":

> The simple combat became at last insipid, and
> every variety of atrocity was devised to stimulate
> the flagging interest. At one time a bear and a
> bull, chained together, rolled in fierce combat a-
> cross the arena; at another, criminals dressed in
> the skins of wild beasts were thrown to bulls,
> which were maddened with red-hot irons, or by
> darts tipped with burning pitch. Four hundred
> bears were killed on a single day under Caligula.
> ...Under Nero, four hundred tigers fought with
> bulls and elephants....In a single day, at the dedi-
> cation of the Colosseum by Titus, five thousand
> animals perished. Under Trajan, the games con-

tinued for one hundred and twenty-three successive days. Lions, tigers, elephants, rhinoceroses, hippopotami, giraffes, bulls, stags, even crocodiles and serpents were employed to give novelty to the spectacle. Nor was any form of human suffering wanting.... Ten thousand men fought during the games of Trajan. Nero illumined his gardens during the night by Christians burning in their pitchy shirts.... So intense was the craving for blood, that a prince was less unpopular if he neglected the distribution of corn than if he neglected the games. [6]

The Western view, and increasingly the *world* view, of other animal species is that they have no soul, are absolutely different from humans in every respect, and that they are "put on earth for us to use." The Christian Church has promulgated this belief since its inception. Even Christ drove 2,000 swine over a cliff into the sea to make a point about his "healing" powers. [7] One undeniable corollary of Christianity is twenty centuries of animal oppression. [8] As late as the middle of the nineteenth century, Pope Pius IX insisted that humans have no duties to animals and refused to allow a society for the prevention of animal mistreatment to be established in Rome. At the end of the nineteenth century a Jesuit lecturer summed up the Christian position which is little changed to this day:

Brute beasts, not having understanding and therefore not being persons, cannot have any rights. ...We have, then, no duties of charity nor duties of any kind to the lower animals, as neither to sticks and stones. [9]

THE MEAT-EATERS' DOMINION

Most of us, particularly women, can deny our actual participation in the savageries of hunting, but few of us, male or female, are completely innocent of the slaughter of billions of "farm" animals each year, animals who live and die at the mercy of the intensive farmer who raises them for our table. Even though men in most cultures are the major meat-eaters, women are by no means incapable of this form of taking dominion. [10]

We may be in touch with our feelings and the feelings of others enough to resist actually killing animals for human consumption, but our natural resistance fails most of us when the flesh is presented to us nicely wrapped in the butcher's case. It is all too easy to forget that this animal would still be alive if it weren't for us.

We may pretend for our childrens' sake, perhaps, that all is well on Old MacDonald's Farm, but most of us know by now that the meat factories which produce what we euphemistically refer to as poultry, pork, and beef more closely resemble Dachau than fairy tale farms. Vegetarians excepted, each year Americans are the cause of billions of animals' grotesque suffering and miserable deaths. Even though they may pay someone else to be the "hit man" they are guilty of murder in the first degree, for it is the blood-lust of the meat-consuming public which pays the animal killers' bounty, without which they could not stay in business.

This is not the place to give a full account of the arguments for vegetarianism. Peter Singer, in his book, *Animal Liberation* [11], has presented the case with the utmost philosophical clarity. Despite my impassioned rhetoric, my purpose here is not to recruit vegetarians so much as to make the point once again that the root of the problem is in our blithely *taking power over* the lives and deaths of other creatures whose suffering is in no way necessary for our survival. If we so easily take the lives of animals who are only a few evolutionary steps removed from us, what is to prevent us from doing the same to humans who are physically very different from us--of a different color, or speaking an unintelligible language, or "primitive" in their customs? Precisely nothing. It happens all the time. And it is the direct result of our unwillingness to draw the line on the needless taking of sentient life. The crime of condoning violence against animals is part and parcel of all human violence. Ask yourself how many people who have chosen to be vegetarians would be willing to kill a "commie" or to snuff a "gook" to "make the world safe for democracy"?

HUMAN HIERARCHY

The urge to overpower, to take dominion, is, as we have seen in the course of this book, an undeniable part of

the male evolutionary inheritance. Just as it didn't take
long for prehistoric men to turn from killing primates to
killing within their own species, so for many men today
the step from hunting wild animals to killing other humans
is all too short.

Human violence, like animal and prehistoric human
violence, is partially controlled by dominance hierarchies,
but human consciousness has come too far to be amenable
to inflexible chains of command based not on merit, but
on physical power or wealth. Although dominance hierarchies such as we find in business, the military, civil
service, etc. may control some everyday outbreaks of
violence, on the whole, the frustration they produce may
cause more violence than they prevent. The growth of the
human population and the world-wide move to cities has
meant that there are fewer positions at the top of the dominance hierarchy. Whereas in a tribe of fifty a man had
one chance in ten of being one of the five big wheels who
made decisions and earned the respect of the tribe, in
urban mass society, the chances of a man's being so rewarded for his efforts, even if he is a genius and a saint,
are almost too small to be calculable. Men compensate
by setting up subsocietal dominance hierarchies; thus we
have the Lions, the Elks, the Rotary, etc. to keep frustrated middle class men quasi-content, and Hell's Angels
for the less amenable members of mass society. And
thus we spend forty-one million dollars per year in this
country on the pseudo-dominance struggle par excellence,
the football game. [12] Football is the phenomenal success
that it is precisely because it satisfies two of the primary
male needs: the need to feel that they can enhance their
positions in the dominance hierarchy, even if only vicariously when "our team" wins, and the need for a challenge
similar to that provided by hunting.

Although perhaps not as weighty as many of the con-
cerns we are exploring in this chapter, games are reveal-
ing metaphors of the origins of male mentality. From
childhood nearly every little boy reenacts the hunt via any
number of games in which he is called upon to chase the
prey, the ball in most cases, but quite often an age-mate.
The struggle to win is every bit as important to junior
hunters as to their beer-gulping fathers vicariously knocking them dead from their tv chair on Saturday afternoons.
The ball-as-prey has occasioned these thoughts from the
author of *The Omnivorous Ape*, Lyall Watson:

In many games a ball is used as a prey substitute. In some cases the ball even has feathers attached to it and is called a bird.
...Sometimes the ball is hit or kicked to give it life, but often a player picks it up and runs with it. When he has the ball, he is the prey. When he is captured or brought down by a pack of players, the ball is said to be dead.... The games were also made more interesting by having several kills take place. After each kill or score the game was stopped and the chase began all over again. The victors (or successful hunters) in many traditional games were awarded a real prey animal. The prize for the Calcio in Livrea football match, which takes place in a Florentine piazza, is a white calf. [13]

Men have come to depend so heavily on "the games" to satisfy their urge for competition and dominance and to escape the meaningless work which they endure five days a week, that we can no longer really describe the function of adult male games as "recreation." It is a far more serious business than that, one in which vicarious identification can lead to fights and brawls and even mass violence such as the soccer matches often occasion in Latin America. The games are not simply recreation, but as Lyall Watson puts it:

They are in fact a re-creation of something that once played an equally large part in our lives--the hunt. A large number of people do their pseudo-hunting by proxy, as spectators. Most of these are men--few women can understand what the fuss is about. But, then they never took part in the hunt. The men who most often play or watch these games are ones whose work is so dull and undemanding that it cannot serve as an adequate substitute for hunting. [14]

Men, although they are loath to admit it, know in their hearts that games are for children, and that such superidentification with "our team" is, at the least, ridiculous, if not pathological. Perhaps they don't admit it even to themselves, but the fact of the matter is that games, or Sunday night poker sessions, or gambling in Vegas, however immediately thrilling, can not really substitute for challenging work and the creative use of their human potential.

The easy wins in the weekend pseudo-dominance struggle do not compensate a man who has been a loser all week and a captive of his particular real-life dominance structure. Those with high mobility on the totem pole are, of course, less obviously disaffected than those who must struggle constantly to just maintain their status quo. But the executive ulcer is more than a metaphor. The problem, whether a man is at the top or the bottom of the social hierarchy, is that to the degree that he is party to such a power structure at all, he is not free. His position inevitably depends on the assent of others and their good will, of which he can never be certain. The abuse of power, one man's wielding power over another, inevitably engenders suspicion, ruthless competition, and a loss of individual freedom.

The upper echelons may delude themselves with a mirage of happiness, but their mental illness, divorce and suicide rates belie the image. The lower echelons, less deluded about their happiness, still, for the most part, feel that it is being denied them because they are not adequate to move up in the dominance hierarchy. Their anger and frustration is, at least temporarily, internalized.

Those truly at the bottom of the heap are disaffected to the point of no longer trying to meet their needs through the established routes. They have little to lose by attacking the hierarchy which refuses them entry. If they cannot get their material needs met and cannot gain the respect of others for the work they can do, they will turn to other means of meeting their needs and earning respect.

And thus, for those sitting atop the totem pole, power has its price; the frustration of those on the bottom inevitably comes to threaten the security of those on the top. When the frustration mounts high enough, we find ourselves with a crime problem such as we are faced with today, when all of us must live in fear of what our fellow humans will do.

According to FBI statistics, there were nineteen serious crimes committed each minute in the U.S. in 1974. [15] Since 1969 there has been a forty-seven percent increase in violent crime. At best, the police are able to solve only 20% of the crimes reported to them. Furthermore, crime surveys have shown that approximately twenty-three times more crimes are committed in the U.S. than are actually reported to the police.

In fact, a Gallup Poll in 1975 found that one household

in every four had been hit by crime sometime in the preceding one year period. According to another Gallup Poll
half of all Americans are afraid to walk in their neighbor-
hoods at night, and that figure rises to 56% in the largest
cities. [16]

Crimes of violence are committed primarily by men of
the lowest stratum of society: the semi-skilled workers,
the unskilled, and the unemployed. In a five year study
carried out by a noted criminologist, Marvin Wolfgang, it
was found that *all* of the homicides in the city of Philadelphia during those five years were committed by blue-
collar, lower social and economic class members. Wolfgang says of this finding that the lowest social class is
the most violent:

> Studies reported since 1958 and in many other
> languages consistently report the same observation:
> namely, that the overwhelming majority of homicides
> and other assaultive crimes are committed by per-
> sons from the lowest stratum of social organization.
> Of course, it must be noted that most crimes in
> general, except the white-collar variety, are at-
> tributed to this same social class. Still, the rate
> difference between the social classes is signifi-
> cantly greater for physically aggressive than for
> purely acquisitive crimes. [17]

Of the members of the lower class in this country,
Blacks commit by far the greatest number of violent
crimes. Statistics on murder and other violent crimes
show that Blacks have rates four to ten times higher than
whites. In 1974, according to FBI statistics, Negroes
made up 57% of those arrested for murder despite the fact
that Blacks are only about 10% of the total population. [18]

"The totem pole phenomenon," as we might call it,
may largely account for striking class and race differences
in violence. Those on the bottom are the most frustrated
and have the least to lose in shooting for broke. Their
basic needs for food, clothing and shelter are often unmet,
and their equally basic needs for recognition and esteem
are almost never met through the traditionally established
dominance hierarchies. Just as middle class men do,
poor man establish pseudo-hierarchies to meet their needs
for esteem and approval, but the nature of the competition
and the acts which are required for them to win are very
different. The result is a sub-culture in this country in

which violence is the approved route to social favor. Permission to commit violence in order to earn social approval or to meet other basic needs is granted by the subculture to each male individual who is a part of it. In some cases, violence may actually be required of a young male before he is accepted as a man. The following selection from *Manchild in the Promised Land* is a graphic example:

> I was growing up now, and people were going to expect things from me. I would soon be expected to kill a nigger if he mistreated me, like Rock, Bubba Williams, and Dewdrop had.
> Everybody knew these cats were killers. Nobody messed with them. If anybody messed with them or their family or friends, they had to kill them. I knew now that I had to keep up with these cats; if I didn't, I would lose my respect in the neighborhood. I had to keep my respect because I had to take care of Pimp and Carole and Margie. I was the big brother in the family. I couldn't be running and getting somebody after some cat who messed with me. [19]

Thus, in addition to the biological contributions of maleness to crime, there is a cultural exacerbation, particularly in the lower classes, where maleness is most often equated with aggression. Middle class males can prove themselves in more cerebral fashion or in culturally approved "recreational" competition. The lower class male at the bottom of the totem pole is driven to instill respect in his peers by one of the few routes open to him-- exaggerated maleness which all too often culminates in violence.

Unable to make it into the traditional hierarchies and to participate in the power games of the establishment, the disaffected create their own. Their dissatisfaction is not with *power*, but with their failing to have obtained it themselves; thus the social orders they create do not eschew power-over tactics and rigid hierarchy. In fact, precisely because they are outside the establishment's protection and the stakes are higher, their dominance structures and the means used to impose them are often more ruthless than the establishment's. The ultimate tool, of course, is violence. Though we may see that men are driven to meet their needs elsewhere when society has not provided

153

for them, in mirroring the establishment's power structure,
and particularly in resorting to violence, those outside the
traditional society are as guilty of the male mistake as
those who wield power within it. We can certainly recognize that they are victims of grave injustice, but no injustice on earth is sufficient to warrant the taking of another
human life. The inherent male drive for power-over is
compounded by the frustration of poverty and rigid hierarchies, but this does not excuse violent men nor change
the basic fact that if any of us are to survive we must
come to understand that no one has the right by any means
whatsoever to take power over another human being.

Crime is completely out of control; all of the police
and government efforts to reduce it have failed miserably.
In 1971, a congressional subcommittee investigating the
success of the multi-million dollar Federal crime prevention program found it to be ineffective and wasteful of
taxpayers' money.

It just may be that crime is "uncontrollable" precisely
because police are trying to control it in another top-down,
power-over action which mirrors the boss overpowering
the man low in the factory hierarchy. Greater control,
stricter laws and punishment, only serve to further frustrate the man on the bottom of the societal totem pole.
His urge to win, to gain the respect of other men, will
out; if this means beating the cops at their own game,
sobeit. Male aggressiveness and dominance seeking can
not be stifled by repressive laws and law enforcement.
If thousands of police were to line all the streets in a city
to prevent assault and rape, the assault and rape would
not end. Statistics on wife-beating and child abuse would
soon point out where the frustration had gone.

The "war on crime" is doomed precisely because it
is a war. We must, rather than continuing to try to
overpower the violent, begin a dispassionate search for an
understanding of what *causes* crime and seek to alleviate
the causes, not to change the person who is already too
frustrated to withstand any more "correction." Some emi-
nent criminologists have suggested that the most direct
way of reducing crime in this country would be to shut
down the prisons where frustration creates more criminals
than it cures. The prisons are not about to be closed
down, but no one in government has any better ideas. In
fact, of all the candidates for the November 1976
presidential election, not one claimed to have a new idea
about how to reduce crime. Politicians are not usually so

154

wont to throw up their hands about an issue of such concern to their constituency, but they know better than to make promises about something there's not a chance of "delivering" on. Their best thoughts on the matter at the moment are to impose stiffer sentences, to reinstate the death penalty, and to deny probation to recidivists...all of which have proven not to work in the past.

Staring us in the face is the fact that 80% of all crime is committed by men--90% of all *violent* crime. Has anyone stopped their "war against crime" long enough to ask why this is? Of all factors influencing crime--crowding, poverty, age, race, geographic locale, etc.--sex is far and away the most significant. The sociologists and environmental criminologists tell us we must decrease the number of poor and hungry, insure equal rights to all, alleviate urban crowding problems, etc., but not one has ever suggested that we should decrease "maleness" in order to stop crime.

BIOLOGY AND CRIME

Maleness is a *biocultural* phenomenon. Obviously males, as a whole, are much more violent than females, but some males are more violent than others. This too is biocultural. Some men's biochemical makeup predisposes them to anger and violence more often than other men's. At least part of the predisposition for violence is known to be genetically influenced. If we are to understand male crime we must understand the biological as well as the cultural factors.

J. Lange, a German psychiatrist, began investigating the genetic contributions to crime almost fifty years ago. [20] He used a method which has since become standard procedure for the assessment of all genetically linked behaviors; he compared the behavior he was interested in, criminality, in fraternal twins and identical twins. If there is a genetic predisposition for criminal behavior, then identical twins should more often *both* have committed criminal acts than fraternal twins whose genetic makeup is no more alike than that of two brothers. The environment is constant in either case, both kinds of twins receiving as close to the same care and experiences as possible. The only difference is that identical twins have 100% of their genetic information in common while fraternal twins have as little as 5%.

J. Lange found when he looked up the twin brothers of men in prison for violent crimes that ten out of thirteen who were *identical* twins had become criminals. Only two of the *fraternal* twin brothers of the seventeen prisoners Lange studied had become criminals. Hans Eysenck in *The Inequality of Man* combined Lange's data with subsequent studies and found that, in a sample of two hundred and thirty-one pairs of identical twins and five hundred and thirty-five pairs of fraternal twins, identical twins were both involved in criminal activity four times as often as are fraternal twins. [21] The genetic contribution to crime was thus strongly supported.

We have seen how the male brain and nervous system predisposes most men to be more violent than most women. We have seen that the XYY chromosome anomaly predisposes some men to be more violent than others. We know then, that biology is an undeniable influence in determining how violent an individual will be. So far we have been speaking of genetic factors, but biology influences violence throughout the life of an individual in less predetermined, irremediable ways.

The impact of health and nutrition on behavior, for example, is just coming to be recognized by criminologists. Scientists have recently found that poor nutrition can be responsible for brain damage which will decrease an individual's impulse control. How many babies of the poor are destined for trouble because their mothers could not obtain sufficient protein, vitamins and nutrients during their pregnancy? How many were damaged by poor delivery techniques? How many by improper diets in childhood? Brain damage need not even be a factor. Poor nutrition at any age can predispose an individual to be violent. Richard Speck who murdered eight student nurses in Chicago in 1966 was a compulsive candy eater. So was Hitler. Dr. Richard Mackarness, a British psychiatrist, reports that delinquent behavior in teenagers dropped significantly when their sugar intake was lowered. [22]

Our hope lies in the fact that there is a constant interaction in any individual between biology and environment and that *humans*, at the pinnacle of evolution, have the power to change the programming, whether biological or environmental, which limits our chances in the future. Maleness is one such program. In the next chapter we will discuss the ways by which males who have become

156

conscious of their biological proclivities can voluntarily seek to bring themselves and their children back into harmony with the ecosystem and their fellow humans. We will also discuss the environmental input in childhood which can minimize the male desire for power-over and violence. We will look at some recipes, then, for alleviating male aggression, some "home remedies," but male violence is more than an *individual* problem, it is a broad *biosocial* problem: we must seek change on the individual level and we must also seek to change the *social* augmenters of male violence.

SOCIAL CHANGE AND CRIME

Our social system exacerbates crime by increasing the frustration of those with little power while at the same time providing models of violence for them to identify with and imitate. We can't even start to lower crime until we deal with both of these factors. To begin with, we must provide for the basic needs of all humans *including* their need for attention, recognition, and power over their own lives and power *with* others. In addition to needing food, shelter, and clothing, everyone blessed with human consciousness has the necessity to use and to share it. Just as basic is our need for recognition and the esteem of others. When a man's consciousness is stifled, when it is not allowed its natural creative outlets, and when he can no longer earn the respect and love of others through work and sharing, then he rebels and turns all his creative force to destroying the impediments to growth. The *crime* is in the limitation of human consciousness which has become institutionalized in the power structure of nearly every culture on earth. The waste of human potential, like the waste of animals' lives, has inevitable consequences which we can not avoid seeing in the headlines each day.

While we know that contemporary men have hunting man's biology, we deny them the harmless rewards that hunter man received for hunting--the respect and appreciation of the primitive group and the opportunity to increase that respect and appreciation at any time by his increased efforts. Lockstep hierarchies do not extinguish men's needs to please, to earn attention, affection (or love if you will); they merely frustrate them. This means that men

157

are forced to find more dramatic ways to feel significant. What gains more public attention than an act of violence? If a man can't earn respect for his mind, for his natural abilities, he can at least win awe for his bravery and aggressiveness.

We must focus on how we can loosen the clamps on human creative consciousness and satisfy every individual's longing to feel necessary and important to his/her neighbors.

MODELS OF VIOLENCE

At the same time that we work to alleviate the sources of class frustration and the antiquated equation of maleness with violence we must seek to change the general societal approval of aggression and the all too available cultural models of violence. In one week in New York City, there are about 6,800 aggressive incidents on television. [23] The culturally approved channel for the release of frustration is clear.

Boys who are escaping their frustration with school, men escaping their frustration with work, sit in front of the tube transfixed night after night by murder, rape, assault, and torture. Could any situation be more conducive to the creation of a criminal? Americans worship violence. If this weren't the case then the television producers would stop including it in their programs, as it would lower their viewing ratings. Rather, every year the incidence of violence on tv increases.

Not only tv mirrors the cultural approval of aggressive behavior--all the media reflect it. "In a recent survey of the all-time best-sellers in the world of fiction," says Desmond Morris, "the name of one author who specializes in extremes of violence appeared seven times in the top twenty, with a total score of over thirty-four million copies sold." [24]

Television is the prime offender, if for no other reason than that it reaches the largest audience, but films are the pioneers with respect to the *degree* of violence which they depict. According to Jack Valenti, head of the Motion Picture Association of America, "there are 2000 different ways to kill.... As for violence, who can tell us how to handle it, what is right or wrong? Is it wrong to kill with a bulldozer but OK if you shove a person off a cliff?" [25] The extent of Mr. Valenti's thinking on the matter is obvious.

The effect of the media is particularly strong on young people who are seeking role models. With the rise of media violence in this country we have seen an unparalleled rise in juvenile crime. In 1974, 47% of all crimes were committed by persons under twenty-one years of age. [26] In the cities, 50% of those arrested were under twenty-one. (By now there should be no need to point out that only a small percentage of those arrested were female.) Yet, who would think of unplugging junior from the tube or picketing the networks to get them to reduce violence? Despite the massive evidence of the connection of tv and real-life violence published by the U.S. Commission on the Causes and Prevention of Violence, the television industry is still quibbling and refusing to accept responsibility. Meanwhile every mother's son is inheriting our violent cultural tradition from a one-eyed monster in the living room.

A few mothers have begun to speak out against such manipulation of their children's minds. Cashing in on male children's attraction to violence, in 1971, the Aurora Toy Company, a subsidiary of Nabisco, introduced a new line of toys for boys--torture toys. There were eight different kits; a typical one included a semi-nude female who was to be strapped to the platform of a guillotine with a razor-sharp pendulum over her throat. Because mothers organized and picketed Nabisco the toy was withdrawn from the market. [27] It is no accident that it was mothers, not fathers, who felt compelled to protect their children from such a glorification of violence.

Women can perhaps more readily see that violence is counterproductive and wasteful, and, consequently, morally reprehensible. As we have seen, women instigated primitive taboos against murder and cannibalism precisely because it made no sense to use their energy to create and nourish life only to have men carelessly destroy it. It is not that females are born with some special "moral turpitude detector," but that we, because we are most instrumental in creating life, have always known that life is sacred. And, too, we must not forget that our biology made us more susceptible to male violence than males are. Feeling the pain and humiliation of male attack, we can identify with all victims.

FEMALE VIOLENCE

Recently the media has taken some pains to point out that, concurrent with the success of the Women's Liberation Movement, female violence has increased in this country. In one year we had Patty Hearst, Lynette Fromme, Sarah Jane Moore, Joanne Little and Inez Garcia. The FBI statistics for 1974 do, indeed, show that the percentage of murders committed by females is on the rise. The media suggests that because women are no longer staying at home with their children they are exposed more often to conditions which elicit violence. It may well be true that we are seeing an increase in female spouse-murder because some women have suddenly come to a full recognition of how they have been oppressed.

But the slight rise in the female violent crime rate in no way alters the fact that 90% of violent crime is still committed by men. Nor does it show that female violence necessarily has anything to do with Women's Liberation. Statistics show that those women whose lives have been least touched by the feminist movement are those who have become more violent. Half of all the females arrested in 1974 were Black. [28] Race and class may be more instrumental in the etiology of female violence than feminism. Without an analysis of the motives of each female who turned to violence we can say nothing about what prompted her actions.

In fact, it is even questionable as to whether the statistics are accurate in telling us that females have become more violent. We must remember that there are many times more crimes committed in this country than those which are reported to the police and the FBI. Women murder primarily within their own families where detection is nearly inevitable. It could very well be that "the mob" or "the gang" is expert enough in hiding the evidence to prevent the arrests and conviction of many of the men who have committed crimes of violence. (Only 80% of murder cases are solved by the police.) [29] And we should not forget that although FBI statistics do not reflect it, every man who killed in Vietnam should be counted among the male murderers. If we understand that the majority of non-spouse murders were undoubtedly committed by men and that we must count the bodies of every man, woman and child felled in Vietnam, then the actual ratio of male to female violent crime in the U.S. would be more on the order of 999 to 1. According to Marvin Wolfgang, criminologist:

> It would appear to be incorrect to claim that, as
> women experience a social status more closely re-
> sembling equality with men, female homicide in-
> creases. If we can judge by the United States and
> other western countries, woman's right to vote,
> her greater participation in the labor force and in
> the family decision-making episodes, and so on,
> have not significantly raised her rate of assaultive
> crime. The anthropological evidence from socie-
> ties with more than the usual amount of female
> responsibility and economic activity does not clear-
> ly indicate woman's greater criminal aggression. [30]

We have been considering only homicide, but we must
remember that among violent crimes is one which no woman ever commits--rape. Once every ten minutes in this
country a woman is forcibly raped. [31] So many excellent
books have been written about this problem that there is
no need to elaborate here. To bring home the true extent
and brutality of rape, readers are advised to read Susan
Brownmiller's *Against Our Will*. [32]

Suffice it to say that *males are the violent sex*; it is
a miracle that women have held back from imitating their
example to the extent that we have. In that reluctance to
take life, to take power over the life of another, may lie
our hope for the preservation of the species and ultimately
the planet.

THE CRIME AGAINST THE PLANET

Not unrelated to rape is the incontinent male sexual
expression which has led to critical overpopulation of the
earth and the plundering of the planet's resources.

Riddle: When is a man most a man? Answer: At
war and sex. The male need to reaffirm masculinity over
and over again (two and a half times per week on the average according to Kinsey) [33] is the root cause of the population problem, a problem which threatens to make life on
this planet so unbearable that children will come to despise
their parents for having created them. Women's sexuality
is so tuned that we prefer sex just before menstruation
and just after--the times when we are certain not to con-

ceive. [34, 35, 36, 37] This pattern of sexual appetite holds true even in cultures where women have no knowledge of the fertile period. If we were allowed to assert our own sexual rhythm rather than being obligated to constantly service insatiable male needs we would have far fewer children. Men think they're off the hook because of birth control pills. They're not. Ultimately women are going to have to make it clear that we will not continue to ingest such unnatural and harmful chemicals. We will have to declare our unwillingness to assume the risk of blood clots and cancer so that men can have full-time access to our bodies. As women wrench free of male domination it may very well be that the population will automatically decrease. Women will learn to say no when they don't want sex and odds are that will be much more often than men, in their vanity, can predict. We will learn to know our body's fertile periods and never allow ourselves to be cajoled into risking pregnancy for "love." Naturally, as sexism subsides and women find new roles and new satisfactions in life besides motherhood, we will want fewer children.

For 99% of the time humans have been on earth, the population remained under one million. After the agricultural revolution the population soared to one hundred million. We now have four billion people on the planet and by the year 2000 there will be approximately seven billion of us. [38]

We are all too painfully aware of how world violence can lead to the death of us all, but world sex has escaped notice as the threat that it is. Lionel Tiger and Robin Fox overcome self-interest as few men ever do to suggest a solution to the population problem:

We are perhaps back in the medieval situation: we see violence and sex as dangerous to us, and rightly, and we seek to control them without thinking that we can or should eliminate them. While we may, with some justification, toy with the idea of eliminating violence, we do not think of eliminating sex. Yet these are closely associated functions in human physiology, and the arousal and control of sex and aggression are intimately linked in the brain and in the glandular and nervous systems. It may well be, therefore, that they are equally intimately linked as social phenomena. It is not simply that men fight over women (in fact, they fight much less over women than over property, for

162

instance), but that the consequences of sex--more
and more people--may in themselves be potent stimuli to violence. [39]

It is no accident that as the population of a city rises
so does the crime rate. There are four times more violent crimes per capita, for example, in U. S. cities of
250,000 than in those with under 10,000 people. Why?
In a phrase: anonymity encourages excess. The larger
the group, the town, the city, the less effective the traditional bonds of kinship which keep people from seeing each
other as "other" and therefore as suitable targets. Desmond Morris says of the bonds which prevent our objecti-
fying and molesting one another:

> ...It is a basic feature of all bonds that there
> is a limit to their extendability. Those holding to-
> gether a community which are already extensions
> of the family ones, cannot be extended to hold to-
> gether more than a certain number of people.
> Aristotle considered that a city could be made up
> of no more citizens than could know each other by
> sight. The Greek city states, which displayed
> some of the features of self-regulating units were
> in fact very small. [40]

The greater the number of people in one area, the
greater the number of controls imposed on them to keep
them from doing each other in. These very controls increase the frustration of mass living to the point that they
may actually increase crime. Whereas a town meeting is
possible with five hundred people, and collective decision-
making, though cumbersome, could work, there is no way
that 500,000 people can participate in their own governance.
The inevitable outcome of city growth is the institution of
rigid hierarchies which attempt to control complexity by
force. Dictatorships are possible precisely because people
fear the consequences of their numbers in mass society
more than they fear the loss of their freedom and their
voice in government. The solution is neither urban anarchy nor dictatorship, but population reduction and smaller
communities which will make some degree of anarchy feas-
ible. Morris says:

> If there is no hierarchy there will be constant
> bickering and fighting. There will also be no mech-

anism for ensuring the perpetuation of those qualities required if the society is to survive. Hierarchy is another word for organization. There are
only two ways of dispensing with it: one is to accept chaos and with it systemic controls such as
dictators, the other is to reduce the size of the society. In an extremely small social grouping such
as the Kalahari Bushmen and the Pygmies of the
Ituri Forest, the requirement for hierarchy is reduced to a minimum, and very stable egalitarian
societies are possible. However, as the size of the
groupings increases, so must the requirement for
hierarchy. [41]

Only by dispersing the multiple cancers called cities
can we hope to find our natural place in the earth's ecosystem. Nature never meant for millions of us to pile up
on a few square miles of earth. The industrial revolution
made it almost inevitable that we would, but we are not
the helpless pawns of our history. The time is upon us
when we must decentralize in order to save the planet and
any semblance of humane social organization. The ecosystem can not support masses of dependent people who
are taking more and more of the resources of the earth
without returning anything to it. We must disperse and we
must work to become self-sufficient...not just for our own
sake (that would be like building a bomb-shelter in the
backyard), but for the sake of us all. As humanity has
"progressed" we have become less and less self-sufficient.
Most of us, if the pipeline of goods and services were cut
off even for a month, would probably not make it if we had
to depend on our own knowledge of survival skills. We
have forgotten our role in the earth's delicate balance system. We have forgotten that everything we use and everything we eat comes initially from the earth. Perhaps if
we more directly perceived that connection we would come
to take greater responsibility for the right use of the
earth's resources.
    As it is, the cities will soon *have* to disperse if for
no other reason than that we will be buried in our own
garbage. It is only through the dispersal of cities that we
can regain our right relation with nature and become even
semi-self-sufficient. The megalopolis is a new institution
--a few moments really in the span of human history. It
is not too late to admit that cities are an unsuccessful experiment and to go on to explore new alternatives.

Ultimately, though, dispersal is not enough. We will have to stabilize, if not reduce, the world's population. The population explosion, like violent crime, is a result of the male impulse toward dominance and the need to feel one-up. Men are going to have to find a less destructive ego-booster and pastime than sex. As they come into balance with the earth and cease taking power over women, the earth and each other, we may be able to reduce crime and the population without imposing unnatural controls.

But all of us, male and female, are also going to have to adjust our conception of what our needs are as well. At the present time it would appear that the U. S. does not truly have a population problem compared to the rest of the world. We have more space per citizen in this country than most other countries in the world, but as the bar graph below indicates, each of us *use* so much more of the earth's gifts than people in the rest of the world that our impact on the environment is comparable to that of a population far greater than our 400 million. [42] Although the U. S. has but 6% of the world's population, we consume more than 40% of the earth's raw materials and energy. This gluttony means that, taken in terms of the ecological impact, we have the most severe population problem of any country in the world. As the chart shows,

Yearly Increase in Population
Expressed in Terms of GNP

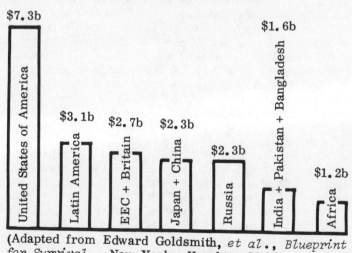

(Adapted from Edward Goldsmith, *et al.*, *Blueprint for Survival*. New York: Houghton Mifflin, 1972.)

India, which we usually think of as the world's most critical population problem, has one of the lowest ecological impacts.

This plundering of the world's resources is violence; it will inevitably lead to violence between humans as we scrabble over the last remaining resources on earth. Within fifty years almost all of the earth's metal reserves will have been exhausted if we continue to use them at our present heedless pace. [43] No one needs to be reminded that the same is true of oil and natural gas, and it is certainly not inconceivable that a world war could be the result of an oil embargo even now.

The rape of the earth is a crime against all of us. All of us are responsible to the degree to which we consume more than we truly need. It is men who mine the earth, cut down the forests, pollute the seas with oil and drain the earth's reserves of natural resources, but women are only slightly less responsible if we encourage their heedlessness by buying their products. We must simplify our needs and thereby cease consuming what the men are producing. Only then will it be profitable for them to stop their violence against the planet.

Ultimately the danger from what men are taking from the earth is far surpassed by the dangerous consequences of the unnatural things they are adding to the earth. There are half a million man-made chemicals. They have been developed so quickly that there has not been time to assess the ecological impact of more than a fraction of these. We experience the effects of pollution--see the dead fish on our scummy lakes, gasp for breath in our smoggy cities, and watch the cancer rates climb as we ingest more and more chemical food and water--but none of us really can begin to know all of the subtle changes we and all creatures are exposed to as a result of random chemical combinations and radiation. We do know that 280 mammalian species, 350 bird species, and 20,000 plant species are now threatened because of the combined threats of pollution and habitat destruction. [44] Who can say how many of us have been the victims of chemical poisoning, cancer, and genetic mutations which have been the result of men's heedless attempts to impose their will on nature.

At the present time the most serious threat to all of us is nuclear radiation; the life of every single living thing in the world is now in the balance. Will we come to our senses before men have pocked the planet with nuclear power stations? This is not the place to really go into a complicated discussion of the hazards of nuclear power. Some scientists tell us we can not afford not to harness nuclear energy--I say that what we can least afford is this ultimate dominion of man over nature. Read *Poisoned Power* [45] and *Time to Choose: America's Energy Future* [46] if you can bear a thorough understanding of what we face. All other expressions of male dominion are, in reality, secondary to this one, the most unnatural of unnatural acts acts. The next five years will probably decide whether we will allow this ultimate rape of the earth or not.

It is not my intention here to add to the ecological doomsday collection available at any public library. We do not work well when we are motivated by hopelessness and terror. The point is that we must all act as if there is still time. Ralph Nader points to the number of nuclear power stations which have been shut down in this country and says that within five years, if the public really gets behind the effort, there will be no functioning nuclear power stations left in the U. S. There is still room for hope, and hope we must. We must also act. We must cease our own individual plundering of the earth's resources: get off the top of the foodchain, stop wasting ten gallons of water every time we use the toilet, stop polluting the atmosphere with chemicals and robbing the atmosphere of its ozone with aerosols, and stop driving our metal monsters. We must raise our voices to appeal to industry and government to follow our example.

But I think we must be clear in our hearts as to the real nature of the problem. We could devote a lifetime to saving the whales, only to have them and all of us destroyed in a moment by nuclear explosion. We could work in the peace movement and prevent war for a decade only to have all of us die of radiation poisoning from power plant accidents. We could free women, free racial minorities, free the poor, only to have us all fighting one another for food and energy. There is no partial solution; there is no one cause which is ours to fight for. There is a universal mistake, predominately a male mistake, which is the root cause of all the problems we face. It is precisely because men have followed the Biblical injunction to TAKE DOMINION (and, of course, the path began long before the Bible was written) that we are faced with such multiple crises today.

We come into the world teeming with energy and a desire to grow and change--to transcend all limitations. The very urge for transcendence, for limitless expansion and creative growth, which is our unique human heritage, has on the whole been misused. Men have mistakenly sought to transcend the very earth herself, not realizing that transcendence can not be physical, but must, ultimately, be a metaphysical goal. In one of the wisest books of our time, E. F. Schumacher, an economist like no other, has summed up this most basic mistake:

> ...Man's needs are infinite and infinitude can be achieved only in the spiritual realm, never in the material. Man assuredly needs to rise above this humdrum "world"; wisdom shows him the way to do it; without wisdom, he is driven to build up a monster economy which destroys the world, and to seek fantastic satisfaction, like landing a man on the moon. Instead of overcoming the "world" by moving towards saintliness, he tries to overcome it by gaining preeminence in wealth, power, science, or indeed any imaginable "sport."
> ...Wisdom demands a new orientation of science and technology towards the organic, the gentle, the non-violent, the elegant and beautiful. [47]

WAR, THE ULTIMATE DOMINANCE GAME

In the last 3,425 years of recorded history, there have been only 268 when men were not at war. [48] Obviously such a cross-cultural phenomenon must answer a very deep need in the human male psyche. Of course it would be impossible to pinpoint *the* cause of war. All wars are different. But one thing is certain--invariably one group of men want power over another group of men or their territory and resources. And invariably when a male fights in a war he earns the respect and esteem of his fellow soldiers and (usually) his peers and countrymen. Thus two prehistoric male programs are fulfilled: the desire to take power over, and the desire to win the respect of others, particularly those higher in station. This respect usually means a higher niche in the totem pole as well.

As Margaret Mead has said, the force that propels men into war is at base biological:

...the young male has a biologically given need to prove himself as a physical individual....In the past the hunt and warfare have provided the most common means of such validation. [49]

Perhaps more than anyone else, Lionel Tiger has searched the male psyche to discover what makes men fight. His first book, *Men in Groups*, broke ground on this very important question. Along with Robin Fox, Tiger extends his study of the pathology behind the male drive to war in a later book, *The Imperial Animal*:

> ...war is not a human action, but a male action; war is not a human problem but a male problem.

> ...*organized predatory violence* has always been a male monopoly, whether practiced against game animals or those enemy humans defined as "not-men" (and hence also a kind of prey animal). This is the important step in the move toward human warfare. It is not that man (or rather *men*) in the course of his evolution either learned to be a killer or lost his capacity to ritualize. He always was a killer--he still ritualizes. What he learned was the use of weapons, the predatory skill, and above all the organization of predation in male bands. He built into his biogram a whole set of satisfactions that did not have to do with killing as such, but with enjoying dangerous and status-enhancing activity in the company of other males. [50]

It is not so much, then, that men enjoy the sight of blood and revel in the suffering of others. What they enjoy is each other's company in a dangerous venture and the prestige they can earn through their acts of violence. We might think that the sight of mangled bodies and the screams of their fallen "enemies" might put a damper on their fun, but, in fact, the uniquely human capacity to symbolize allows them an escape from the guilt they should feel. By an act of definition, a North Vietnamese fellow human becomes a "gook" and can be seen as non-sensate, non-conscious, and, ultimately, non-human. Of course, men can also mythologize what they are fighting *for* to the point of excusing the bloodshed. The point is that by virtue of this uniquely human ability to symbolize and mythologize, men can commit mass interspecies murder without a twinge of the natural guilt inherent in the taking of life. And what's more they are amply rewarded for their violence.

Usually men do require some myth to fight for—democracy, Protestantism, "purification of the race." Of late these myths have become so abstract that Kissinger could hie the troops to "maintain the balance of world power." In his 1975 pleas before congress for military and financial aid for Angola he warned that the U. S. was "emasculating itself" by not sending help to this African country. There seems to be no limit to the absurd things men can be inspired to fight for, or the lengths to which they will go to achieve their purpose.

But there *must* be a limit if any of us or our children are to survive. When men invented nuclear weapons they unwittingly imposed a limit on their own game and cramped the style of all would-be warriors to come. War is no longer an arena of bravery, the showcase for the manhood of a nation, in a nuclear age. Manhood is not an issue when he who can push a button holds the life of the planet in his hands. Nixon, a pathetic though despicable shell of a man in the last days before his forced resignation, rattled his sabers to Senator Alan Cranston, saying that even now he could just walk into the next room and lift the special red phone and 60,000 people would die instantly.

An estimated thirty-six countries will have nuclear power stations by 1980 and therefore will have the means to make nuclear warheads. [51] Unless men rapidly discard the prehistoric program of taking dominion and we stop rewarding those who do, we, all of us, will have no future. Unless men can be persuaded to go a step further in human evolution where the capacity to symbolize is used for *life*, not death, we do not have a chance. The misuse of the power intrinsic in the complexity of the human brain will have finished us:

> The human animal is hoist on its own cerebral petard. The brain that was good enough to produce the skilled hunter who excelled and found satisfaction in his male-group predatory activities was also good enough to produce huge empires, noble causes to die for, vast armies, and megadeath. With all these at his disposal, he goes on behaving as if he were still a hunter-warrior, in a war party, on a raid for scalps, glory, and honor among equals. It is obvious to anyone that all the pomp and pano-

ply of war, which may have served splendidly to boost the morale of the war party, is completely ridiculous when the outcome is not a few scalps and a feather in the war bonnet, but the annihilation of the species. [52]

The question is whether we can convince males that the war game is for keeps now, that the stakes are not just high, but total, and that even the "victor" will be vanquished. Buckminster Fuller, Lionel Tiger, Lyall Watson, and many other men who have given thought to the problem have concluded that the only hope might be to turn the world over to women:

> Buckminster Fuller, on a television broadcast in 1968, shocked his studio audience into nervous giggles when he suggested that society might be saved by restoring women to their age-old leadership in government while men confine themselves to their gadgetry and games. [53]

> ...a simple prediction. So long as the use of nuclear weapons could be banned for one year, if all the menial and mighty military posts in the world were taken over by women, there would be no war. Of course, this is an unrealistic surmise, because for this to happen politics would have to change markedly, along with the control of force. But were we to continue this unfortunately frivolous proposition, we would well find that all the elaborately pious ritual, all the quietly insane military rigamaroles, all the puzzling hauteur of admirals huffing about their autonomy and their advancement, and finally all the energetic killing of the troops at the front would be more intimate, less presumptuous about the outside world, more realistic, occasionally more vicious in small doses, but never initiating the vast episodes of poisoning that the wars of men are now and have been. [54]

> I have this vision of an army of pseudo-mothers (whose potential membership is already about one billion) taking on the whole human species as a child substitute. Organizing themselves into squads of superadministrators and painstakingly supervising the emergence of a completely new social order.

The type of system that many men have dreamed of, but none have had the patience or the skill to put into practice. 55

An Iroquois brother tells me that female control of war has long been a reality in his nation:

The Iroquois peoples have long recognized that there is a basic difference in the propensity of men and women for aggression, and for that reason gave to the women the sole right to declare war of their nation against another. The ancestor people and the elders today still recognize that the men are too likely to lead their nation away from peace, and thus that authority must remain vested in the women alone. 56

OUR CULTURAL MIRROR

For at least a century some men have been aware of the pathology of the Western cultural tradition. For the most part they have been and are intellectuals--writers and artists--those in our culture least subject, one would think, to the machismo ethic; yet they have failed, almost to a man, to discern that the degeneration and corruption of the culture is largely due to its being a reflection of male values. Had they perceived this, they would have deduced something about what must be done. As it is, they, the brightest and most creative men, have acceded to and compounded the moral bankruptcy of the culture by yielding to its negative power rather than seeking to change it. The result is the *Weltanschauung* of the Twentieth Century: despair, meaninglessness, absurdity, anomie. These are the cultural blessings to which we in our time are heir.

The point of any culture is that it passes on the knowledge and wisdom of one generation to the next. It should teach us how to live in harmony with ourselves, each other, and the planet. Now we must learn to live *in spite of* the culture men have created, for they have little to tell us about wisdom and their knowledge is corrupted by power.

Culture is the mirror in which we see ourselves; without it we lose our consciousness of ourselves as a species, a society, as individuals within that society. Our understanding is distorted to the degree that our culture is distorted. It is imperative that we throw out distorted mirrors and create new ones if we are to have any idea of where we are and where we are going.

As we help men change their behavior, their uses of each other and the planet, we must, at the same time, inspire them with hope, with a *reason* to change, and, ultimately, with a new cultural mirror. If we do not we may all find ourselves counting down to the apocolypse just waiting for Godot.

Though it would be an overstatement to say that revitalization of literature and the arts is as urgent as the dismantling of nuclear weapons, it is necessary to deal with both since they create each other. As we seek to change we must work from both ends: 1) to remove the material nightmare that has created a degenerate culture and 2) to inspire that culture with new values and new vision to help us change that material reality.

It is painful to go into the vacuum of contemporary culture, but in this section we will explore it in hopes that we will realize how urgent it is that we create a new vision for the future. We must take a long hard look at our cultural tradition, for ultimately, it is what's in our libraries, our theaters, our museums and concert halls which will most influence the ideas of generations to come. Let us hope that we can leave them a legacy superior to the one which we are heir to--let us hope that we can muster the wisdom and the love to do so.

What is our cultural mirror telling us when we go to a museum and find it filled with tomato soup can "sculpture," blank canvases, and rotting fruit dubbed "art"? What do we learn about how to live from concerts composed by computers, or at a rock concert where the performance is climaxed by the lead guitarist smashing his guitar as he jerks off into the audience? What values do we absorb from black comedies when we are insulted and intentionally bored by the players?

If we take it all together, the music, the art, the literature, we can not help but find that our age is very much under the sway still of the Despair and Absurdity Zeitgeist which is now almost a century old. We can not help noticing that the "Great Artists" (*men*) are describing a very unendearing world.

In poetry, in literature, in philosophy, we are led to

173

expect a life of frustration, meaninglessness, despair--
Nothingness. Where there is not violence and degrading
sex, there is a bleak absence--waiting for Godot, or the
bomb, for the fall of the government, or simply one's
own death.

The list of those male writers and artists in this century with an essentially negative world view reads like a
list of who's who in arts and letters. It would include
the "Great" (male) prose writers like Joyce, Dreiser,
Fitzgerald, Sartre, Camus, Genet, Henry Miller, Heming-
way (some later works mitigate this), Mailer, Faulkner,
Graham Greene (with some exceptions), Burroughs, Albee,
Styron, Malamud, Salinger, Joseph Heller, John Hawkes,
John Barth, Donald Barthelme, Alain Robbe-Grillet, Stan-
ley Elkin, Thomas Pynchon, etc.

Anais Nin in *The Novel of the Future* explored the
effects of a writer's negative vision:

> Callousness in a writer creates the equivalent
> of cataracts in the eyes. It not only clouds or
> deforms his vision but may end in total blindness.
> Callousness is not operable. It breeds callousness.
> What makes us human is empathy, sympathy.
> The novels born of revulsion, repulsion, hatred
> are those I consider war novels. They encourage
> war among human beings, and consequently, uni-
> versal war.
> The *cult of ugliness* is distinct from the ac-
> ceptance that there is ugliness, just as taking
> pleasure in cruelty is distinct from the acceptance
> that there is cruelty in the world. But an obses-
> sion with ugliness lies ultimately in the writer's
> vision of the world, and when the writer loses his
> perspective and balance, he adds to the ugliness. [57]

In poetry the negativity is even more pervasive, as
evidenced by the works of Eliot, Pound, Auden, Kenneth
Patchen, John Berryman, Robert Creeley (with some miti-
gating exceptions), W. S. Merwin, Phillip Levine, James
Wright, etc. Your average modern poetry anthology
reads like a Doomsday Book.

Kenneth Patchen strikes me as one of the most defi-
antly and violently negative. This from *The Journal of
Albion Moonlight*:

```
I am
sick
as a buggered pig
with all this
mess.  I can't
go on with the
farce.  "Quality"--
I hope some
smart fool tears
this book apart
and throws it
in the toilet and
then does his little
function even as
you and I  58
```

Here the outward negativity has turned in on him...
but it is really the same thing. Inner and outer loathing
are as inextricably united as a moebius strip. Another
good example of the writer caught up in his own negative
cultural mirror:

```
Man's heart is the rotten yolk of a black snake egg
Corroding, as it is just born, in a pile of dead
Horse dung.
I have no use for the human creature.
He subtly extracts pain awake in his own kind.
I am born one, out of an accidental lump of chemistry
I have no use.  59
```

Ugly as this is, it doesn't even have the virtue of
shock appeal, since the Dadaists had already gone as far
in this direction as it is possible to go. James Wright
still, apparently, sees some worth in writing his poems--
at least he is still publishing them. The Dadaists sought
to destroy everything: the establishment, their audience,
art, even Dada itself. As Louis Aragon put it in a manifesto read at the second Dada manifestation in 1920:

> No more painters, no more writers, no more
> musicians, no more sculptors, no more religions,
> no more republicans, no more royalists, no more
> imperialists, no more anarchists, no more social-
> ists, no more Bolsheviks, no more politicians, no
> more proletarians, no more democrats, no more
> armies, no more police, no more nations, no more

no more of these idiocies, no more, no more,
NOTHING, NOTHING, NOTHING. [60]

"All writing is garbage," proclaimed Artaud, the play-
wright. [61]

Jacques Vache was one of several Dadaists who acted
on these nihilistic convictions. He had begun to view life
as black humor, so that nothing had any more value than
anything else. Violence, death, torture--a great cosmic
joke. This passage about Vache from *The Savage God* by
A. Alvarez describes the ultimate male violence perpe-
trated in the name of art:

> "I object to being killed in the war," he had
> written from the front, "...I shall die when I want
> to die, and then I shall die with somebody else.
> To die alone is boring; I should prefer to die with
> one of my best friends." He did precisely that.
> In 1919, when he was twenty-three years old, he
> took an overdose of opium; at the same time, he
> administered the same lethal dose to two friends
> who had come along merely for the trip and had
> no suicidal intentions. It was the supreme Dada
> gesture, the ultimate psychopathic joke: suicide
> and double murder. [62]

The tangible results of Dada were almost nil. In 1917,
Marcel Duchamp presented as his sole work at the Exhibition of Independent Painters in New York a signed urinal.
If a Dadaist actually made something he took pains to destroy it--or more cleverly yet, many of the sculptures of
this time were designed so they would self-destruct.

We could, with tongue in cheek, at least credit them
with humility. Humility has been one of the most notori-
ously lacking elements, it seems to me, in visual art
since then. Following the masculine territorial imperative,
avante-garde male sculptors and painters in the last century had one thing in common: whatever their ugly contribution it is *big*. One can't avoid the towering, sprawl-
ing mass of it.

Tony Smith's junk metal monstrosities are a case in
point and his work since the Twenties has been widely imi-
tated. That these fellows actually sell these hulks of cor-
roding iron and sheet metal is testimony to the whole Em-
peror's-new-clothes syndrome, where anything, if touted
loudly enough as *Great Art*, is accepted as such.

And of course there are the action painters, like Jackson Pollock, whose metaphor of spurting all over the canvas could not be clearer. That the resulting product could have been created by any itinerant ape is beside the point--and that it is *ugly* we are told is beside the point. The point is never to ask what the point is.

Then there's the whole pop-op phenomenon, with Andy Warhol selling his tomato soup cans for as much as $17,000, gigantic sexist cartoon murals, whole bowling alleys and service stations reproduced in the museums, etc., to truly insure that we never, not even in the art museums, get away from the perversity of the American supermarket culture. True, the boys are satirizing--but how many years of one's life must one spend proving that advertising and tomato soup cans are ugly?

The sad fact is that pop art is much more of a testament to the passivity of its creators than effective social criticism, as Anais Nin has said:

> When we decided to believe only what was visible, we lost the faculty for apprehending what might be. Out of such a distorted view of what is came the monstrosities of pop art. Accepting what is (a complete service station in a museum, Campbell's soup cartons and billboards in our living rooms) is an act of passivity, an act of resignation, of impotence, lack of invention and transformation, also an inability to discard *what is* and create *what might be* .... The artist has surrendered. The mad-man who went about tearing down the billboards for their ugliness was closer to being a hero than the pop artist. He might have become the hero-artist if he had redesigned them. 63

More recently, the galleries are filling up with the giant canvases of neo-realism, with its concentration on tract houses, cars, ugly cityscapes, service stations, etc. Satire? No, they tell us that this is a serious exploration of things-as-they-are and for accuracy's sake many of them paint from a slide projected onto the canvas.

All this seems mild compared to the newest in male art. In 1973 Lucas Samaras took over a gallery and built a solid platform three or four feet above the floor. When the crowds came and strolled up the ramp into the empty room they could hear moanings and pantings underneath them as Samaras crawled about "jerking off" under their

177

feet. This was dubbed "body art" and there are sure to be plenty of followers.

And then there's Christo, the curtain-hanger and fence builder, who, in one of the grossest assertions of the phallic territorial imperative and alienation from nature ever, encased a canyon in a curtain of plastic which cost $750,000 to hang.

The ultimate male art hype is called *earth works*. Dennis Oppenheimer and a score of others have actually talked millionaires out of tons of money in order to tear up the desert. They hire bulldozers, make a few wriggly ditches, and then the millionaire can fly over the area in his private plane to look at his very own "work of art."

As long ago as 1967, Valerie Solanas had this to say about "Great Art":

> Ugliness: Being totally sexual, incapable of cerebral or aesthetic responses, totally materialistic and greedy, the male, besides inflicting on the world "Great Art," has decorated his unlandscaped cities with ugly buildings (both inside and out), ugly decors, billboards, highways, cars, garbage trucks and, most notably, his own putrid self. [64]

If we care to sum it all up, I think we could safely say that the touchstones of literature, art and philosophy proclaim that this is the Age of Absurdity and Despair (which many, many historians and critics have already declared). The turning point into this age was about the end of the French Revolution or about the time of Whitman's death in America, or the end of the Age of Romanticism. It was about then that the cockiness over man's discovery that there was no God (or ordained social order) began to wear off. Man was free. Free to do what? The old sense of universal order had vanished and he had to make up the rules *and the goals* as he went along. If there was no god, no ordained social order, then he must look elsewhere.

At first there was a cocky kind of joy in the new god-defiance, with the roustabout antics of the *fin d'siecle* boys and the Surrealists (in art *and* literature), which wound down eventually into a frantic quest for Meaning. Some tried to fuck their way into it, some sought it by joining up with *The Cause* of whatever persuasion, and some simply stared at their own navels. But whenever the men really stopped for reflection (and of course few did) they were faced with the *Emptiness* . Man felt his "contingency." Cut off from the supreme license that the belief in the patriarchal god had once afforded him to act in His image in superiority over all nature's creatures, Man cast about here and there trying to justify his own paltry existence. And he felt *Absurd*. Out of relation. Cut off.

Sartre wrote a whole cartload of books about it, but in this passage from his autobiography he lays out his own life as example:

> My retrospective illusions are all in pieces.
> Martyrdom, salvation, immortality: all are crumbling; the building is falling in ruins. I have caught the Holy Ghost in the cellars and flung him out of them. Atheism is a cruel, long-term business: I believe I have gone through it to the end. I see clearly, I am free from illusions...for about ten years, I have been a man who is waking up, cured of a long, bitter-sweet madness, who cannot recall his old ways without laughing, and *who no longer has any idea what to do with his life.* I have become once again the traveller without a ticket...65

Valerie Solanas put it this way:

> Most men, utterly cowardly, project their own inherent weaknesses onto women, label them female weaknesses and believe themselves to have female strengths; most philosophers, not quite so cowardly, face the fact that male lacks exist in men, but still can't face the fact that they exist in men only. So they label the male condition the Human Condition, pose their nothingness problem, which horrifies them, as a philosophical dilemma, thereby giving stature to their animalism, grandiloquently label their nothingness their "Identity Problem," and proceed to prattle on pompously about the "Crisis of the Individual," the "Essence of Being," "Existence preceeding Essence," "Existential Modes of Being," etc. etc.
> ... The male's inability to relate to anybody or anything makes his life pointless and meaningless (the ultimate male insight is that life is absurd)...66

Though it is certainly true that Man can look out on
the state of affairs he has created in the world and rightly
proclaim it absurd, and although when he looks inward he
may indeed be truthful in reporting Nothingness, the lie is
in the acceptance that it must always be so. It would be
possible to write of Ugliness and Despair in a way that
would not perpetuate them, but the caricature that men re-
sorted to (from lack of connection with their own emotions,
each other, nature) has accelerated the plunge into meaninglessness. Caricature, with its own logic, destroys itself and those who create it.

The male cultural mirror is, for the most part, *the*
cultural mirror. It will take a labor of love to show the
world another view. It is up to any of us who have seen
beyond the nightmare, who have to some degree cured ourselves of the Twentieth Century malaise of despair and
meaninglessness, to point the way, however we can, to
others. Our values need not be identical; the important
thing is that we have values at all.
We who grew up in the shadow of philosophical nihil-
ism have had to wrest values and meaning from life, since
none were bestowed on us. It is our task now to share
this process and to educate all who will hear. We needn't
create a new ethic from scratch; all world religions contain the essentials of wisdom with which we may start.
But begin we must, for though our enemy is only ignorance, it is a mighty wind howling at our door.
One thing is certain: MEN MUST CHANGE. Even if
women *could* orchestrate the world, this would depend on
men relearning their part in nature's harmony. Unfortunately, women are faced with the thankless and difficult
job of teaching men what this might be. As much as we
might think that men aren't worth it, that we have our own
goals to attend to, that, perhaps, they are too thick-head-
ed to hear anyway, WE MUST TRY TO HELP THEM
CHANGE.
If there is one lesson to be learned from the way men
have botched the job of living on this planet, it is that *we
can not take power over men* in order to save them and
ourselves. If there is one message which I would like to
convey in this book it is that, *ipso facto,* taking power
over others inevitably leads to disharmony and destruction.
We will have to help men change, but we can not force
them. We can make them excruciatingly aware of their
limitations, both biological and cultural, and suggest the

180

path to their absolution. We can set an example which they can not help but be drawn to. But, in the end, the choice must be up to them. Will they forsake their prehistoric programs in order to spare the planet--or will they, like lemmings, rush on to their own destruction? Whatever the answer to that question, we must *act* on the assumption that they can and will change. Despite the odds, even if they are a million to one, it is, for the moment, the only choice open to us. All our action, if we would not act in total absurdity, must be based on the hope that the very flexibility of the human brain which allowed us to get into such a mess can also be used to get us out. We must speak to the highest idealism men are capable of; we must reward them generously when they show signs of understanding; and ultimately, although we may rightly hate almost everything they do, we must love them as we help them change.

To close on a hopeful note, I will tell you about a modern-day Johnny Appleseed who, in his humble way, is seeding the planet with wisdom. Ernest Mann was a well-off middle-aged Midwestern businessman who one day woke up to realize that he didn't like how his life was going. He decided to give away all the possessions that were tying him to wrong ways of living and to seek a righteous relationship with himself, his neighbors, and nature. He kept only as much as he could carry on his back and set off travelling to learn more about the world.

He has been travelling and thinking and talking out his ideas for years now. From time to time he sends out progress reports on the wisdom he has found in a little paper he sells for 2¢ and calls *The Little Free Press* . Reprinted from an issue of the paper is the following time schedule for changing the world. You may find it helps to hang it on your wall.

There is no enemy only ignorance.

Learn what's natural and teach it.

(If you want a better world to live in.)

What can one person do?

Teach 2 of your friends, in one week so well that they _each_ teach 2 more people the next week to do the same.

THEN

in 30 weeks, one billion people will understand the simple natural alternative.

1st week →	2
	4
	8
	16
	32
	64
	128
	256
	512
10th week →	1024
	2048
	4096
	8192
	16,384
	32,768
	65,536
	131,072
	262,144
	524,288
20th week →	1,048,576
	2,097,152
	4,194,304
	8,388,608
	16,777,216
	33,554,432
	67,108,864
	134,217,728
	268,435,456
	536,870,912
30th week →	1,073,741,824

Reprinting Permissable

182

Chapter Five

HOME REMEDIES

We are free to choose the course of our own evolution; part of that freedom has included the freedom to be wrong --to act out of a desire for power over others, to deny our basic interdependence with all life, to disrupt the evolution of consciousness. Such action inevitably leads to its own demise: for the first time in the history of our planet men have the capability to almost instantly destroy themselves and all life. The evolutionary mandate has never been clearer--we can either choose to change or to die. The choice is ours and it is imminent. We must find a cure for violence, for the unnatural imposition of one creature's will over another's, for the plundering of the earth, if we are to survive on this planet.

In the previous chapter we discussed the macrocosmic disease and the necessity for social and cultural change. In the final analysis, however, each of us must start with ourselves and our relationships with those closest to us. We must learn how to interact peaceably and equitably with each other; for most of us this will require *unlearning* much of what we have been taught about how we should live. Our culture, as we have seen, provides few models for the kind of changes we must begin to make.

The changes required of us will not be easy. Males, as we know, are doubly handicapped--both by what they've been taught about "what makes a man a man" and by their psychobiological inheritance. It will not be an easy task, but I believe that a man who truly wants to change will be able to do so.

In this chapter we'll take a look at some possibilities for decreasing the effects of adverse psychobiological programming. We can not, of course, change the fact that a male's brain is androgenized during gestation and that he has certain emotional proclivities as a result. Men can, however, learn to minimize their expression.

The focus here is on the possibilities for changing that part of masculine behavior which has its roots in *physiology*. Remedying adverse *conditioning* is equally important, but this, it seems to me, is more a matter of common sense; ie. we reward peaceful, loving, sharing behavior while making it clear that aggressive, dominating, destructive actions will not win our approval or love. We'll consider a potpourri of ways that we can have a positive influence on the physiological components of masculine behavior. Not magical cures, not guaranteed to work, they are, at best, "home remedies" for the individual problem of aggressiveness and dominance assertion which are worth a try.

Like any other disease, obsessive male behavior is best controlled early on, before a male is entrenched in his ways. Old dogs can learn new tricks, but our best efforts will be directed toward helping new generations to live peaceably and responsibly from the beginning. I begin this chapter, then, with suggestions for parents who are assuming the responsibility of raising male children. In the second half of the chapter we will go on to explore a few psychobiological "remedies" for adult males.

PARENTING FOR PEACE

To really begin at the beginning we will have to start with conception. It is up to the mother to decide who will contribute his genetic material to her child. When she makes that choice she may be deciding more than she knows about the personality of her future child. Lower animal experiments suggest that the old adage "like father like son" may be true, particularly with respect to aggressiveness. [1] Though the evidence is far from conclusive, there is at least a strong possibility that hirsute, ectomorphic, macho fathers are likely to father sons who will grow into men of the same description *and* that they, like their fathers, will be more aggressive than less obviously masculine men. So one of the simplest and most effective of "home remedies" may be for women to choose their children's fathers with care. An even surer remedy, of course, would be to have only girls.*

THE PRENATAL ENVIRONMENT

The first nine months of life, from conception to delivery, are far more important to a child's psychological development than most people realize. In fact, the prenatal environment may have as much influence on the personality of the child as the environment during the first few months after birth. Our tradition of counting age from the day of birth obscures the fact that a child is born with nine months of experience behind him/her. There is no reason to trust to "luck" during this time for the wellbeing of the child any more than we would after the child is born. It is time we realize that motherhood begins at conception.

Physical complications of pregnancy, many of which are within a mother's control, have been found to contribute to aggressive and antisocial behavior in childhood. [2] Children whose mothers suffered toxemia during pregnancy and/or who are premature or small for their age at birth all run a higher risk of behavior problems than children whose mothers had little difficulty during pregnancy and who carried them full term. [3, 4] Toxemia, in particular, has a damaging effect on the personality of the child.

Indications are that minimal brain damage which may be clinically undetectable often results from the fetal anoxia associated with mothers' toxemia. This brain damage is thought to contribute to hyperactivity, aggressiveness, and antisocial behavior. Mothers who are carrying boys are more likely to suffer toxemia. [5, 6] This may partially explain why the majority of behavior-disordered children are male. Nevertheless, there are constructive steps a woman can take to lower her chances of toxemia. Weight, for example, has been found to be directly cor-

*Appendix I, page 215, tells you how.

185

related with toxemia. [7]   The more overweight a woman is
during her pregnancy, the more likely she is to suffer
from toxemia.

PRENATAL DIET,
SMOKING AND ALCOHOL CONSUMPTION

   Most women know that they should pay extra attention
to their diet during pregnancy, but few would suspect that
what they eat may have a direct influence on their susceptibility to toxemia and the kind of personality their child
will come to have.   Antonio Ferreira in an excellent book,
Prenatal Environment , reviews numerous studies which
show that an inadequate diet leads to toxemia. [8]   He says
that "the incidence of toxemia has been found to increase
in direct proportion with the inadequacy of the maternal
diet."   A study which Ferreira reviews found that only 5.6
per cent of women who had an "excellent diet" suffered
toxemia while 42.1 per cent of women on a "very poor"
diet did. [9]
   The amount of protein a woman includes in her diet
during early pregnancy is predictive of the amount of complications she will experience *and* the risk of her child's
being mentally or emotionally disturbed.   Researchers have
found that 6.4 per cent of women who get pregnant in October, November or December experience complications
during their pregnancies while 8.4 per cent who get pregnant in April, May or June do. [10]   This puzzle is explained by the fact that people tend to lower their protein
intake during the hot summer months, and protein deficiency causes some complications of pregnancy.
   Related to this is the fact that children who are conceived in June are at significantly higher risk of mental
deficiency than children conceived in the winter months.
A sufficient maternal protein intake during the first three
months of pregnancy is vital to the normal brain development of the fetus; when these first three months fall during
June, July and August, this usually means that the fetus
receives less protein than a child conceived in winter.
During particularly hot summers when women tend to eat
even less protein, the mental abnormality rate increases
dramatically. [11]
   A special report issued in 1973 by the Food and Nutrition Board of the National Academy of Sciences emphasizes

the strong connection between maternal diet and brain development:

> Anatomically, various indices of the brain struc-
> ture, including brain weight, cell number, cell
> size, cellular organization, and myelin formation,
> have been found to be decreased by moderate to
> severe malnutrition occurring early in develop-
> ment.... Numerous biochemical features have been
> found to be reduced or altered by early malnu-
> trition. This has been shown by measurements of
> RNA, DNA, proteins, glycosides, lipids, activity
> of a variety of enzymes, and neurotransmitters. [12]

Diet, in addition to its influence on toxemia and fetal brain development, also has an influence on two other factors which correlate with behavior disorders: prematurity and low birth weight. Children who are born prematurely or who are of lower than average birth weight have been found to be at significantly higher risk for behavior disorders than children who are full term and of average weight. [13, 14] For over forty years it has been known that premature children are subject to greater emotional difficulties than full term children. [15] One early study gave the following description of premature children:

> ...Emotionally the premature child is more irasci-
> cible, petulant, and more often shy and negativistic
> than the term child. Prematures are upset by
> slighter stimuli; they are capable of standing just
> so much, then they explode in a tantrum or a
> panic.... Often they are enraged at having a toy
> taken away from them, even though they are of-
> fered an equally attractive one at the same time. [16]

The unborn child's brain is adversely affected by a poor maternal diet. Whether this is because of the direct problem of insufficient nourishment for cellular metabolism or as a result of toxemia, prematurity or low birth weight associated with poor diet, the effect is the same: an increase in retardation, lower IQ, and behavior disorders.

One prevention for antisocial aggressive behavior may be a good prenatal diet. Just what this is is open to question. Seemingly no two nutritionists have the same story on how many calories a pregnant woman needs, how much protein, how many units of vitamins and minerals, etc. Every country has its own version of "minimum daily requirements." The variety is overwhelming. In West Germany, for example, the adult protein recommendation is twice as much as in any other country. Countries where the economy is very dependent on meat production, like Argentina and New Zealand, tend to argue for a higher protein need. This is not the place to go into the specifics of. diet, but certainly every pregnant woman should read up on this and try to make intelligent choices about her food intake.

Poor nutrition is very much a factor of socioeconomic class, of course. Middle-class and upper-class women tend to have better diets and have proven to have significantly fewer complications of pregnancy (and fewer behavior-disturbed children) than lower-class women. [17] Though certainly there are numerous class-related factors which are sociological, not nutritional, it is fair to say that at least *some* of the problem of class-related violence could be alleviated by insuring that *every* woman gets a good diet during pregnancy.

A good diet need not necessarily be an expensive one, as *Diet for a Small Planet* and several other recent books have shown. [18] Knowledge of food and how it works in our bodies may be more important than the amount of it we can buy. Low-budget foods like bean sprouts, green leafy vegetables, eggs, milk, nutritional yeast, etc. can provide better nutrition than expensive processed foods and fatty meats. Diet is really as much a factor of education as economics. Our schools do little to encourage an awareness of the importance of nutrition to physical and psychological development.

Since the thalidomide tragedy, most pregnant women have become a bit more wary about the chemicals they send through the placenta to their child, but, curiously, there has been very little mention of the five pounds of unprescribed chemicals the average American ingests per year in the form of food additives. Since food additives are now being linked with hyperactivity in children, it is a good bet that they also have a negative influence on the unborn child. [19]

Smoking definitely has an adverse effect on the fetus. When all other factors are controlled for, it has been found that women who smoke have 30% more stillbirths than women who do not smoke during their pregnancies. [20] Smoking also causes babies to be born premature and to have a lower than average birth weight, both of which we know to be associated with learning and behavior disorders.

In 1957, W. J. Simpson found, in a study of 7,500 patients, that women who smoked had twice as many premature babies as women who did not. [21] A study of 2,000 women in 1963 found that smokers' babies weighed an average of eight ounces less than nonsmokers', that there was a prematurity rate two and one half times as high among smokers, and that they had a higher number of stillbirths. [22] At least thirty studies since these have found that smoking definitely contributes to low birth weight, prematurity, and fetal death. [23]

A major national study in Britain involving 17,000 births has shown a direct correlation between maternal smoking and a child's development and learning ability:

> The effect of smoking in pregnancy on reading ability is to reduce the "reading age" by about three months at the age of seven years, after allowing for all other variables, including birth weight. If birth weight is excluded, the deficit almost doubles. A similar "retarding" effect is seen on the child's height at the age of seven, where the average "retardation" in the children of smokers is about one cm., or 0.5 cm. after allowance has been made for birth weight.... [24]

Of most interest to us here, however, is the fact that British mothers who smoked were found to have children with more behavioral disturbances:

> The effect of smoking in pregnancy on the child's behavior was adverse, when an analysis of covariance was carried out, using the child's social adjustment score in the school situation as the dependent variable. This is a marked "smoking" effect on social adjustment, even after allowance has been made for all other variables.

Smoking mothers are more subject to toxemia and this could account for the differences described above, but some researchers feel that most of the problem may come from a direct lowering of oxygen in the fetal blood supply which smoking causes. Carbon dioxide increases while oxygen decreases in the smoker's blood. Oxygen lack (anoxia) and carbon monoxide poisoning can cause fetal brain damage.

189

Pregnant women should, of course, stop smoking.
The British study mentioned above found, however, that
there is a "grace period"; women who stop smoking by the
fourth month of pregnancy do not endanger their babies.

The effect of alcohol on the fetus is not as certain as
that of tobacco. In mice, alcoholism causes smaller lit-
ters and a higher percentage of stillbirths. [25] Rats born
to alcoholic mothers are emotionally labile and have significantly lower learning abilities. [26] Brown and Davis
found that alcohol may have an influence on behavior since
it interferes with the metabolism of norepinephrine and epinephrine. [27]

The effect of heroin addiction on the fetus has long
been known. The newborn child undergoes withdrawal immediately after birth with all the physiological repercus-
sions of "going cold turkey." Mothers who are heroin ad-
dicts have a higher number of stillbirths and their children
are very likely to be premature. [28]

It is best to assume that all drugs have some effect
on the fetus. Too few studies have been done to really
trace specific abnormalities to drug intake, but all pregnant women should be extremely careful about what they
put into their bodies. One study has shown that 92% of
pregnant women in America had taken at least one drug
and that 3.9% had taken ten or more which were prescribed by their doctors. [29] Many of these drugs are
mood alterers and tranquilizers which affect the brain of
the fetus just as they do the mother's brain. It is certainly possible that they could cause brain damage.

The placenta has been found to be permeable to nearly
everything a woman takes into her body, plus many of the
hormones which she secretes. In this way, the physiological and psychological state of the mother is directly communicated to the fetus. Even more amazing than this direct line of communication *within* the fetal environment
is the fetus's ability to know what is going on *outside* the
mother's body. As early as 1935 researchers found that
the fetus in the last two months of pregnancy can actually
hear and respond to noises in the mother's environment. [30]
Sontag and Wallace put a buzzing doorbell to a woman's
abdomen and found that the fetus's heart rate rapidly increased and that it became "hyperactive." Sontag warned
in 1944 that fetuses might be adversely affected by the
bombings they could hear during World War II, and he
suggested that these loud sounds could lead to the develop-

ment of an unstable nervous system in the fetus. [31] He later ascertained that fetuses can hear and react differentially to a wide range of tones. [32]

Animal studies have shown that noise has a definitely adverse effect on the developing fetus. Mothers exposed to high noise levels have more stillbirths and higher rates of prematurity and malformation than controls. Noise can also cause women to give birth to smaller than normal babies. A study done in Osaka, Japan, found that the closer a woman lived to the airport the smaller her newborn was likely to be. [33] Babies who are small for their age are at considerably greater risk for all manner of emotional and learning difficulties than normal size babies. One research team has suggested that behavioral changes which are associated with noise during gestation may result from alterations in the functioning of the adrenal glands. [34]

One of the most amazing studies of the effect of sound on the fetus was carried out by L. Salk in the 1960's. [35, 36] Salk noticed that both monkey and human mothers have a strong tendency to hold their newborn infants on the left side of their bodies. He thought that this might be connected with the fact that the heart is on that side, and that somehow the mother intuited the infant's need to continue to hear the heartbeat pattern which it had been hearing during prenatal life. In order to test the idea that the infant needs to hear this sound he made a tape recording simulating the continuous heartbeat and had it played in a nursery full of newborns. When compared with controls, the babies exposed to the heartbeat were found to be calmer, to cry less, and to breathe more deeply. Salk then increased the rate of the heartbeat to that which would correspond to what a mother's heartbeat might be if she were suddenly frightened or very anxious. The babies immediately became more restless and cried more. The infants in prenatal life had come to expect a certain kind of sound and their sense of wellbeing depended on it. Alterations in that sound, especially loud noises and indications of a mother's fear, have an emotional impact on the fetus. More studies should be done to determine if noise has any long-range effect on the emotional state of the child.

MOTHERS' EMOTIONS DURING PREGNANCY

Many cultures, including our own, have held the belief

that a woman's thoughts during pregnancy influence the personality of her child. Relegated to the status of superstition, this "old wives' tale" has in the last few decades proven to be scientifically valid.

Women's anxiety level throughout their pregnancies correlates with the amount of difficulty they experience during delivery and the likelihood of their child's being premature. [37, 38] Women who are apprehensive about bearing a child are more subject to toxemia and other complications during pregnancy. How a woman feels about having a child seemst to have a direct bearing on the likelihood of her having a miscarriage, the likelihood of a full term delivery, and the likelihood of birth complications and birth defects.

The emotional state of the mother during the pregnancy definitely influences the emotional balance of the child during infancy. Mothers who regret their pregnancy, or mothers who have suffered hardship, fear, or psychological disturbance during their pregnancy, tend to have emotionally volatile babies. They cry more, are less easily comforted, and generally require more attention than babies born to calmer and more stable mothers. Dr. Antonio Ferreira has published an extensive survey of the research on prenatal emotional influences and finds that:

> The importance of emotional factors in the course and outcome of pregnancy requires...no further demonstration. By now, it has become apparent that the mother's negative emotions, if not always sufficient to destroy the fetus ("infertility," miscarriage, stillbirth, abortion, neonatal death) may conceivably interfere with its normal development and lead to or predispose to congenital malformations or perhaps other abnormalities of a more subtle and less obvious nature. [39]

Sontag and co-workers have found that the mother's emotional stress can cause hyperactivity of the fetus, which after birth may:

> ...continue postnatally as irritability, crying, food intolerance, loose stools, etc., which could persist for months after birth, or give way to a pattern of conspicuous "social apprehension" detectable at the age of two and one half years, in the nursery school. [40]

192

Another researcher who noted the behavioral effects on the child of prenatal maternal stress concluded that:

> ...prenatal stress might affect the reactivity of the fetal nervous system and alter the whole pattern of postnatal behavior. [41]

The question, of course, is how the mother's emotions are communicated to the fetus, and how they can have such a long-term effect. The prevailing theory is that the mother's psychological imbalance alters her level of catecholamines and that this imbalance in her bloodstream causes a corresponding imbalance in the fetal bloodstream which may alter the fetus's sensitivity to or production of catecholamines. One research team has found that toxemia considerably increases a woman's norepinephrine level. [42] Another group found that infants who undergo a very stressful birth or who are delivered with forceps secrete higher than normal amounts of norepinephrine in their first urine. [43] As we have seen in chapter one, norepinephrine is very much related to aggressive behavior. At this point we can only speculate that this early imbalance in catecholamines is one mechanism whereby children are marked during gestation with different emotional proclivities. Clearly, more research is needed.

In addition to the catecholamines, other maternal hormones which are altered by stress also have an effect on the fetus. Of particular interest are animal studies by Ingeborg Ward in which she found that maternal stress had a feminizing effect on male newborn mice. [44, 45] We can not extrapolate to humans, but certainly there are indications that maternal stress may play some role in human psychosexual differentiation and gender-related behaviors.

We have seen in this section on prenatal influences that there are choices open to a woman which may have a bearing on the personality of her child. Even though we know of course that the strongest "marker" for aggressivity is that of genetic sex, there are good indications that this proclivity can be somewhat ameliorated by a good psychological and physiological environment during gestation. Many more studies will be required before we can know just how the prenatal environment may alter sex-linked behavior in childhood. What we have are a few suggestions worth trying: 1) good diet, 2) no drugs (except those parsimoniously prescribed by a knowledgable physician), 3) no smoking, 4) as little stress as possible, and 5) a positive psychological state during pregnancy.

Dr. Antonio Ferreira, to whose book this chapter is much in debt, believes that even with what little we now know we can begin to make definite changes for the better in the prenatal environment of our potential citizens:

... even at this point in our knowledge, it is apparent that a more systematic practice of prenatal care, a less enthusiastic or better regulated use of drugs, a more determined attempt to improve socioeconomic conditions, and, above all, some definite steps to prevent further defilement of Nature by chemicals, radioactive materials, noise, crowding, etc., could go a very long way to safeguard the normality of prenatal life. [46]

BIRTH AND BEHAVIOR

Some people have known for a long time that natural childbirth techniques, like the Lamaze method [47], are better for the mother than the technological circus of the contemporary delivery room, and better for the child as well. In the last couple of years, Dr. Frederick Leboyer, a French obstetrician, has taken up where the Lamazists leave off, and popularized a revolutionary new way of handling the newborn in the hours after birth. [48] Used together, the Lamaze method and the Leboyer method may have a considerable impact on the emotional development of children.

Several books are available to assist parents who want to have a natural birth. [49] Midwives, despite legal sanctions, are becoming more numerous, and many women are choosing to have their babies at home. There are always risks attendant upon home birth, but early reports indicate that contemporary midwives have a better infant survival rate than the majority of hospitals.

There is one technique of assisting a woman with delivery which is not so widely known as the methods we have been discussing. O. S. Heyns, a South African doctor, has invented an abdominal decompression technique which assist the mother during delivery and decreases her need for pain-killers. [50] An airtight plexiglass bubble is fitted over the mother's abdomen during labor. A hand-controlled air evacuation pump is attached to the bubble.

When the woman feels a labor pain coming on she can lower the air pressure over her abdominal region, which causes the fetus to rise in her body cavity. This technique has been found to greatly reduce pains and to significantly shorten the labor time. Additionally and most importantly, it has been found that the decompression technique affords the baby a better oxygen supply during contractions. Early infancy tests on the children who have been born using the decompression bubble indicate that they are "developmentally advanced" when compared to children born via the usual methods. [51] The reason suggested is that they were not subject to the brain damage that oxygen loss during hospital deliveries is associated with. What effect, if any, this has on the emotional balance of the child is open to question, but we have seen that behavior problems are definitely correlated with difficulties in pregnancy and birth, and that anoxia (oxygen loss) is thought to be related to emotional disorders. The plexiglass bubble, now marketed as "Birtheez," might turn out to be a most valuable "home remedy." (A full illustrated account of one woman's experience with the device is available. [52])

One "home remedy" which could make a big difference in the number of children born premature as well as the number who suffer brain damage as a consequence of anoxia is vitamin E. Maternal deficiency of this vitamin actually causes premature birth. [53] If mothers have sufficient vitamin E during pregnancy it helps the fetus to withstand the stress of birth because it enables its body to make better use of the oxygen available to it. In other words, vitamin E could prevent some of the destruction of brain cells which oxygen deprivation causes during pregnancy and birth.

EARLY INFANCY

As we noted earlier, much of human brain development takes place after birth. Good nutrition is vital to the full development of a child's mental potential. Malnutrition definitely causes psychophysiological damage to the infant. Brain size, the number of cells and how well they communicate with one another all are affected by diet. [54, 55]

It has been known for some time that postnatal malnutrition can cause learning deficiencies or retardation. Recently it has become clear that emotional problems also result from poor diet.

Without going too far afield into a complicated discussion of dietetics, suffice it to say that every parent should become aware of what an infant's nutritional needs are. Most people assume that only the children of the poor are suffering from malnutrition. Not so. For example, it has been found that all babies who are not breast-fed suffer certain vitamin and mineral deficiencies. Several trace minerals, zinc and magnesium in particular, vital to intellectual and emotional development are undersupplied by cow's milk. Colostrum, the clear fluid produced by a woman's breasts before her milk comes in, is rich in these trace minerals. It contains three to ten times the amounts found in cow's milk. A pioneering study on the effect of trace minerals on behavior has this to say about the possible consequences of deficiency in infancy:

> This early neonatal period is...the period of rapid development of the brain and nervous system, and conceivably marginal depletion of one or more trace elements during this period may also contribute to behavioral problems in later life. This important problem has not received the attention of investigators to date.
> ...bovine dried skim milk has been used experimentally to produce deficiencies of iron, copper, manganese, and magnesium and should not, therefore, be considered an adequate diet for growing children. [56]

Cow's milk is also deficient in vitamin E which is known to be vital in the prevention of anemia. Human breast milk contains as much as twenty times more vitamin E than cow's milk. [57, 58, 59] It is some researchers' opinion that most infants who are bottle fed are deficient in vitamin E, and that anemia and poor muscle development can result from this deficiency.

This is not the place to go into the relative merits of breastfeeding and bottlefeeding; there are psychological as well as physiological factors to consider which are beyond the scope of this book. The point here is simply to emphasize that diet in infancy can have a long-range effect on a child's behavior.

SUGAR, SPICE AND PUPPY DOG TAILS

Severe malnutrition has definitely been found to influence the physiological mechanisms of children's brains.
Dr. Joseph Wilder, specialist in psychiatry and neurology,
has warned that the impact of malnutrition on the brain
may be much more severe for children than adults:

> The importance of nutrition for mental function-
> ing is much greater in children than in adults. In
> adults, faulty or insufficient nutrition may alter or
> impair specific or general mental functions, and
> eventually cause reparable or even irreparable
> structural damage of the central nervous system.
> In children, we face a grave additional factor. The
> development of the brain may be retarded, stopped,
> altered, and thus the mental functions may become
> impaired in indirect and not less serious ways....
> The child may be neurotic, psychopathic, and be
> subject to anxiety, running away tendencies, ag-
> gressiveness, a blind urge to activity and destruc-
> tiveness, with impairment of moral sensibilities....
> In its simplest form, it is a tendency to deny
> everything, contradict everything, at any price. [60]

Estimates are that about one quarter of American children go to school without having eaten breakfast. [61] Teachers report that these children are listless, nervous, and
disruptive. Controlled studies on wide samplings of young-
sters have shown that when schools provide a mid-morning
snack of milk and cookies the children are better able
to concentrate on their lessons and are less irritable, ex-
citable and nervous. Teachers also report fewer behavior
problems when children are given fruit juice at mid-morning. Obviously, children should have breakfast every day
and schools should be encouraged to provide supplementary
nutrition during the school day.

All the vitamin and mineral deficiencies which have
been found to affect the emotional states of adults have an
impact on children also. B vitamins, magnesium, calcium,
trace minerals--all play a part in insuring the mental and
emotional stability of the child.

Some researchers have found that children, particularly
adolescents, are more subject to hypoglycemia than adults.
(See page 203.) Obviously one thing parents can do is
see to it that children eat frequently enough to keep their

blood sugar levels stable and that they stop eating empty carbohydrates which bounce the blood sugar level up only to cause a rebound effect a short time later.

The most extensive nutritional problem for children in the U.S., however, is iron deficiency anemia. One out of three pre-school children in the U.S. is anemic. [62] These children are disruptive; they are irritable and likely to be aggressive. They do not concentrate well on their studies and are likely to fall far behind their classmates if they are anemic over an extended period of time. Parents concerned with their children's emotional and intellectual development need to do some research on the foods that prevent anemia. It is much more complicated than popping an iron pill; anemia has many causes, and usually all of a child's vitamin and mineral intake needs to be considered. See Adele Davis's book, *Let's Get Well* [63], for a concise and readable summary. [64]

Good nutrition involves far more than we can go into here. Suffice it to say that what little most of us learned about nutrition in school is not sufficient to raise a child. Much of the "seven basic foods" dogma is just plain wrong and at best it is an inadequate guide to food planning. What we don't know can be dangerous. For example, there's the newly discovered connection between food additives and hyperactivity in children. A recent book by Dr. Ben F. Feingold, head of Etiology at Kaiser-Permanente Health Center in San Francisco, details his studies with hyperactive children. Dr. Feingold has been able to cure hyperactive children or at least slow them down without the use of drugs just by excluding food additives from their diets. An estimated five million children in this country are hyperactive. This level has been climbing at an alarming rate ever since the 1950's when hyperkinesia was first defined as a clinical entity. Dr. Feingold has found that this enormous rise in hyperkinesia correlates strongly with the rise in the use of food additives in America. [64]

Adults in the U.S. eat an average of five pounds of unprescribed chemicals each year; children who are fond of candy bars and soft drinks may far surpass this level. Today there are over 3,800 chemicals used to preserve, flavor, and lend eye appeal to our foods. [65] The number of chemicals and the amount of them we eat increases dramatically each year. This country's runaway food additive problem is highlighted by the fact that there are 750 legal synthetic flavors used in the U.S., while in

198

France this number is restricted to seven.

Although Dr. Feingold does not say that normal children become hyperkinetic from eating food additives, it is clear that some children are genetically predisposed to be overly sensitive to them. They definitely do not do anyone any good. Few of the chemicals we eat have been rigorously tested; none, according to Feingold, have received the careful scrutiny that all prescription drugs receive, even though we ingest far more food additives than drugs. Until every additive receives thorough testing, and therefore F.D.A. approval really means something, it would certainly seem best to withdraw processed foods from children's diets. [66]

ADULT MALES

Since much has been made of the connection between testosterone level and male aggressiveness, it seems important to allay men's castration anxieties at the outset. Nothing in this chapter can be imposed on a man without his consent. All of the recipes for the reduction of aggressiveness depend on a man's desire to change his ways. There are no secret potions to slip into coffee, no hints about dropping saltpeter into the stew. What is here are some suggestions for men who sincerely want to become gentler, more loving people, and who realize that as males they are working with a handicap both of biological and cultural origins.

ALCOHOL, ANDROGENS, AND AGGRESSION

As we've noted several times, alcoholics have androgen levels five to ten times higher than normal men. The reason for this is not certain, but indications are that alcoholism causes severe liver damage which in turn causes an increase in androgen levels. Normally the liver inactivates much of the androgen in the bloodstream, but a severely damaged liver is unable to perform this function; thus androgen levels rise precipitously.

Alcoholism and violent crime are strongly correlated. Androgen levels, as we have seen, are correlated with aggressiveness. We can not say with certainty that alco-

holics are more violent because of increased androgen
levels; there may be many ways that alcohol damages the
human nervous system and increases the likelihood of violent reactions. Nevertheless, whether because of its effect
on androgen or of other effects on the central nervous system, alcohol lowers the human threshold for violent reaction. A four-year study in Philadelphia found, for example, that alcohol was involved in 70% of all physical assault murders and 50% of all other murders. [67]

For our purposes here it is not necessary to find that
androgen is the culprit. Men interested in decreasing
their aggressiveness should cut down on alcohol, period.
In addition to lowering alcohol intake, some men may want
to switch to beer if they are currently hard liquor drinkers. Several studies have found that the same amount of
alcohol causes less aggression when a man drinks beer
than when he drinks distilled liquor. [68] The chart below

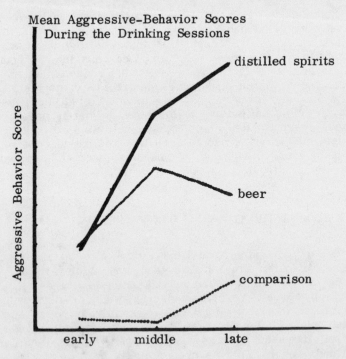

(Adapted from R. E. Boyatzis, "The Effect of Alcohol Consumption on the Aggressive Behavior of Men," *Quarterly
Journal of Studies of Alcohol* 35: 959, 1974.)

shows the results of one study which compared the aggressive behavior of men given distilled liquor to drink at a four hour "party" to that of men given beer to drink and men who drank only nonalcoholic beverages. [69] The men's blood level of alcohol was tested several times during the evening; even when beer drinkers' levels were the same as distilled liquor drinkers they were not nearly as aggressive. Although the reason for this is not clear, it is possible that beer minimizes the alcohol's effect because it contains a greater amount of vitamins, minerals and proteins than do distilled spirits.

MARY JANE AND SIR JOHN THOMAS

Fortunately all that's fun is not verboten. Marijuana has been found to decrease men's potential for aggressive behavior as well as plasma testosterone levels. [70] It has been suggested that the active ingredient in marijuana, THC, has a chemical structure very similar to estrogen and that it works as an antiandrogen in men who are heavy smokers. [71]

Animal studies have shown conclusively that THC reduces aggression. [72] Human studies have characterized marijuana users as "apathetic and sluggish," and have warned of "diminished drive, lessened ambition, and decreased motivation." [73, 74] Indications are that marijuana may be a valuable "herbal remedy" for aggressiveness.

Scientists believe that marijuana smoking causes the testicles to secrete less testosterone and also causes decreased spermatogenesis. [75] Heavy marijuana use has led to impotence and lowered sexual desire, but on the other hand, most male users declare that marijuana increases sexual pleasure. It could be that this will be a real breakthrough in the population problem; men who smoke marijuana will enjoy sex more but want it less... the more they smoke the less they will feel like having sex ...the less likely they will be to impregnate their mate.

At the present time scientists are unable to find any physiologically damaging effects, short-term or long-term, of marijuana smoking. The worst side-effect so far reported was breast development, but this occurred in men who had been chronic smokers from four to six years and for whom smoking marijuana "was the major life activity." [76]

If for no other reason than that it would reduce alcohol consumption, it seems that increased male use of marijuana would be a real asset. Laws are changing and in time, perhaps, men will willingly (and joyfully) put a damper on their machismo with Mary Jane.

CIGARETTES

The information on cigarette smoking and aggressiveness is equivocal. Some studies report that cigarette smoking increases aggressiveness and others report a "tranquillizing effect." Several researchers have documented the effect of smoking on brain catecholamines and serotonin. [77], [78]

Barbara Brown, noted pioneer in biofeedback research, has found that heavy smokers have distinctly different EEG patterns than light or non-smokers. [79] She believes, however, that people are born with EEG patterns and personality traits which predispose them to become heavy smokers. In other words, the case may be that smoking is not the cause of aggression, but that aggressive personalities may most often choose to smoke.

Researchers are agreed that cigarette deprivation in habitual users causes them to be more aggressive. [80] The behavioral descriptions as well as exacting tests of EEG and involuntary muscle activity have shown that men who are trying to stop smoking are behaviorally more reactive than non-smokers or men who are continuing to smoke. This effect appears to diminish in about one month's time, however.

NUTRITION

Diet definitely influences emotional reactivity. The most severe emotional problems associated with diet result from hunger and malnutrition. A hungry person is less able to cope with stress and more likely to overreact to mildly irritating stimuli. During World War II an experimental study of starvation was carried out with thirty-six normal young men who lived together for one year. [81] During the first six months of the study they reduced their intake of calories to 1570 per day and, as a consequence, lost about 24% of their body weight. As the study progressed and they became more severely malnourished their personalities underwent dramatic changes. The men, themselves, were aware of being unable to control themselves:

> It became "too much trouble" or "too tiring" to have to contend with other people. With the decline in the interests which had previously been held in common with others and with the growth of feelings of social inadequacy the men became self-centered. Because of this egocentricity and...irritability, of which the subjects were well aware, it required at times a real effort for them to maintain socially acceptable behavior. [82]

After three months of nutritional rehabilitation these men's personalities were returned to normal.

Another example of the effects of malnourishment on emotional behavior is provided by the Siriono Indian culture of Bolivia which was studied by A. R. Holmberg. [83] These people live in a constant state of malnourishment and hunger. Holmberg found that they refused to share food with one another and quarreled frequently over food. They are aggressive, individualistic, and uncooperative, forming no social bonds outside the immediate nuclear family.

These, of course, are extremes. Nevertheless it is clear that hunger has a definite effect on people's ability to interact with one another.

Many people are malnourished without being aware of being hungry. Hypoglycemia, low blood sugar, can have dramatic emotional effects without alerting a person with hunger pangs. [84] As with hunger, a person suffering from hypoglycemia becomes more sensitive to irritation and less able to control his/her responses. [85] The cure recommended by some nutritionists is a high protein diet, low intake of carbohydrates, particularly sugar, no caffeine, and no alcohol. One point to remember is that *all* alcoholics are hypoglycemics.

In addition to hypoglycemia, many vitamin and mineral deficiencies are associated with aggression, even violence. Severe vitamin B-12 deficiency, for example, is said to produce "violent maniacal behavior." [86] People with pellagra, a disease caused by a niacin deficiency, were thought to be insane and institutionalized before the connection with vitamins was discovered. Their symptoms were indistinguishable from schizophrenics'. Magnesium and calcium deficiencies have also been linked to aggressive unpredictable behavior. There's no point in reeling off a list here; the idea is that a person concerned about controlling a violent temper should definitely do some reading about nutrition. Megavitamin research, in particular, appears to have exciting new implications for the gentle reduction of violent behavior. See *Mega-Nutrients for Your Nerves* by Dr. H. L. Newbold [87], and *Supernutrition* by Richard Passwater. [88]

MEAT-EATING AND AGGRESSION

Although scientific analysis of carnivorousness and aggression is scarce, there are many reports from anthropology about the connection "primitive" people make between the two. Similarly, folk wisdom has always connected meat-eating and masculine potency and behavior. The *Bhagavad Gita* warns that meat-eating makes one aggressive and irritable. [89] In 1957, J. S. Walters, the director of the National Academy of Nutrition, found that when vegetarians with low hormone levels began to include meat in their diet there was a substantial rise in their sex hormones and adrenocortical hormones. [90]
Two researchers have recently found that the kind of food one eats has an influence on the production and turnover of serotonin in the brain. [91] (See chapter one.) A diet which is too high in protein causes a reduction in brain serotonin. Hopefully in the near future many more studies will be done relating specifics of diet to differences in neurochemistry and behavior. This has been a much overlooked area of research, partially accounted for by the fact that research on human nutrition receives only one-third the amount of money spent in this country on researching the nutrition of livestock.
Admittedly, few men will be willing to change the lifetime habit of meat-eating in order to become less aggressive. Nevertheless, many people have given up meat-eating for spiritual reasons and rumor has it that one can not get high with a stomach full of cow flesh. Hopefully spiritual, ecological, and humanitarian concern for animals will coalesce with the desire to reduce masculine aggressiveness and some men will give up the meat-eating habit.

CITY LIFE

Intuitively most of us know that crowded, noisy, smoggy cities are not good for us. Some recent studies indicate that noise level alone has a definite bearing on aggressivity. People who work around high-intensity sound have been found to be more irritable, distrustful and aggressive than those who work in a quieter environment. [92] One research team found that they could increase subjects' aggressiveness in the laboratory by exposing them to constant but nonirritating noise. [93]

Airport noise has been indirectly implicated as a cause of mental illness. Mental hospital admission rates for people who live in close proximity to airports are significantly higher than for people who live in quieter areas of the city. [94]

Some preliminary reports indicate that air quality may have a bearing on human emotions. A certain balance of negative air ions to positive air ions is essential for emotional stability. [95] Jet emissions and aerosol sprays deplete our air of negative ions. Though negative ion counts are decreasing over the entire face of the earth, generally the problem is worse in urban areas.

Of course these physiological considerations don't touch the real anathema of city life: the competitiveness, the alienation, the perpetual frustration of knocking elbows with our fellows in the rat race. Suffice it to say that most of us could decrease our blood pressure as well as our tempers by living in less-crowded, less-polluted environments.

PSYCHOBIOLOGICAL SELF-HELP

There are a number of promising new techniques whereby men can alter both psychological and physiological components of their behavior. Biofeedback, for example, teaches a person to gain control over his/her autonomic nervous system and, therefore, to control his/her temper. Blood pressure, heart rate, body temperature, brain waves--nearly every function of the human body can be brought under conscious control. Read Barbara Brown's *New Mind, New Body* for a good account of the potential for change which biofeedback affords us. [96]

Yoga, meditation, mind-control techniques, self-hypnosis--all have been found to have profound psycho-physiological effects. The importance of these techniques is that they so dramatically emphasize that our evolution is in our own hands, that we can consciously decide to change and do so, whether that change involves attitudes and beliefs or the physiological substrates of behavior. A good overview of these techniques and their potential for psychobiological change can be found in *The Nature of Human Consciousness* [97], edited by Robert E. Ornstein.

BEYOND HOME REMEDIES

Unfortunately, the men most in need of "passivity training" are the men who are least likely to voluntarily undertake home remedies. Medical science now provides us with a wide range of techniques for taming these recalcitrants, but most people are rightfully wary about their use. In effect, most of what we have discovered to be wrong with men's psychobiology can now be rectified. Testosterone levels can be decreased with hormone injections, drugs which alter neurotransmitter levels can be administered, brain surgery can cancel the effects of brain damage, tranquilizers can tame overly reactive nervous systems and shock treatments can joggle them into "behaving better." Doctors can manipulate the degree of "maleness" of a fetus by giving a pregnant woman hormone injections during the critical period for brain differentiation. Conceivably genetic engineering could even come up with a solution for the genetic propensity for aggressiveness connected with the Y chromosome.

Despite the urgency of the problem, despite the absolute catastrophe that will result if men do not change, I believe that we should not resort to these methods of dealing with male aggressiveness as they are themselves unnatural, aggressive interferences with nature which could be used to take power over others and to do violence to the human potential. At any rate, they are beyond the scope of this book. You will find a short bibliography on this antiviolence technology in the chapter notes. [98]

WOMEN, MEN AND CHANGE

We can only hope that men will soon recognize the
urgency of taking personal responsibility for changing their
aggressivity and dominance behavior. Although women can
not force them to change, we can exert tremendous pressure on men to undertake self-help programs by simply
withdrawing approval and (need I say it?) sex. Men may
perceive this as violence, a low blow worthy only of radical feminist harpies, but it is a form of *passive* resistance
which I believe should have a rightful place among other
nonviolent tactics for social change.

Similarly, women can exert control over the genetic
makeup of future generations. We have a tremendous
responsibility to consider the genetic material a man will
contribute to our children as well as the kind of conditioning he will provide. Eugenics may be one of our most
powerful home remedies.

As we have seen, women play a major role in both the
physiological and psychological components of their child's
personality. The first crucial nine months of development
are completely within our control. Diet, smoking, emotional states during pregnancy--these are up to us. We
can decide how our children will be born and how we will
handle them in infancy. Women decide what children will
eat, and, as we know, this has a definite influence on
personality. Since children are still primarily in the care
of women, we can also exert a strong influence in their
conditioning for peacefulness. What I'm saying here is
that women need not lie back and wait for men to come to
their senses. We have a responsibility to do everything
we can to wake them up and to change our own behavior
which may contribute to their aggressiveness and dominance
behavior.

As well as our responsibility to those closest to us,
we also have a responsibility to do all we can to facilitate
peacefulness in the world at large. We have been considering individual remedies, which, of course, become collective remedies when widespread, but some conditions
like poverty, racial injustice, etc. do not have immediate
individual solutions. We must work to insure that all
people have access to the earth's bounty and that as we
work to end dominion--of one person over another, one
group or nation of people over another--we at the same
time try to redistribute what has been unnaturally hoarded.
We must heal the earth of all the harm we have caused

through ignorance and greed. In other words, we must go far beyond "home remedies"--we must rectify the mistakes men have been making for at least a half million years. In my opinion we are in a better position to do this than ever before; at the same time that science has given us the weapons with which we can destroy the world it has given us an understanding of how it can be saved. The choice is ours.

It's up to us to learn all we can about nature's balances within ourselves and within our spaceship earth so that we can assume our rightful place in the ecosystem. We will do this or we will die--the evolutionary imperative is as clear as that and ineluctably final.

Chapter Six

New Paths

A revolutionary is motivated not by hate, but
by love.   --Gloria Steinem

It has been my purpose in this book to show how men
came to take dominion, how that program persists in male
psychobiology, and how men can, by becoming conscious
of the consequences of such a course, choose not to follow
it. But it is not enough to only give up maladaptive male
behavior. Inaction will solve nothing; to be alive is to
produce and expend energy. When men give up their
power-over (other creatures, people, the earth) they can
not just dam up that energy. It must be diverted to another course. That course is by no means arbitrary. It
will take all the tracking skill our nouveau hunter posses-
ses to find his path and to follow it. Yet there are sign-
posts.

It seems to me that there is a moral imperative in a
book such as this, which at great length has called attention to what is *wrong* with men, to suggest more than
"home remedies" for their redemption. To do otherwise
may be to empower the status quo, if only by making it
more clearly visible. What follows are suggestions about
the uncharted territory ahead for all of us--both male and
female. At this point we venture beyond documentation and
deductive logic. We enter the realm of metascience or
metaphysics, literally beyond science, where we focus on
those ultimate questions of how we shall live: how we shall

use our energy, and for what purpose.

By looking outward and learning the lessons of nature, and inward at the physical processes of our own bodies, we can discern our place in the ecosystem and what our action within it should be. This knowledge of how we must interact in the physical universe in order to preserve its balance I call ecoethics.

In order to answer the ultimate questions about how to live we must also look inward for what some might call racial memories, the collective unconscious, cosmic consciousness, or just plain "God." I believe that what we can find are more than "relative truths." By looking inward we can discern values which transcend both the cultural limitations on our perception and the limitations of our physical existence. Literally, metaphysical truths = truth beyond the power of our senses, but accessible at the deepest levels of our consciousness.

The two ways of knowing, physical and nonphysical, are by no means mutually exclusive, as contemporary physicists and extrasensory perception researchers have discovered. There is one system, both physical and metaphysical in its entirety, but we are only beginning to be able to perceive it as such. We might call this interface of the physical laws of the universe (cosmic "ecology") and the spiritual laws (metaphysics) the mecosystem.

All of us are infants in the invisible. The following view of how we might proceed in the mecosystem is offered as a toddling beginning:

The first step is to transmute power-over to power-with. Power-with comes from an understanding of the synergy we have with the earth, earth's creatures, other humans. Power-with is love. With the understanding that love brings, we stop doing what harms and seek to do what helps--within ourselves, in relation to others, in relation to the planet. An action, in order to be right, must be right with all three.

Love, like everything in the mecosystem, constantly evolves. Love must be in the process of becoming more conscious in order to be. With the power of love we can move toward truth, which is itself ever-becoming. Love propels our conscious evolution. With greater truth (higher consciousness) we become ever more aware of the power of love. It is the mecosystem spiral. The starting point is love. Love must expand, create, seek higher

210

consciousness. The higher our consciousness, the greater our awareness of the power of love. We can start by seeking truth, but, ultimately, we must still power the search with love. The search for truth alone can be counter-evolutionary, as we have seen to be the case with much of what man has made of science. Truth is not, nor can it ever be, value-free. There is no objective short-cut to higher consciousness. To know the mecosystem we must experience our power-with. Power-with equals love.

The evolution of consciousness is the ultimate human goal. It is at once a biological and a spiritual pursuit for which we, by virtue of millions of years of physical evolution, have been prepared. Implicit in the laws of the mecosystem is the certainty that all evolution progresses from less to more conscious and that we, as humans, are always on this continuum. When we cease to take dominion and begin to experience power-with, we become aware of our place in the continuum and of how best to proceed.

We gain consciousness in many different ways, at different speeds. There are others "higher" and "lower" on the continuum--that is, less conscious and more conscious. Throughout the continuum, the will to greater consciousness is God in action. We respect God by never subtracting from consciousness as a whole more than we need to continue our own evolution. This means that we, like all the members of a balanced ecosystem, find our rightful place in nature's continuum of consciousness. It means that we don't eat one another (physically or metaphysically) nor the beings close in consciousness to ourselves. *And* it means thoroughly understanding that everything is a valued and necessary part of the evolutionary continuum. Nothing can be plundered without disrupting the whole.

We choose social-political systems, methods of production, living situations, educational methods, etc. all on the basis of how best to preserve the creative synergy of the planet while increasing our own contribution to the evolution of consciousness.

Love and truth are the touchstones. But how do we learn to love? The first step is to give up *all* dominion. Nature abhors a vacuum. When violence and the power-over uses of the brain are diminished we begin to feel our affinity and creative synergy with others, the planet, the universe. Once we free ourselves to feel it, we can not help but be drawn to the feeling of Power-With = Love --

211

power with ourselves, with others, with nature.

How will we learn to overcome feelings of emptiness, meaninglessness, contingency? The creative force of love will empower us to see ourselves and all life as members of the continuum of evolving consciousness. We have a place on this continuum and we are moving toward the highest goal of all--greater consciousness. We are not accidental, "only a lump of chemistry," futile experiments; we are the apotheosis of millions of years of evolution. Each of us is unique by virtue of our genetic heritage and our experience--each of us has a path to follow that is uniquely our own. We feel "contingent" only when we forget our synergy with all life, our interdependence in our growth toward consciousness. As we choose our actions by the touchstones of Love's truth we cease to feel contingent. We, in the process of earning our neighbors' love, make ourselves indispensable. Our greatest security is in knowing that our contribution to a relationship, a community, a planet would be sorely missed.

How do we find purpose, meaning, the reasons for living? Our purpose we share with all life--to become more conscious. Each of us will do that in different ways, but we do have a map, which is essentially our racial memories. As we come to truly love ourselves and others we begin to know our maps, to be able to follow them, and to create new ones for ourselves.

But how do we know that any of this is true? Truth is the collective reality of all who participate in making it. Nonstatic, nonfinal, ever-emerging. It is at once the goal and the product of the power of love. All we read here is as true as we would make it. The "highest truth" we will ever know is that we create truth by virtue of the power of love.

We know that human males have developed peculiarities of body and mind, with us for at least half a million years, which are maladaptive to earth's synergy and to the evolution of consciousness. We could attempt to eliminate these propensities. But nature is never wasteful; we needn't assume that these qualities can only be used for harm. With consciousness comes the power of transmutation. We are not stuck with a biological "given" but can choose to adapt the maladaptive at any point. Unlike pterodactyls, we can consciously choose to change in order to survive. How then can men's maladaptive traits be transformed?

212

Some of the abilities which men have developed to take
power-over can be useful in the epoch of power-with.
Male bonding, for example, minus the dominance structure,
can be a useful proclivity for human cooperation. The
hunt gave men an awareness, though misplaced, of cooper-
ative action, in that men came to understand that certain
men were the best with weapons, others were most able
to spot the prey, and still others could most readily perceive the route the animal would be likely to follow. Men
learned that success comes with the unification of such
diversity. Both individuality and cooperation assisted the
hunt--men will find these same qualities essential in a new
epoch of power-with.

Men's desire for progress, to push ahead, to hunt and
to find, was at least half a million years in the making.
There is no need to extinguish this urge, but again, the
task at hand is to transmute it. The desire to "get somewhere," "to be somebody," to "win" will be useful in pow-
ering men's search for a biospiritual evolutionary path.
With an understanding of Power-With these traits can become useful.

Males, we are told, are on the whole more independent and perhaps less fearful than females. This may be
an asset at the inception of an epoch of power-with. Men
can fearlessly begin to find their path on their own if need
be. All, however, must be tempered with the constant
awareness of how their actions affect other humans, fellow
animals, and the planet as a whole.

Men have evolved to have greater physical strength
than women. This too may have a right use. The work
of production, now accomplished by the unconscious violence of machinery which has come to take power over its
very creators, can be successfully transferred back into
the hands of men. This is not to say that women will not
participate in the process of physical work, nor that all
machinery need be abandoned, but that men, because of
their adaptation for greater strength, can assume a goodly
share of the physical labor necessary for a more peaceful
interaction with the ecosystem.

The male urge toward winning a place in the dominance
structure, gaining prestige and status, can be put to use
when transmuted. Men will have a strong natural pull toward earning their neighbor's love. When men realize it
is love and respect which can give them the most secure
place in a community, their desire to dominate by evoking
others' fear can be transmuted to a desire to synergize by

213

evoking others' love.

In short, with the change from power-over to power-with no male propensity need be stifled. It is the *use* of male power, not the power itself, which men must change.

What would a Power-With human society be like? Whatever we like so long as it will meet three crucial tests: that it do no harm to the planet, to the balance of life on it, or to any any human consciousness.

Obviously it would require another book to even begin dreaming about a Power-With society. This one ends, then, with the suggestion that you write it, or that you at least begin now to live in a way consistent with your vision. There are as many books, as many visions possible, as there are of us. May Love guide you.

Appendix I

HOW TO HAVE A GIRL

I suspect that some of you who are reading this book have about decided that you will not burden the world with any more males if you can help it. Or perhaps pure self-interest tells you that you are not up to the challenge of raising a boy. In this section we'll take a look at what determines the conception of a boy or a girl and how we can now *choose* the sex of our children.

There are two kinds of sperm: female-producing and male-producing. Although there is much information which indicates that the female's egg *enables* one or the other to enter it and is *the* deciding factor, a sperm either carries the genetic information X or Y and it is, ultimately, which of these that fertilizes the egg that determines the sex of the fetus. These two kinds of sperm behave differently and can be distinguished from each other under the microscope. Female-producing sperm (X-bearing or gynogenic) have oval-shaped heads, they are heavier, and they are slower swimmers than Y-bearing (male-producing or androgenic) sperm. Gynogenic sperm are sturdier and survive longer than androgenic sperm.

In the last decade research teams around the world have been working on a way to use what we know about the difference between gynogenic and androgenic sperm to enable parents to choose the sex of their offspring. One of the simplest and most effective techniques for conceiving girl babies was discovered by Dr. Sophia Kleegman. She found in her research at New York University that if a woman has intercourse thirty-six to forty-eight hours before her egg is released from the ovary there is about an 80% chance that she will conceive a girl. The closer the time of intercourse to the time of ovulation the greater the likelihood of conceiving a boy.

Dr. Landrum B. Shettles was the first person to actually detect the difference between androgenic and gynogenic sperm under the microscope. Working with Dr. Kleegman, he has figured out the reasons behind the importance of the timing of intercourse. Working together, the doctors have been able to advise patients on how to reproduce the sex of their choice.

In 1970 David M. Rorvik, a free-lance journalist, wrote a popular book with Dr. Shettles, *Your Baby's Sex: Now You Can Choose*, which includes the recipes for sex selection and a clear explanation of why they work. [1] Readers who are seriously

215

interested in this are advised to read the book; here we can only summarize Dr. Shettle's findings.

Approximately 400 million sperm are released into a woman's vagina whenever a man ejaculates during intercourse. About twice as many of these are androgenic as gynogenic. The vaginal environment is very hostile for sperm of either kind, but it is particularly difficult for the Y-bearing androgenic sperm who are constitutionally less able to survive than gynogenic sperm. Whatever the difficulties encountered, the male-producing sperm will suffer the most casualties.

So, common sense tells us that whatever a woman can do to make life difficult for sperm will increase her chances of having a girl. Androgenic sperm live, on the average, only one-third as long as gynogenic sperm. This accounts for Dr. Kleegman's findings that the longer the interval between intercourse and ovulation the better the chances of having a girl. Since the Y-bearing sperm live only about twenty-four hours there would be few of them left to fertilize the egg cell two or three days after intercourse. The X-bearing sperm, on the other hand, live from two and one-half to three days in the cervix and fallopian tubes.

Another factor which creates more difficulties for androgenic sperm than gynogenic is an acidic environment in the vagina. Acid is hostile to either kind of sperm, but since androgenic sperm are less physically viable, they are more likely to die than gynogenic sperm when the vagina is very acidic. The acidity of the vagina naturally changes during the course of the menstrual cycle. The closer to ovulation a woman gets the lower the acidity level of her vagina and the more alkaline her cervix. Hence for this reason too, a long interval between intercourse and ovulation is recommended for the conception of females.

Knowing the exact timing of ovulation is crucial to sex determination. The most widely-used method of predicting ovulation involves making a chart of daily temperatures for a few months. Normally a woman's temperature drops about two-fifths of a degree on the day she ovulates. A woman with a fairly regular cycle could predict that she would ovulate on the fourteenth day following the onset of menstruation, for example, by observing the day her temperature had dropped in previous months. But many things can cause a woman's ovulation to be delayed or to be early. For this reason, Dr. Shettles has worked out a more certain method of determining when ovulation will take place, based on the knowledge that as a woman gets closer to ovulation her cervical mucous gets progressively more alkaline and contains more glucose. On the day of ovulation the mucous is more alkaline than at any time during her cycle.

Dr. Shettles suggests that women buy a package of Tes-tape from the local pharmacy to determine the state of their cervix. The tape is readily available because it is the same as that used by diabetics to test their urine. Each day women are advised

216

to take a three-inch strip of the tape, wrap it around their finger, and secure it with a rubber band. The finger is inserted into the vagina just like a tampon, but the object is to actually touch the cervix with the fingertip. The tape is left in place for ten to fifteen seconds and then withdrawn for color observation. Early in the cycle the tape does not change color much at all. But as ovulation approaches it will begin to turn green. A deep bluish-green indicates that ovulation is at hand. If a woman makes these daily observations for several months, she will eventually be able to recognize the darkest color the tapes turn, and thus she will be able to accurately predict her ovulation.

Working from the simple fact that acidity is more lethal to androgenic sperm than to gynogenic sperm, Dr. Shettles has been able to concoct a "recipe" for having a girl: 1) He suggests that you use an acidic douche of two tablespoons of *white* vinegar in a quart of water just before having intercourse, which as we know should be two to three days before ovulation. 2) You should avoid having an orgasm since orgasm greatly decreases the acidity of the vaginal environment. 3) The missionary face-to-face position is recommended because the penis does not come as close to the mouth of the cervix from this angle as it would in some other positions. The longer the sperms' trip up the vagina before making it to the alkaline safety of the cervix, the more Y-bearing sperms will die. 4) For the same reason, Shettles recommends shallow penetration by the male at the time of orgasm. 5) Frequent intercourse, or male masturbation, is recommended before the attempt to conceive a girl, since a lower sperm count facilitates the conception of a female.

Dr. Shettles' and Dr. Kleegman's patients who have used this recipe have enjoyed an 85% success rate. That this is not 100% suggests that other factors are at work. Some of these have recently come to light.

In 1972 Donald Schuster and Locky Schuster published the first report on psychological factors which have an effect on a woman's conceiving a girl or a boy. [2] They found that the psychological state of the parents at the time of intercourse influences which sex will be conceived. This mind-over-matter phenomenon attracted some attention in the scientific community and there have been follow-up studies which have confirmed the initial report.

Basically what they found is that the sex of a child is influenced by which of the parents is the most uptight at the time of intercourse. If the father is under a great deal of stress the child is likely to be a girl. If the mother is under more stress than the father, then she is likely to conceive a boy. When both parents are under extreme stress the chances of conceiving a child at all are reduced.

The Schusters are not absolutely certain why this is so, but they have some theories which have stood up in the studies so far. They have found, for example, that androgenic sperm are more susceptible to heat and that high temperatures favor the survival of gynogenic sperm. They suggest that acute anxiety may raise the overall body temperature of a man. If the father's scrotum is abnormally warm for a period of time, the Y-bearing sperm would die, leaving mostly X-bearing sperm to fertilize the female's egg.

Another research team had earlier discovered that men who wear insulating underwear have a scrotum temperature one degree centigrade higher than men who do not. [3] After two weeks of wearing this kind of underwear, the men studied had sperm counts which were as low as men who are considered infertile. When they stopped wearing the underwear their sperm counts returned to normal within three to eight weeks. Indications are that men who wore this kind of underwear would be more likely to father girls if they were able to father children at all.

If a man is not under stress (nor wearing insulating underwear) then the mother's psychological state may determine the sex of the child. The Schusters suggest that Y-bearing sperm have a higher metabolic rate--or, as they put it, they are "hyperactive"--compared to X-bearing sperm. If the sperm encounter a warm temperature on the woman's cervix then the Y-bearing sperm are better adapted, because they can swim up out of danger and fertilize the egg faster than can the X-bearing sperm. So, if a woman is under stress and has a warmer body (and cervical) temperature as a result, then Y-bearing sperm will be favored and she is more likely to conceive a boy.

Records at a fertility clinic have supported the Schusters' theory about women's temperatures and sex determination. Rectal temperatures were recorded for fifty women in the week prior to conception. Those women with lower body temperatures had more girls, while women with higher body temperatures had more boys.

The Schusters summarize their findings:

> The personality test studies with people showed that knowing which parent was under the less anxiety (stress) could be used to predict the sex ratio of the progeny. [4]

A very interesting follow-up study has found a connection between rape and the sex of the child who is conceived. [5] A woman who has been raped (and who, obviously, has undergone severe stress) is very likely to conceive a boy. Researchers have found that nine out of ten children who were conceived as a result of rape were boys. In contrast, it has been found that women who truly want a child are more likely to have girls. Single women who make the decision to have children despite societal proscriptions have been found to have more girls than boys.

Other influences besides anxiety and temperature are likely to be involved in sex determination. One researcher has found that ten mothers who took LSD during early pregnancy all had girls. [6] Similarly, women who have certain chemicals in their blood which are associated with schizophrenia always have girls. The theory is that the biochemical alteration induced by LSD and schizophrenia causes male fetuses to abort.

At any rate, it is now definite that psychological as well as physiological factors influence sex determination. Women seriously interested in conceiving girls should probably add at least one more direction to Dr. Shettles' recipe and that is RE-LAX. And perhaps you might suggest that your partner wear a jockey strap or insulating underwear for a few weeks. To ask a man to enter a state of stress so his scrotum will get hot is perhaps going too far, but maybe a heating pad would be acceptable.

Women who are not content with the 85 - 90% chance of having a girl via the Kleegman-Shettles method do have more certain options open to them. These do not, however, fall under the category of home remedies. Even the Catholic church has given its blessing to the Kleegman-Shettles method, but the morality of these lower risk methods is open to question. For 100% accurate sex selection a pregnant woman can have a few ounces of the fluid surrounding her fetus withdrawn in a process called amniosentesis. Recently this procedure has been simplified so that the fluid can be taken through the vagina with little or no risk to the mother or the fetus. A simple staining process reveals whether the fetus is female or male. A woman may decide to have an abortion if she learns that the fetus is not the sex of her choice.

Another method of sex selection which will eventually have 100% accuracy involves selective artificial insemination. Several techniques for sorting out the "sex" of sperm have been developed in the last few years. Dr. R. T. Ericsson and colleagues, working at the A. G. Schering Co. in Berlin, reported in the British journal *Nature* that they had centrifuged sperm, separated out the Y-bearing sperm, and produced live male rabbits. [7] The centrifuge is like an automatic washer on the spin dry cycle. The lighter and skinnier Y-bearing sperm have a lower density than the fatter and genetically richer X-bearing sperm which allows them to be separated in the centrifuge. Once Ericsson and comrades had separated out what they thought to be primarily Y-bearing sperm, they put them in a hard-to-swim-in liquid inside a test tube. They waited a bit and then simply decanted the ones at the bottom of the tube, reasoning that only the fast swimmers would have made it that soon. So far their technique has been 85% effective; there is every indication that within a few years it will be perfected to 100% effectiveness.

A woman at Cornell University, Dr. Dorothea Bennett, and a colleague, Dr. Edward Boyse, have reduced the conception of male mice by 8% by another method which relies on the use of antibodies. [8] They extracted blood from females who had recently had a skin graft from male mice and dipped the sperm in it before pumping it into the females' vaginas. The blood carried antibodies resulting from the attempted skin grafts which, for some reason, discriminated against Y-bearing sperm. Obviously this technique has a long way to go, but researchers are confident that techniques will be perfected which will eventually make this an efficient method of sex selection.

At the moment these artificial insemination techniques are mostly at the experimental stage. But early in 1976 a Chicago hospital announced that it is in the business of producing boys on demand. Using a sperm separation technique and artificial insemination, Michael Reese Hospital can now insure a couple that their chances of having a girl are extremely low. In typical fashion, the media (and perhaps even the hospital) automatically assumes that everyone will want a boy when sex selection is possible. No mention is made of their ability to produce females; the article I came across in the local daily was entitled "One Boy, Please." But the time is not far off when women will similarly be able to ask for a girl and be assured of having one.

This is, of course, not really a practicable solution to the problem of violence in our society. Few people would want all female offspring and even fewer would be willing to painstakingly follow the "recipes" to insure female babies. Much as we might like to send them all beyond the Northern Sea sometimes, the fact is that males are here to stay and we probably had better learn to make the best of it.

Appendix II

FEMALE PRIMACY
& THE MALE MUTATION

There is a theory abroad that all males, of whatever genetic makeup, are mutations. The assertion that nearly half the human race are mutants can not, of course, be made lightly. Proof has yet to be established, but enough of a factual framework already exists to make this a compelling theory. All of the credit for such a stunning jab to the male ego goes to Jerome Cobb who has done the research necessary to establish to his satisfaction, at least, that the male of all species is a genetic blunder and one which threatens the life of the planet.

It is so extraordinary that a male should expound a theory which would call for his own and all men's extinction that it seems a shame not to let him speak for himself. What follows is a condensation of Jerome Cobb's article, "Philogyny: 'Men's Liberation,' Female Primacy, and the Biology of Sexism," part of which was originally printed in *The Village Voice* under the auspices of Jill Johnston. 1

The Y chromosome which makes us males is a damaged X, the female chromosome. I used to think that "X & Y" were arbitrary designations which would have been served equally well by "A & B" or "1 & 2," but not so. Under the microscope chromosomes actually look like X's and Y's, and a Y is obviously an X with a leg broken off or severely crippled. Isaac Asimov refers to it as 'stunted' in *The New Intelligent Man's* (natch) *Guide to the Biological Sciences*, and Ashley Montagu relates that the Y chromosome "really is a sad affair":

> It is as if in the evolution of sex a fragment at one
> time broke away from an X chromosome, carrying with
> it some rather unfortunate genes (creating) an incom-
> plete female, the creature we call the male!

These "unfortunate genes" were formerly thought to transmit the traits of "over-hairy ears (hypertrichosis), horny, scalelike, or barklike skin (ichthosis hystrix), nonpainful hard lesions of the hands and feet (keratoma dissipatum), and webbing between the second and third toes." By 1956, however, it became doubtful that the Y carried even *these* genes! An "empty affair" indeed.

Throughout the animal "kingdom" the male of any species is the sexual adjunct to the female, an anomaly whose only purpose is the production of sperm. How, then, could females have ever existed without them?

One hint is the fact that the male mutation was not universal among life forms on earth. As we go down the evolutionary scale, and hence closer to the oldest established life forms, sex differentiation becomes less common. Here we find "asexual" creatures who reproduce by mitosis or budding (hence, by definition these animals are all *females*, as only females may give birth by whatever means); "hermaphroditic" animals which fuse briefly to exchange chromosomal material, *both* individuals of whom later reproduce by various means (again, all females); "advanced hermaphrodites" such as the earth-worms (annelids) where each animal produces both sperm and ova, and after cross-fertilization *both* give birth; as well as certain maverick species such as the Artemia "sea monkeys" who reproduce at least five different ways, certain shrimp which begin life as females and *mutate later* into males; and crustaceans such as Daphnia ("water fleas") which are all parthenogenic (capable of "virgin birth") females *until times of genetic disaster* (temperature change, solar radiation, mineral imbalances in the water, etc.) when males appear among the offspring. These fuck the females to again produce parthenogenic females.

All this goes to show that dual sexuality is by no means nature's only way, and that there may well have been one or several primeval genetic disasters which introduced among the "higher" animals (which are more susceptible to gene damage due to greater complexity) the freak occurrence we call maleness. In some phyla the mutation didn't "take" because the original females later regained their fertility, rendering the new males "obsolete" and useless; in some the mutation was eventually assimilated into the individual creating hermaphroditism where separate "males" would be genetically intolerable; while in other phyla, most notably the very complex Chordata, the genetic disaster *permanently* disabled the original females, simultaneously creating mutant males who became indispensable for procreative purposes. Undoubtedly other mutations were produced as well, but these must have been infertile or sexually incompatible with the female and therefore were selected out. Males, on the other hand, retaining one undamaged X chromosome were adaptive regarding the now damaged female. (Could females have been originally XXX? This would explain what males are "filling in for," as well as explain the nature of the damage to the female. Perhaps parthenogenesis requires an additional X chromosome?)

I am presently writing a paper suggesting a possible mechanism for monosexual evolution: triploidism. As Darwin's theory has been largely discarded as an explanation for anything *but* extinction (V. L. Kellogg, *Darwinism Today* ; Henry Fairfield Osborn, *The Origin of Evolution and Life*, etc.) some radical approach is clearly called for. Very briefly, my paper will propose that all plants and animals were originally monosexual females. The triploid model I'm presenting for these organisms is only one possibility, admittedly a precarious one, but it is useful. The third chromosome in the gonads of a triploid organism would be sensitive to prolonged stimuli from other cells in the body including the sensory organs, and would act as an internal, controlled mutation catalyst in the germ cells. This would facilitate genetic inheritance not of "acquired characteristics," but of fetal adaptations to a changed environment *by the very next (F1) generation*. This, of course, would be the true origin of species, not taking place gradually over millions of years as Darwin postulates, but, as the geological record seems to indicate, even within a single generation. A construct for the emergence of immediately viable species has been the holy grail of biological theorists from Lamarck through the Orthogenesists and Vitalists (not to mention adherents to Divine Creation) to Darwin himself. (Darwin once offered a theory he called "pangenesis" in which cells in the parent body sent "gemmules" to the sex cells to "instruct" them in the formation of the embryo.) As attractive as some of these theories have been, they have all failed for lack of an acceptable mechanism. This includes the once vaunted theory of "natural selection" (popularly called "survival of the fittest" after Spencer) which never could explain the giraffe's neck any more plausibly than theories of the inheritance of acquired characteristics. Darwinism fails too in its explanation of how species originate--the very question the theory set out to answer. Assuming the standard "sexual" model, why wouldn't a mother pterodactyl (for this illustration's sake) kill her archeopteryx offspring as soon as it hatched, as mother birds (or cats) kill young whose deformities are so subtle as to escape our detection? Or, supposing it was allowed to survive, as an isolated freak (as Darwin would insist it must be) what would it mate with? As a true separate species and the first of its kind, it would be sexually incompatible with its siblings and/or its contemporary pterodactyls. The chances of another mutant archeopteryx having been coincidentally hatched nearby and both allowed to safely reach sexual maturity are slim. Complicate matters with the need for both to also be healthy members of the opposite sex, and the already infinitesimal odds are halved. Yet such is the contention of Darwinian evolution; further, that these lucky coincidences have occurred successfully for *all* species, extant and extinct, literally *trillions* of times since the first amoeba! If, then, Darwin is to be accepted as gospel this *must* have happened, for here we all are, right?

Darwin was on the right track when he proposed "pangenesis," but his "gemmules" are clearly lacking. What can "modern science" substitute for "gemmules" to achieve similar ends? I propose a hormone or hormone-enzyme chemical similar in effect to that of the chameleon which can sense the pattern of colored stripes under its belly and transfer these, via the bloodstream, to its back. A similar hormone may have transferred information of a radically altered environment to the germ plasm of any creature possessing the complementary third chromosome, or "variable factor." The problem of finding a mate would be non-existent as such creatures would necessarily be parthenogenic (or in the case of plants "parthenocarpic") fe-males, both parent and offspring.

The global and semi-global catastrophes which several times created maleness (the term used for any separate heterogametic sex) were the same catastrophes that wiped out the dinosaurs and, much later, many perfectly adapted Pleistocene mammals. Because active triploidism would permit thousands of variegated species and sub-species to exist simultaneously (with reproduc-tively complete females, freed of the need for male mates, the variety of distinct body types could be tremendous (as was in-deed the case in the Pleistocene) with natural selection acting only to keep the overall population in line with the food supply), relatively few found compatible mates when the third chromo-some was obliterated, females lost their powers of self-genera-tion, and males first appeared. Hence the decimation of species which occurred toward the close of the Ice Age; gone from the Americas were the horses, mammoths, mastodons, sabre-tooth tigers, (in North America: the llama being a survivor to the south), rhinos and other exotic species, many of whom exist nowhere on earth today. In the case of the horse, at least, it is immediately evident that Equus was in no way unfit to survive here, as its rapid refilling of its former ecological niche after the Spaniards reintroduced them to America in the 1500's attests. Why then did they die out here 10,000 years ago in such num-bers that the plains on which their Spanish-ancestored cousins graze today were literally covered with their bones? The same might be asked of the woolly mammoth, an animal more highly evolved than today's tropical elephants and perfectly adapted to both icy tundra and temperate meadows. Why did it die while the bison and deer remain to this day? Standard texts will either state honestly that they don't know, or plunge into absurd extra-Darwinian theories such as intense competition for food supplies (which actually were on the increase as the glaciers melted), climate (but this too was improving, not to mention that the animals in question had already survived a million-year win-ter...why should they be exterminated by the spring?), plague, and even Man the Hunter (obvious nonsense...we're discussing tens of thousands of species, *billions* of individuals; no plague on record comes near this capability numerically, geographically, or with such specificity, and North America's human population at the time has been estimated to have been around 28,000... quite a feat to have wiped out three-quarters of the continent's fauna!). Even Velikovsky's answer, cataclysmic evolution, is not enough. Yes, these creatures were wiped off the face of the earth by catastrophe, but not of the usual sort Velikovsky proposes. Physical violence did accompany the phenomenon in question, but its nature was primarily of genetic import. Tidal waves, hurricanes and earthquakes would have had to attack, in this case, the whole of North America to account for the *total* annihilation of whole orders of mammalia which occurred. Yet this would clearly have destroyed *all* life on the continent, which was demonstrably not the case. The catastrophe must then have been some stripping away of earth's protective ionosphere, perhaps by violent solar activity or even by Velikovsky's passing comet. In any case, the effect would be the same; the admittance of hard radiation through the atmosphere to the surface of the earth, causing widespread mutations of the sex-splitting variety already discussed, leaving as survivors only those who could find a viable mate in time. Among these was Homo sapiens, now a two-sexed race; among the losers, the closely related Neanderthal, Steinham "Man," Swanscombe "Man," Fontechevade "Man," Predmost "Man," Kanam "Man," Kanjera "Man," and a host of other related humans as yet undiscovered, all of whom were parthenogenic women who failed to find similar males to mate with (or who refused the indignity) and were either absorbed (raped by Cro-Magnon males) or terminated.

Since the last genetic disaster when the males appeared and mammalian females were damaged into needing them, little intra-species evolution has occurred and not one new species has emerged, not even under highly favorable conditions such as dog breeders have attempted to realize for hundreds of concerted years. Much extinction has been taking place right under observers' noses for as long as records have been kept, with or without our "help." This is because evolution is no longer possible now that the true triploid females are gone.

As the fossil record clearly shows, evolution has progressed in great leaps in the past and sometimes has leaped, as it were, into instant oblivion. Darwinism cannot account for this, nor can it be shown to be creating new species today, in violation of its own belief in Uniformity.

However, neither can *this* theory be adequately tested in the laboratory using existent gendered diploid subjects. Obviously these damaged organisms can only give rise to exactly their own kind, without regard to their environment except through chance mutations over long periods of time. (This, of course, is what Darwinism states, and it is an accurate observation of how "evolution" plods along *today* in diploid (XX or XY) organisms.) Nor would testing artificially mutated XXX "super female" subjects (as is frequently done with the common fruit- or vinegar-fly), as they lack the anatomy of the original triploid females, including the all-important environment-sensitive hormone which produced adaptive offspring. Chopping the tails off successive generations of diploid mice does not produce evidence that triploid animals would not then be born tailless *if the environment made taillessness important for survival.* In order to test the theory of triploid (female) evolution it will first be necessary to *genetically engineer* a physiologically and anatomically complete XXX subject, which I'm sure would indeed reproduce parthenogenically and whose offspring (always female)

225

would display marked adaptations to an induced environment. The present state of the art is far too primitive to accomplish this, and so evidence must be sought in today's flora and fauna, some few of which I previously cited.

Some examples of living organisms have been cited, as was the evidence of the damaged state of the Y chromosome. But what of woman's third X...what has become of it? Perhaps its vestige still exists in the mysterious Barr body, or sex chromatid. This is a deeply staining intracellular structure made, it is believed, of the same material which makes up full chromosomes (chromatin) found only in females. It does not appear to serve any active purpose, but its existence in a cell is known by geneticists to be proof positive its owner is female, despite any seemingly contradictory evidence. I propose this body is all that remains of the destroyed third X chromosome in females, just as the Y is the remnant of a once healthy second X in males (the damage having gone so far in the incomplete female we call the male that there remains no trace of the third X). As I am presently researching this phenomenon I can offer no more information at this time, presenting it only as an exciting possibility in the quest for the original nature of the female.

In any case, I believe men fairly recently appeared among women, much to the latter's detriment. In my research of early Homo I have not come across any bona fide accounts of skeletal remains being definitely *male*. Perhaps patriarchal, male chauvinistic paleoanthropologists only mention the sex of their finds if it is female, and thus "odd" to their way of thinking; but the only times I've seen remains older than Neanderthal documented as male they invariably turn out to be infants whose skulls were smashed--perhaps by a horrified parthenogenic mother?...

MORE ON FEMALE PRIMACY

It is possible that the female was "The First Sex," as Jerome Cobb and Elizabeth Gould Davis have insisted. In Davis's book of that name, she extensively documented the belief that the female sex was self-sufficient and auto-reproductive until a cataclysmic accident created the male mutation. [2] She cites classical mythology's description of female primacy and Plato's assurance that auto-reproductive females (male and female in one body) preceded the separation of the sexes into two bodies. She also points out that the female of all mammalian species is the product of a longer evolution:

> Woman's reproductive organs are far older than
> man's and far more highly evolved. Even in the lowest
> mammals, as well as in woman, the ovaries, uterus,
> vagina, etc., are similar, indicating that the female
> reproductive system was one of the first things perfec-

226

ted by nature. On the other hand, the male reproductive organs, the testicles and the penis, vary as much among species and through the course of evolution as does the shape of the foot--from hoof to paw.

Esther Milner, a highly-respected psychologist and author of *Human Neural and Behavioral Development* , which is the result of twenty years of research, has found evidence that would substantiate the Davis-Cobb theory:

> According to evolutionary criteria of morphologically higher and lower forms (degree of organ specialization, particularly), the human male organism is slightly less advanced phylogenetically than the human female organism. [3]

In *Hormones and Evolution* , E. J. W. Barrington tells us that male hormones were rather late in making their appearance on the evolutionary scene. [4] "This implies," he says, "that they must have been introduced relatively late into living systems that were already fully functional." A female without hormones is still a female, but as we have seen, it takes testosterone to make a male. It is at least conceivable, then, that the first sex was in fact female if for no other reason than that it couldn't have been male.

Estrogen was the first sex hormone synthesized by living systems. Its history predates the evolution of humans or any vertabrate species, for that matter. Estrogen is found not only in very primitive organisms, but also in rudimentary plant life. It has been detected and extracted from palm kernels and the female catkins of the willow, according to Barrington. Estrogen preceded the birth of the human species by millions upon millions of years. It is quite likely that our earliest foremothers were well-endowed with the chemical as Barrington assures us:

> ...it is safe to say that there is no evidence that the extensive reproductive specializations of female mammals have involved any marked evolutionary specialization in their oestrogen equipment. On the contrary, in relying primarily upon oestradiol they are using a molecule that has a history longer than their own, and probably longer than that of the whole of the vertebrate group. [5]

Only a minor alteration in the chemical structure of estrogen is necessary to transpose it into an androgen. It is not impossible that further back in the eons of time than we can imagine an extraordinary natural disaster caused the genetic instructions for the creation of estrogen to be transposed in some percentage of the animals and plants alive then so that an androgen was produced. And lo, the first males.

This is, of course, only theory, but it certainly is more

believable than the hokum of the female being created out of the male rib which a goodly portion of the earth's population believed until the last hundred years or so. And it is consistent with myths about female primacy which have come down to us from the earliest recorded history--from people who were, after all, in a better position to know than we are since they were two to four thousand years closer to the events in question.

THE MALE MUTATION AND MEAT-EATING

There is biochemical evidence to support the theory of the male mutation. Barrington tells us that vitamins are necessary to every form of life, plant or animal. Plants can synthesize their own vitamins as can all lower animals, but the higher up the evolutionary scale you go the more dependent the organism is on outside help with vitamins. The larger and/or more highly evolved it is, the more it must find its vitamins in the other plants or animals which it eats. Barrington views this as a consequence of regressive evolution which was the result, originally, of a mutation which "involved the loss of the capacity for synthesizing certain clearly defined agents of cell metabolism." "Genetic mutations," he continues, "led to the loss of the capacity for synthesizing one or other of the B vitamins."

The mutation which limits the ability to synthesize B vitamins is readily instigated in the laboratory by submitting an organism to excessive heat or radioactivity. In fact, with no external inducement at all, many mutant variations of neurospora develop spontaneously which are unable to synthesize B vitamins. They die within a short time because they do not have the ability to crib their B vitamins from other species.

Now, it will probably take a leap of faith to imagine this, but I am suggesting that this B vitamin mutation may have been the original reason why men began to crave meat, and I am also suggesting that they began to kill it in order to satisfy their need. Vitamin B-12, absolutely essential to human health, can only be obtained through animal products like eggs, milk, cheese or meat, according to Adelle Davis, noted nutritionist. [6]

A cataclysm like a gigantic meteor striking the earth or hundredfold doses of radioactivity caused by years of intense solar storms could have caused a vitamin deficiency which would eventually necessitate humans' gaining power over the animal sources of at least one of the B vitamins, B-12.

The mutation caused by such a cataclysm could have had some beneficial effects and those might have insured its continuance via natural selection, despite the negative part of the package, the B-vitamin deficiency. The mutation need not have been advantageous to all of the animals on earth at the time in order for it to become established in their genetic pools. Barrington reminds us of the slim margin of advantage which is necessary to insure that a mutation will influence evolution:

Mathematical analysis has shown, in fact, that a favorable mutation may be expected to become established in a population if its selective advantage is no more than 1%, by which is meant that 101 offspring carrying the mutation will survive for every 100 offspring that survive without it. [7]

As a final outrageous note, I will suggest that since men are known to need at least twice as much of certain B vitamins, their mutation was differentially linked with the X and Y chromosomes. Part of the male genetic package may very well be a vitamin impotence which caused the ruthless meat-eaters to outsurvive those men in prehistory who were known to be vegetarians. The only certain prehistoric vegetarians, *Australopithecus robustus*, became extinct while their meat-eating neighbors thrived.

Of course, this is not to say that females didn't need an external source of vitamin B-12. They did. But, the fact of the matter is that they needed far less of it than males did. Females could well have met their need for B vitamins by stealing the eggs from birds' nests, or even by drinking their own breast milk. Males, on the other hand, would have been led to find other animal sources. The need for B vitamins is greatly increased by stress, so eventually, in circular fashion, the tremendously taxing hunt for animals created an even greater disparity between the males' needs for meat (B vitamins) and females'.

There are strong indications that males are a genetic afterthought. We have seen that pregnant women tend to reject the male fetus, that there is a histoincompatability between mother and conceptus. The adaptation that allowed women to birth males is less than complete as evidenced by the fact that four times more males are miscarried than females. We have also seen that the Y chromosome is not fundamental to the development of the organism. There is no genetic information on the Y chromosome which contributes anything of significance to the creation of a human being. The X chromosome, five times larger than the fragmented Y chromosome, is responsible for everything that makes us human. Males of all species are more susceptible to disadvantageous mutations. This would indicate that they are a more recent development which has not yet learned to really fill its niche. In all measures of physical durability the human female outshines the male.

No doubt in the next decade, as scientists improve their techniques of mapping the chromosomes, we will learn more about why the Y chromosome is so small and broken and, perhaps, how it came to be this way. For now, the evidence suggests that the boys are the newcomers and less suited to life on the planet than their older and more experienced sisters. Perhaps when they come to realize this they will lend a humble ear to what women are telling them.

NOTES

Preface:

1. Kate Millet, *Barnard Alumnae*, Spring, 1970.
2. J. A. Gray and A. W. H. Buffery, "Sex Differences in Emotional and Cognitive Behavior," *Acta Psychologica*, 1971, 35: 89.

Chapter One:
PSYCHOBIOLOGICAL SEX DIFFERENCES & AGGRESSION

1. J. E. Garai and A. Scheinfeld, "Sex Differences in Mental and Behavioral Traits," *Genetic Psychology Monographs*, 1968, 77: 169.
2. F. R. Pauly, "Sex Differences and Legal School Entrance Age," *Journal of Educational Research*, 1951, 45: 1.
3. Garai, *op. cit.*
4. *Ibid.*
5. R. Q. Bell and N. Costello, "Three Tests for Sex Differences in Tactile Sensitivity in the Newborn," *Biologica Neonatorum*, 1964, 7: 335.
6. P. H. Wolff, "Observations on the Early Development of Smiling," in *Determinants of Infant Behavior*, ed. by B. M. Foss. London: Methuen, 1963.
7. A. F. Korner, "Neonatal Startles, Smiles, Erection and Reflex Sucks as Related to State, Sex and Individuality," *Child Development*, 1969, 40: 1039.
8. D. G. Freedman, "Genetic Variations on the Hominid Theme: Individual, Sex, and Ethnic Differences," in *Determinants of Behavioral Development*, ed. by J. Dewit, W. W. Hartup and F. J. Monks. New York: Academic Press, 1972.
9. R. Q. Bell and J. F. Darling, "The Prone Head Reaction in the Human Neonate: Relation with Sex and Tactile Sensitivity," *Child Development*, 1965, 36: 943.
10. June Reinisch, "Fetal Hormones, the Brain, and Human Sex Differences," *Archives of Sexual Behavior*, 1974, 3: 51.
11. Esther Milner, *Human Neural and Behavioral Development*. Springfield, Ill.: Charles C. Thomas, 1967.
12. J. Kagan and M. Lewis, "Studies of Attention in the Human Infant," *Merrill-Palmer Quarterly*, 1965, 11: 95.
13. M. Lewis, "Infants' Responses to Facial Stimuli During the

First Year of Life," *Developmental Psychology*, 1969, 1: 75.

14. M. L. Simner, "Newborns' Response to the Cry of Another Infant," *Developmental Psychology*, 1971, 5: 136.
15. Howard A. Moss, "Early Sex Differences and Mother-Infant Interaction," in *Sex Differences in Behavior*, ed. by Richard C. Friedman, *et al.* New York: Wiley, 1974.
16. Anneliese F. Korner, "Methodological Considerations in Studying Sex Differences in the Behavioral Functioning of Newborns," in *Sex Differences in Behavior*, ed. by Richard C. Friedman, *et al.* New York: Wiley, 1974.
17. *Ibid.*
18. R. W. Goy, "Organizing Effects of Androgen on the Behavior of Rhesus Monkeys," in *Endocrinology and Human Behavior*, ed. by R. P. Michael. Oxford: Oxford University Press, 1968.
19. H. Harlow, "Sexual Behavior of the Rhesus Monkey," in *Sex and Behavior*, ed. by F. A. Beach. New York: Wiley, 1965.
20. Julia A. Sherman, "The Problem of Sex Differences in Space Perception and Aspects of Intellectual Functioning," *Psychological Review*, 1967, 74: 290.
21. Eleanor Emmons Maccoby and Carol Nagy Jacklin, *The Psychology of Sex Differences.* Stanford: Stanford University Press, 1974.
22. E. Maccoby and C. N. Jacklin, "Sex Differences and Their Implications for Sex Roles," unpublished paper presented to the American Psychological Association, Washington, D. C., 1971.
23. Maccoby and Jacklin, 1974, *op. cit.*
24. C. Landreth, "Factors associated with Crying in Young Children in the Nursery and the Home," *Child Development*, 1971.
25. F. L. Goodenough, *Anger in Young Children.* Minneapolis: University of Minnesota Press, 1931.
26. Corinne Hutt, *Males and Females.* Middlesex, England: Penguin Books, 1972.
27. C. Pope and B. Whiting, "A Cross-cultural Analysis of Sex Differences in the Behavior of Children Aged Three to Eleven," *Journal of Social Psychology*, 1973, 91: 171.
28. Richard Green, "The Behaviorally Feminine Male Child," in *Sex Differences in Behavior*, ed. by Richard C. Friedman, *et al.* New York: Wiley, 1974.
29. *op. cit.*
30. Frances Bentzen, "Sex Ratios in Learning and Behavior Disorders," *American Journal of Orthopsychiatry*, 1963, 33: 92.
31. Judith M. Bardwick, *Psychology of Women: A Study of Bio-Cultural Conflicts.* New York: Harper and Row, 1971.
32. E. H. Erickson, "Sex Differences in the Play Configurations of Preadolescents," *American Journal of Orthopsychiatry*, 1951, 21: 667.
33. *Ibid.*

34. Bardwick, *op. cit.*
35. Jeffrey A. Gray and Robert F. Drewett, "The Genetics and Development of Sex Differences," unpublished paper.
36. Maccoby and Jacklin, 1974, *op. cit.*
37. Arnold H. Buss, "Aggression Pays," in *The Control of Aggression and Violence*, ed. by Jerome L. Singer. New York: Academic Press, 1971.
38. Roy G. D'Andrade, "Sex Differences and Cultural Institutions," in *The Development of Sex Differences*, ed. by E. E. Maccoby. Stanford University Press, 1966.
39. Beatrice B. Whiting and John W. M. Whiting, *Children of Six Cultures: A Psychocultural Analysis.* Cambridge: Harvard University Press, 1975.
40. E. W. Goodenough, "Interest in Persons as an Aspect of Sex Differences in the Early Years," *Genetic Psychology Monographs*, 1957, 55: 287.
41. Hutt, *op. cit.*
42. *Ibid.*
43. Thomas Detre, et al., "The Nosology of Violence," in *Neural Bases for Violence and Aggression*, ed. by Wm. S. Fields and Wm. H. Sweet. St. Louis, Missouri: Warren H. Green, Inc., 1974.
44. Alan B. Rothballer, "Aggression, Defense and Neurohumors," in *Aggression and Defense*, ed. by Carmine D. Clemente and Donald B. Lindsley. Berkeley: University of California Press, 1967.
45. W. C. Allee, *et al.*, "Modification of the Social Order of Flocks of Hens by the Injection of Testosterone Propionate," *Physiological Zoology*, 1939, 12: 412.
46. Mary A. Bennett, "The Social Hierarchy in Ring Doves: the Effect of Treatment with Testosterone Propionate," *Ecology*, 1940, 21: 148.
47. R. M. Rose, *et al.*, "Plasma Testosterone, Dominance Rank and Aggressive Behaviour in Male Rhesus Monkeys," *Nature*, 1941, 231: 366.
48. W. D. Joslyn, "Androgen-induced Social Dominance in Infant Female Rhesus Monkeys," *Journal of Child Psychology and Psychiatry and Allied Disciplines*, 1973, 14: 137.
49. Murray S. Work and Hilliard Rogers, "Effect of Estrogen Level on Food-seeking Dominance Among Male Rats," *Journal of Comparative and Physiological Psychology*, 1972, 79: 414.
50. Harold Persky, *et al.*, "Relation of Psychologic Measures of Aggression and Hostility to Testosterone Production in Man," *Psychosomatic Medicine*, 1971, 33: 265.
51. H. F. Meyer-Bahlburg, *et al.*, "Aggressiveness and Testosterone Measures in Man," *Psychosomatic Medicine*, 1974, 36: 269.
52. A. Kling, *et al.*, "Testosterone and Aggression," paper presented to American Psychological Association at annual meeting, Hawaii, 1973.

53. Leo Kreuz and Robert M. Rose, "Assessment of Aggressive Behavior and Plasma Testosterone in a Young Criminal Population," *Psychosomatic Medicine*, 1972, 34: 321.

54. Joel Ehrenkranz, *et al.*, "Plasma Testosterone: Correlation with Aggressive Behavior and Social Dominance in Man," *Psychosomatic Medicine*, 1974, 36: 469.

55. L. LeMaire, "Danish Experience Regarding the Castration of Sexual Offenders," *Journal of Criminal Law and Criminology* 1956, 47: 294.

56. C. C. Hawke, "Castration and Sex Crimes," *American Journal of Mental Deficiency*, 1950, 55: 220.

57. H. F. Meyer-Bahlburg, "Aggression, Androgens and the XYY Syndrome," in *Sex Differences in Behavior*, ed. by Richard C. Friedman, *et al.* New York: Wiley, 1974.

58. D. E. Sands, "Further Studies on Endocrine Treatment in Adolescence and Early Life," *Journal of Mental Science*, 1954, 100: 211.

59. E. B. Strauss, *et al.*, "Use of Dehydroisoandrosterone in Psychiatric Treatment," *British Medical Journal*, 1952: 64.

60. R. M. Rose, *et al.*, "Plasma Testosterone Levels in the Male Rhesus: Influence of Sexual and Social Stimuli," *Science*, 1972, 178: 643.

61. Maccoby and Jacklin, 1974, *op. cit.*

62. Seymour Levine, as quoted in *The Brain Changers: Scientists and the New Mind Control*, by Maya Pines. New York: Harcourt Brace Jovanovich, 1973.

63. Maccoby and Jacklin, 1974, *op. cit.*

64. John Money and Anke Ehrhart, *Man and Woman, Boy and Girl*. Baltimore and London: Johns Hopkins University Press, 1972.

65. *Ibid.*

66. *Ibid.*

67. *Ibid.*

68. Richard Greene, *op. cit.*

69. Money and Ehrhart, *op. cit.*

70. Anke Ehrhart and S. W. Baker, "Prenatal Androgen, Intelligence and Cognitive Sex Differences," in *Sex Differences in Behavior*, ed. by Richard C. Friedman, *et al.* New York: Wiley, 1974.

71. Louis F. Fabre, "Discussion: Hormones and Aggression," in *Neural Bases for Violence and Aggression*, ed. by Wm. S. Fields and Wm. H. Sweet. St. Louis, Missouri: Warren H. Green, Inc., 1974.

72. "Effects of Sexual Activity on Beard Growth in Man," *Nature*, 1970, 226: 869.

73. R. L. Dorfman and R. A. Shipley, *Androgens*. New York: Wiley, 1956.

74. J. M. Tanner, *Growth at Adolescence*. Oxford: Blackwell, 1962.

75. E. E. Joss, *et al.*, "Effect of Testosterone Propionate and Methyl Testosterone on Growth and Maturation in Rats,"

Endocrinology, 1963, 72: 123.
76. Money and Ehrhart, *op. cit.*
77. I. Bieber, *Homosexuality*. New York: Basic Books, 1962.
78. R. C. Kolodny, *et al.*, "Plasma Testosterone and Semen Analysis in Male Homosexuals," *New England Journal of Medicine*, 1971, 285: 1170.
79. J. A. Loraine, *et al.*, "Patterns of Hormone Secretion in Male and Female Homosexuals," *Nature*, 1971, 234: 5331.
80. M. S. Margolese, "Homosexuality: A New Endocrine Correlate," *Hormones and Behavior*, 1970, 1: 151.
81. L. Starka, *et al.*, "Plasma Testosterone in Male Transsexuals and Homosexuals," *Journal of Sex Research*, 1975, 2: 134.
82. Ray B. Evans, "Physical and Biochemical Characteristics of Homosexual Men," *Journal of Consulting and Clinical Psychology*, 1972, 39: 140.
83. M. Diamond, "A Critical Evaluation of the Ontogeny of Human Sexual Behavior," *Quarterly Review of Biology*, 1965, 40: 147.
84. M. Diamond, "Genetic-Endocrine Interactions and Human Psychosexuality," in *Perspectives in Reproduction and Sexual Behavior* , ed. by M. Diamond. Bloomington: Indiana University Press, 1968.
85. Reinisch, *op. cit.*
86. F. J. Kallman, "Twin and Sibship Study of Overt Male Homosexuality," *American Journal of Human Genetics*, 1952, 4: 136.
87. W. S. Schlegel, "Die Konstitutionsbiologischen Grundlagen der Homosexualitat," *Zeitschrift fur Menschliche Vererbungs-und Konstitutionslehre* , 1962, 36: 341.
88. L. Gedda, "Aspetti Genetici dell'osmosessuality," *Medicae et Gemellologiae*, 1963, 12: 213.
89. Christopher Ounsted and David C. Taylor, "The Y Chromosome Message: A point of view," in *Gender Differences: Their Ontogeny and Significance* , ed. by Christopher Ounsted and David C. Taylor. London: Churchill Livingstone, 1972.
90. *Ibid.*
91. *Ibid.*
92. Milton Diamond, *et al.*, "High Affinity Binding of Progesterone, Testosterone and Cortisol in Normal and Androgen-treated Guinea Pigs During Various Reproductive Stages: Relationship to Masculinization," *Endocrinology* , 1969, 84: 1143.
93. P. A. Jacobs, *et al.*, "Aggressive Behavior, Mental Subnormality and the XYY Male," *Nature*, 1965, 208: 1351.
94. P. A. Jacobs, *et al.*, "Chromosome Studies on Men in a Maximum Security Hospital," *Annals of Human Genetics* , 1968, 31: 339.
95. Lissy F. Jarvik, *et al.*, "Human Aggression and the Extra Y Chromosome: Fact or Fantasy?," *American Psycholo-*

gist, 1973, 28: 674.
96. M. Goldstein, "Brain Research and Violent Behavior," *Archives of Neurology* , 1974, 30: 1.
97. Jarvik, *op. cit.*
98. *Ibid.*
99. *Ibid.*
100. Goldstein, *op. cit.*
101. *Ibid.*
102. J. P. Welch, *et al.*, "Psychopathy, Mental Deficiency, Aggressiveness and the XYY Syndrome," *Nature*, 1967, 214: 500.
103. B. T. Rudd, *et al.*, "Testosterone Excretion Rates in Normal Males, and Males with an XYY Complement," *Journal of Medical Genetics*, 1968, 5: 286.
104. A. A. A. Ismail, *et al.*, "Effect of Abnormal Sex Chromosome Complements on Urinary Testosterone Levels," *Lancet*, 1968, 1: 220.
105. W. H. Price and H. J. Van de Molen, "Plasma Testosterone Levels in Males with the 47 XYY Karyotype," *Journal of Endocrinology*, 1970, 47: 117.
106. H. F. Meyer-Bahlburg, "Aggression, Androgens and the XYY Syndrome," in *Sex Differences in Behavior* , ed. by Richard C. Friedman, *et al.* New York: Wiley, 1974.
107. Ounsted and Taylor, *op. cit.*
108. Richard F. Daly, "Neurological Abnormalities in XYY Males," *Nature* , 1969, 221: 472.
109. *Ibid.*
110. G. W. Fenton, *et al.*, "The EEG and Sex Chromosome Abnormalities," *British Journal of Psychiatry* , 1971, 119: 185.
111. Johannes Nielsen and Takayuki Tsuboi, "Electroencephalographic Examination in the XYY Syndrome and in Klinefelter's Syndrome," *British Journal of Psychiatry*, 1974, 125: 236.
112. Fenton, *et al.*, *op. cit.*
113. Goldstein, *op. cit.*
114. Jarvik, *op. cit.*
115. P. L. Pearson, "Technique for Identifying Y Chromosome in Human Interphase Nuclei," *Nature*, 1970, 226: 78.
116. Geoffrey Raisman and Pauline M. Field, "Sexual Dimorphism in the Preoptic Area of the Rat," *Science*, 1971, 173: 731.
117. B. S. McEwen, *et al.*, "Factors Influencing Sex Hormone Uptake by Rat Brain Regions," *Brain Research* , 1970, 21: 29.
118. E. M. Gruenberg, "Epidemiology of Mental Illness," *International Journal of Psychiatry*, 1966, 2: 78.
119. David C. Taylor and Christopher Ounsted, "The Nature of Gender Differences Explored Through Ontogenetic Analyses of Sex Ratios in Disease," in *Gender Differences: Their Ontogeny and Significance* , ed. by Christopher Ounsted

and David C. Taylor. London: Churchill Livingstone, 1972.

120. M. Kramer, *et al.*, "Studies of the Incidence and Prevalence of Hospitalized Mental Disorders in the U.S.," in *Comparative Epidemiology of the Mental Disorders*, ed. by P.H. Hoch and J. Zubin. New York: Grune and Stratton, 1961.

121. Kay Weiss, "Birth: Suffering for Science," *Off Our Backs*, 1975, September-October: 14.

122. Taylor and Ounsted, *op. cit.*

123. Margaret Ounsted, "Gender and Intrauterine Growth," in *Gender Differences: Their Ontogeny and Significance*, ed. by Christopher Ounsted and David C. Taylor. London: Churchill Livingstone, 1972.

124. *Ibid.*

125. *Ibid.*

126. A. Anastasi, *Differential Psychology*. 3rd. ed.; New York: Macmillan, 1958.

127. "Wraparound," *Harper's*, 1975, July: 7.

128. Commission on Professional Hospital Activities as quoted in Kay Weiss, *op. cit.*

129. Weiss, *op. cit.*

130. *Ibid.*

131. *Ibid.*

132. William F. Windle, "Brain Damage by Asphyxia at Birth," *The Nature and Nurture of Behavior.* San Francisco: W.H. Freeman, 1973.

133. U.S. Public Health Service Study, completed in 1972 but not yet released to the public, as quoted in Weiss, *op. cit.*

134. Weiss, *op. cit.*

135. Suzanne Arms, *Immaculate Deception*. Boston: Houghton Mifflin, 1975.

136. Vernon H. Mark and Frank R. Ervin, *Violence and the Brain*. New York: Harper and Row, 1970.

137. Esther Milner, *Human Neural and Behavioral Development*. Springfield, Ill.: Charles C. Thomas, 1967.

138. Beatrice Hamburg, "Development of Sex Differences in Behavioral Functioning," a discussion in *Sex Differences in Behavior*, ed. by Richard C. Friedman, *et al.* New York: Wiley, 1974.

139. Gene P. Sackett, "Sex Differences in Rhesus Monkeys Following Varied Rearing Experiences," in *Sex Differences in Behavior*, ed. by Richard C. Friedman, *et al.* New York: Wiley, 1974.

140. "Stress and Early Life Experience in Nonhumans," a discussion in *Sex Differences in Behavior*, ed. by Richard C. Friedman, *et al.* New York: Wiley, 1974.

141. *Ibid.*

142. Mark R. Rosenzweig, *et al.* "Brain Changes in Response to Experience," in *The Nature and Nurture of Behavior* ed. by William T. Greenough, San Francisco: W.H. Freeman and Company, 1973.

143. Mark and Ervin, *op. cit.*
144. *Ibid.*
145. Anthony W. H. Buffery and Jeffrey A. Gray, "Sex Differences in the Development of Spatial and Linguistic Skills," in *Gender Differences: Their Ontogeny and Significance.* ed. by Christopher Ounsted and David C. Taylor. London: Churchill Livingstone, 1972.
146. Eleanor E. Maccoby and Carol N. Jacklin, *op. cit.*
147. Beatrice Hamburg, "The Psychology of Sex Differences: An Evolutionary Perspective," in *Sex Differences and Behavior*, ed. by Richard C. Friedman, *et al.* New York: Wiley, 1974.
148. Buffery and Gray, *op. cit.*
149. *Ibid.*
150. *Ibid.*
151. *Ibid.*
152. T. G. R. Bower, "Development of Reaching," a paper presented to the New England Pscyhological Association, 1969, as quoted in Buffery and Gray, *op. cit.*
153. Buffery and Gray, *op. cit.*
154. John L. Dawson, "Effects of Sex Hormones on Cognitive Style in Rats and Men," *Behavior Genetics*, 1972, 2: 1.
155. Christopher Ounsted and David C. Taylor, "The Y Chromosome Message: A point of View," in *Gender Differences: Their Ontogeny and Significance*, ed. by Christopher Ounsted and David C. Taylor. London: Churchill Livingstone, 1972.
156. S. D. Porteus, *Porteus Maze Test: Fifty Years Application.* Palo Alto, California: Pacific Books, 1965; as quoted in Beatrice Hamburg, *op. cit.*
157. J. Van Lawick-Goodall, "The Behavior of Free-living Chimpanzees in the Gombe Stream Reserve," *Animal Behavior Monographs*, 1968, 1: 161.
158. Beatrice Hamburg, *op. cit.*
159. P. Flor-Henry, "Psychosis, Neurosis and Epilepsy: Developmental and Gender-related Effects and their Aetiological Contribution," *British Journal of Psychiatry*, 1974, 124: 144.
160. M. C. Goodall, "Studies of Adrenaline and Noradrenaline in Mammalian Heart and Suprarenals," *Acta Physiologica Scandinavica*, 1951, 24: Supplement 85.
161. U. S. Von Euler, "Adrenal Medullary Secretion and its Neural Control," in *Neuroendocrinology*, vol. 2, ed. by Luciano Martini and Wm. F. Ganong. New York and London: Academic Press, 1967.
162. J. Ruesch, "The Physiology of Fear and Anger," *Scientific American*, 1955, 192: 74.
163. B. T. Donovan, *Mammalian Neuroendocrinology.* London: McGraw-Hill, 1970.
164. Donald J. Reis, "Central Neurotransmitters," in *Neural Bases of Violence and Aggression*, ed. by Wm. S. Fields

and Wm. H. Sweet. St. Louis, Missouri: Warren H. Green, Inc., 1975.

165. J.W. Mason, *et al.*, "Concurrent Plasma Epinephrine, Norepinephrine and 17-hydroxycorticosteroid Levels During Conditioned Emotional Disturbances in Monkeys," *Psychosomatic Medicine*, 1961, 23: 344.

166. Joseph Brady, "Emotion and the Sensitivity of Psychoendocrine Systems," in *Neurophysiology and Emotion*, ed. by David C. Glass. New York: Rockefeller University Press and Russell Sage Foundation, 1967.

167. J.J. Schildkraut and Seymour S. Kety, "Biogenic Amines and Emotion," *Science*, 1967, 156: 21.

168. M.C. Goodall, *op. cit.*

169. F. Elmadjian, *et al.*, "Excretion of Epinephrine and Norepinephrine in Various Emotional States," *Journal of Clinical Endocrinology and Metabolism*, 1957, 17: 608.

170. U.S. Von Euler and U. Lundberg, "Effect of Flying on the Epinephrine Excretion in Air Force Personnel," *Journal of Applied Physiology*, 1954, 6: 551.

171. F. Elmadjian, *et al.*, *op. cit.*

172. B. Hokfelt, "Noradrenalin and Adrenalin in Mammalian Tissues: Distribution under Normal and Pathological Conditions with Special Reference to the Endocrine System," *Acta Physiologica Scandinavica*, 1951, 25: Supplement 92.

173. D.M. Shepherd and G.B. West, "Noradrenaline and the Suprarenal Medulla," *British Journal of Pharmacology*, 1951, 6: 665.

174. G.B. West, *et al.*, "Adrenaline and Noradrenaline Concentrations in Adrenaline Glands at Different Ages in Some Diseases," *Lancet*, 1951, 261: 966.

175. S. Funkenstein, "The Physiology of Fear and Anger," *Scientific American*, 1955, 192: 74.

176. B.J. Fine and D.R. Sweeney, "Socio-economic Background, Aggression and Catecholamine Excretion," *Psychological Reports*, 1967, 20: 11.

177. *Ibid.*

178. *Ibid.*

179. *Ibid.*

180. *Ibid.*

181. David G. Gil, *Violence Against Children: Physical Child Abuse in the United States*. Cambridge, Mass.: Harvard University Press, 1970.

182. Wm. J. Goode, "Force and Violence in the Family," in *Violence in the Family*, ed. by Suzanne K. Steinmetz and Murray A. Straus. New York and Toronto: Dodd, Mead and Co., 1974.

183. Murray A. Straus, "Some Social Antecedents of Physical Punishment: A Linkage Theory Interpretation," in *Violence in the Family*, ed. by Suzanne K. Steinmetz and Murray A. Straus. New York and Toronto: Dodd, Mead and Co., 1974.

184. A. Bergsman, "Urinary Excretion of Adrenalin and Nor-adrenalin in Some Mental Diseases," *ACTA Psychiatrica Acta Psychiatrica et Neurologica Scandinavica*, 1959, Supplement 34.

185. N. T. Karki, "The Urinary Excretion of Noradrenaline and Adrenaline in Different Age Groups, its Diurnal Variation and the Effect of Muscular Work on it," *Acta Physiologica Scandinavica*, 1956, 39: Supplement 132.

186. W. W. Lambert, *et al.*, "Catecholamine Excretion in Young Children and their Parents as Related to Behavior," *Scandinavian Journal of Psychology*, 1969, 10: 306.

187. G. Johansson, "Sex Differences in Catecholamine Output of Children," *Report of the Psychology Laboratory University of Stockholm*, 1971, No. 326: 1.

188. *Ibid.*

189. Lennart Levi, "Sympathoadrenomedullary activity, diuresis and emotional reactions during visual sexual stimulation in females and males," in *Stress and Distress in Response to Psychosocial Stimuli* , ed. by Lennart Levi. Oxford and New York: Pergamon Press, 1972.

190. *Ibid.*

191. Bruce L. Welch, Discussion of A. B. Rothballer's "Aggression, Defense and Neurohumors," in *Aggression and Defense: Neural Mechanisms and Social Patterns*, ed. by C. D. Clements and D. B. Lindsley. Los Angeles and Berkeley: University of California Press, 1967.

192. B. T. Donovan, *op. cit.*

193. Wm. E. Bunney and Dennis L. Murphy, "The Behavioral Switch Process and Psychopathology," in *Biological Psychiatry*, ed. by Joseph Mendels. New York: John Wiley and Sons, 1973.

194. Donald J. Reis, *op. cit.*

195. J. J. Schildkraut and Seymour S. Kety, *op. cit.*

196. *Ibid.*

197. Joseph Mendels and James L. Stinnett, "Biogenic Amine Metabolism, Depression and Mania," in *Biological Psychiatry*, ed. by Joseph Mendels. New York: Wiley, 1973.

198. Wm. E. Bunney and Dennis L. Murphy, *op. cit.*

199. *Ibid.*

200. *Ibid.*

201. Donald J. Reis, *op. cit.*

202. *Ibid.*

203. B. L. Welch and A. S. Welch, "Aggression and the Biogenic Amine Neurohumors," in *Aggressive Behavior*, ed. by S. Garattini and E. B. Sigg. New York: Wiley, 1973.

204. W. Ladosky and L. C. J. Gazir, "Brain Serotonin and Sexual Differentiation of the Nervous System," *Neuroendocrinology*, 1969, 6: 168.

205. H. Shimada and A. Gorbman, "Long Lasting Changes in RNA Synthesis in the Forebrains of Female Rats Treated with Testosterone soon after Birth," *Biochemical and*

Biophysical Research Communications, 1970, 38: 423.
206. C. V. H. Clark and A. Vernadakis, "Sex Differences in Brain Deoxyribonucleic Acid and Cholinesterase Activity in Rats," *American Journal of Physiology*, 1971, 220: 1775.
207. E. L. Klaiber, "The Automatization Cognitive Style, Androgens, and Monoamine Oxidase," *Psychopharmacologia*, 1967, 11: 320.
208. B. L. Welch and A. S. Welch, *op. cit.*

Chapter Two:
VIOLENCE BEGETS VIOLENCE

1. Gene P. Sackett, "Sex Differences in Rhesus Monkeys Following Varied Rearing Experiences," in *Sex Differences in Behavior*, ed. by Richard C. Friedman, *et al.* New York: John Wiley and Sons, 1974.
2. Gordon D. Jensen, "Human Sexual Behavior in Primate Perspective," in *Contemporary Sexual Behavior: Critical Issues in the 1970's*, ed. by Joseph Zubin and John Money. Baltimore and London: Johns Hopkins University Press, 1973.
3. Howard A. Moss, "Early Sex Differences and Mother-Infant Interaction," in *Sex Differences in Behavior*, ed. by Richard C. Friedman, *et al.* New York: John Wiley and Sons, 1974.
4. Jensen, *op. cit.*
5. Sackett, *op. cit.*
6. Moss, *op. cit.*
7. M. Lewis, "State as an Infant-Environment Interaction: An Analysis of Mother-Infant Behavior as a Function of Sex," *Merrill Palmer Quarterly*, 1972, 18: 95.
8. Howard A. Moss, "Sex, Age and State as Determinants of Mother-Infant Interaction," *Merrill Palmer Quarterly*, 1967, 13: 19.
9. L. J. Yarrow, *et al.*, "Dimensions of Early Stimulation: Differential Effects on Infant Development," paper presented at the meeting of the Society for Research in Child Development, 1971, as summarized by Eleanor Maccoby and Carol Jacklin in *The Psychology of Sex Differences*. Stanford: Stanford University Press, 1974.
10. R. J. Tasch, "The Role of the Father in the Family," *Journal of Experimental Education*, 1952, 20: 319.
11. Jules Henry, *Culture Against Man*. New York: Random House, 1963.
12. Eleanor Maccoby and Carol Jacklin, *The Psychology of Sex Differences*. Stanford: Stanford University Press, 1974.
13. Rodney Stark and James McEvoy III, "Middle Class Violence," *Psychology Today*, November 1970, p. 52.
14. J. N. Butcher, "MMPI Characteristics of Externalizing and and Internalizing Boys and Their Parents," paper presented at the First Conference on Recent Developments in the Use

of the MMPI, Minneapolis, March, 1966. Reviewed in "Parent Personality and Childhood Disorders: A Review of MMPI Findings," in *MMPI: Research Developments and Clinical Applications*, ed. by James Neal Butcher. New York: McGraw-Hill, 1969.

15. Thomas Detre, *et al.*, "The Nosology of Violence," in *Neural Bases for Violence and Aggression*, ed. by Wm. S. Fields and Wm. H. Sweet. St. Louis, Missouri: Warren H. Green, Inc., 1974.

16. L. M. Anderson, "Personality Characteristics of Parents of Neurotic, Aggressive, and Normal Preadolescent Boys," *Journal of Consulting and Clinical Psychology*, 1969, 33: 575.

17. Suzanne K. Steinmetz and Murray A. Straus, editors' introduction to "When Parents Hit Out," by Myrna Blumberg, in *Violence in the Family*, ed. by Suzanne K. Steinmetz and Murray A. Straus. New York and Toronto: Dodd, Mead and Co., 1974.

18. Myrna Blumberg, "When Parents Hit Out," in *Violence in the Family*, ed. by Suzanne K. Steinmetz and Murray A. Straus. New York and Toronto: Dodd, Mead and Co., 1974.

19. Marvin E. Wolfgang, "Delinquency and Violence from the Viewpoint of Criminology," in *Neural Bases for Violence and Aggression*, ed. by Wm. S. Fields and Wm. H. Sweet. St. Louis, Missouri: Warren H. Green, Inc., 1974.

20. Leonard D. Eron, *et al.*, *Learning of Aggression in Children*. Boston: Little, Brown and Co., 1971.

21. S. Gluech and E. Glueck, *Unravelling Juvenile Delinquency*. Cambridge: Harvard University Press, 1950.

22. Stuart Palmer, *The Psychology of Murder*. New York: Thomas Y. Crowell, 1960.

23. Wesley C. Becker, "Consequences of Different Kinds of Parental Discipline," in *Review of Child Development Research*, ed. by Martin L. Hoffman and Lois W. Hoffman. New York: Russell Sage Foundation, 1964.

24. Seymour Feshback, "Aggression," in *Carmichael's Manual of Child Psychology*, Third Edition, ed. by Paul H. Mussen. New York: John Wiley and Sons, 1970.

25. Martin L. Hoffman, "Moral Development," in *Carmichael's Manual of Child Psychology*, Third Edition, ed. by Paul H. Mussen. New York: John Wiley and Sons, 1970.

26. Lawrence Kohlberg, "Development of Moral Character and Moral Ideology," in *Review of Child Development Research*, ed. by Martin L. Hoffman and Lois W. Hoffman. New York: Russell Sage Foundation, 1964.

27. Murray A. Strauss, "Some Social Antecedents of Physical Punishment: A Linkage Theory Interpretation," in *Violence in the Family*, ed. by Suzanne K. Steinmetz and

Murray A. Straus. New York and Toronto: Dodd, Mead and Co., 1974.

28. Maccoby and Jacklin, *op. cit.*
29. *Ibid.*
30. L. A. Serbin, *et al.*, "A Comparison of Teacher Response to the Pre-Academic and Problem Behavior of Boys and Girls," *Child Development*, 1973, 44: 796.
31. Stark and McEvoy, *op. cit.*
32. Eron, *op. cit.*
33. Sepp Shindler, "Family Constellation and Aggressive Conduct," *Zeitschrift fur Klinishe Psychologie und Psychotherapie*, 1974, January: Vol. 22.
34. David G. Gil, *Violence Against Children*, Second Edition. Cambridge: Harvard University Press, 1973.
35. *Ibid.*
36. Suzanne K. Steinmetz, "Occupational Environment in Relation to Physical Punishment and Dogmatism," in *Violence in the Family*, ed. by Suzanne K. Steinmetz and Murray A. Straus. New York and Toronto: Dodd, Mead and Co., 1974.
37. Suzanne K. Steinmetz and Murray A. Straus, ed., *Violence in the Family*, editors' introduction. New York and Toronto: Dodd, Mead and Co., 1974.
38. Suzanne K. Steinmetz and Murray A. Straus, editors' introduction to "Physical Frustration and Murder," by Stuart Palmer, in *Violence in the Family*, ed. by Suzanne K. Steinmetz and Murray A. Straus. New York and Toronto: Dodd, Mead and Co., 1974.
39. Leopold Bellak and Maxine Antell, "An Intercultural Study of Aggressive Behavior on Children's Playgrounds," *American Journal of Orthopsychiatry*, 1974, 44: 503.
40. *Ibid.*
41. Leonard D. Eron, *et al.*, "How Learning Conditions in Early Childhood--Including Mass Media--Relate to Aggression in Late Adolescence," *American Journal of Orthopsychiatry*, 1974, 44: 412.
42. Robert M. Liebert, "Television and Children's Aggressive Behavior: Another Look," *American Journal of Psychoanalysis*, 1974, 34: 99.
43. Eron, *et al.*, *op. cit.*
44. *Ibid.*
45. *Ibid.*
46. Robert F. Baker and Sandra J. Ball, *Violence and the Media*, a Staff Report to the National Commission on the Causes and Prevention of Violence. Washington, D. C.: United States Government Printing Office, 1969.
47. G. S. Lesser, "Designing a Program for Broadcast Television," in *Psychology and the Problems of Society*, ed. by F. F. Morten, *et al.* Washington, D. C.: American Psychological Association, 1970.
48. Baker and Ball, *op. cit.*

49. *Ibid.*
50. *Ibid.*
51. Kenneth Moyer, "A Physiological Model of Aggression," in *Neural Bases for Violence and Aggression*, ed. by Wm. S. Fields and Wm. H. Sweet. St. Louis, Missouri: Warren H. Green, Inc., 1974.
52. Jeffrey H. Goldstein and Robert L. Arms, "Effects of Observing Athletic Contests on Hostility," *Sociometry*, 1971, 34: 83.
53. *Ibid.*
54. Albert Bandura and Richard H. Walters, "Catharthis--A Questionable Mode of Coping with Violence," in *Violence in the Family* ed. by Suzanne K. Steinmetz and Murray A. Straus. New York and Toronto: Dodd, Mead and Co., 1974.
55. General Bibliography:
Ruth Benedict, *Patterns of Culture*. Boston: Houghton Mifflin, 1934.
Leonard Berkowitz, *Aggression: A Social Psychological Analysis*. New York: McGraw-Hill, 1962.
Konrad Lorenz, *On Aggression*. New York: Harcourt, Brace, World, 1966.
Margaret Mead, *Growing Up in New Guinea*. New York: Wm. Morrow, 1966. First Edition, copyright 1930.
Ashley Montagu, ed., *Man and Aggression*. New York: Oxford University Press, 1974.
Desmond Morris, *The Naked Ape*. New York: McGraw-Hill, 1967.
and *The Human Zoo*. New York: McGraw-Hill, 1969.
J. P. Scott, *Aggression*. Chicago: University of Chicago Press, 1958.

Chapter Three:
THE EVOLUTION OF THE SEXES

1. Roy G. D'Andrade, "Sex Differences and Cultural Institutions," in *The Development of Sex Differences*, ed. by Eleanor Maccoby. Stanford: Stanford University Press, 1966.
2. Lewis Richardson, *Statistics of Deadly Quarrels*. London: Stevens and Sons, 1960.
3. Louis B. Leakey, "Development of Aggression as a Factor in Early Human and Pre-Human Evolution," in *Aggression and Defense*, ed. by Carmine D. Clemente and Donald B. Lindsley. Berkeley and Los Angeles: University of California Press, 1967.
4. *Ibid.*
5. David Pillbeam, "Man's Earliest Ancestors," *Science Journal*, 1967, Vol. III, No. 2.

6. Louis B. Leakey, "Bone-Smashing by Late Miocene Hominid," *Nature*, 1968, 218: 528.
7. Leakey, *Aggression and Defense*, *op. cit.*
8. *Ibid.*
9. Sherwood L. Washburn and C. L. Lancaster, "The Evolution of Hunting," in *Man the Hunter*, ed. by Richard B.
   Lee and Irven DeVore. Chicago: Aldine, 1968.
10. Leakey, *Aggression and Defense*, *op. cit.*
11. Kenneth P. Oakley, "On Man's Use of Fire, with Com-
    ments on Tool-making and Hunting," in *The Social Life
    of Early Man*, ed. by Sherwood L. Washburn. Chicago:
    Aldine, 1969.
12. Washburn, *op. cit.*
13. *Ibid.*
14. *Ibid.*
15. Robert Ardrey, *The Social Contract*. New York: Dell,
    1970.
16. S. L. Washburn and Irven DeVore, "Social Behavior of Ba-
    boons and Early Man," in *The Social Life of Early Man*,
    ed. by Sherwood L. Washburn. Chicago: Aldine, 1961.
17. Washburn and Lancaster, *op. cit.*
18. Lyall Watson, *The Omnivorous Ape*. New York: Coward,
    McCann and Geoghegan, Inc., 1971.
19. Washburn and Lancaster, *op. cit.*
20. Elizabeth Gould Davis, *The First Sex*. New York: G. P.
    Putnam's Sons, 1971.
21. Lionel Tiger, *Men in Groups*. New York: Random House,
    1969.
22. Wm. S. Laughlin, "Hunting: An Integrating Biobehavior
    System and Its Evolutionary Importance," in *Man the
    Hunter*, ed. by Richard B. Lee and Irven Devore. Chi-
    cago: Aldine, 1968.
23. J. A. Gray and A. W. H. Buffery, "Sex Differences in Emo-
    tional and Cognitive Behavior in Mammals Including Man:
    Adaptive and Neural Bases," *Acta Psychologica*, 1971,
    35: 89.
24. Adriaan Kortlandt and M. Kooij, "Protohominid Behavior
    in Primates," *Symposium of the Zoological Society of
    London*, 1963, 10: 61.
25. Tiger, *op. cit.*
26. Washburn and DeVore, *op. cit.*
27. Ardrey, *op. cit.*
28. Evelyn Reed, *Woman's Evolution*. New York: Pathfinder
    Press, 1975.
29. Carleton Gajdusek, "Physiological and Psychological Char-
    acteristics of Stone Age Man," *Engineering and Science*,
    1970, 33: 26.
30. Raymond Dart, *Adventures with the Missing Link*. New
    York: Harper and Row, 1959.
31. Watson, *op. cit.*
32. Reed, *op. cit.*

33. *Ibid.*
34. *Ibid.*
35. Frank Byron Jevons, *An Introduction to the History of Religion*, New York: MacMillan, 1911. As quoted in *Woman's Evolution*, by Evelyn Reed. New York: Pathfinder Press, 1975.
36. Hulton Webster, *Taboo: A Sociological Study*. Stanford: Stanford University Press, 1942. As quoted in *Woman's Evolution*, by Evelyn Reed. New York: Pathfinder Press, 1975.
37. Davis, *op. cit.*
38. Tiger, *op. cit.*
39. Robert Bigelow, *The Dawn Warriors*. Boston: Little, Brown and Co., 1969.
40. Ardrey, *op. cit.*
41. D. Hamburg, "Recent Evidence on the Evolution of Aggressive Behavior," *Engineering and Science*, 1970, 33: 15.
42. *Ibid.*
43. "Study Leads to New Perspective on Sexual Politics Among the Primates," *Harvard Gazette*, 1975, October 17.
44. *Ibid.*
45. Gordon D. Jensen, "Human Sexual Behavior in Primate Perspective," in *Contemporary Sexual Behavior*, ed. by Joseph Zubin and John Money. Baltimore and London: Johns Hopkins University Press, 1973.
46. Kenneth Moyer, "A Physiological Model of Aggression," in *Neural Bases for Violence and Aggression*, ed. by Wm. S. Fields and Wm. H. Sweet. St. Louis, Missouri: Warren H. Green, Inc., 1974.
47. Robert Briffault, *The Mothers" A Study of the Origin of Sentiments and Institutions*. New York: Macmillan, 1952.
48. B. Beit-Hallahmi, "Sexual and Aggressive Fantasies in Violent and Non-violent Prison Inmates," *Journal of Personality Assessment*, 1971, 35: 326.
49. Briffault, *op. cit.*
50. P.D. MacClean, "New Findings on Brain Function and Sociosexual Behavior," in *Contemporary Sexual Behavior*, ed. by Joseph Zubin and John Money. Baltimore and London: Johns Hopkins University Press, 1973.
51. Gajdusek, *op. cit.*
52. *Ibid.*
53. P.D. MacClean, *op. cit.*
54. P.D. MacClean, *A Triune Concept of Brain and Behavior*. Toronto: Toronto University Press, 1972.
55. Gajdusek, *op. cit.*

245

Chapter Four:
MAN'S DOMINION: THE HUNTER TODAY

1. Lionel Tiger and Robin Fox, *The Imperial Animal.* New York, Chicago, San Francisco: Holt, Rinehart and Winston, 1971.
2. J.P. Scott, "Theoretical Issues Concerning the Origin and Causes of Fighting," in *The Physiology of Aggression and Defeat,* ed. by Basil E. Eleftheriou and J.P. Scott. New York and London: Plenum Press, 1971.
3. Cleveland Amory, *Man Kind? Our Incredible War on Wildlife.* New York: Harper and Row, 1974.
4. Genesis 1: 28.
5. Genesis 9: 2-3.
6. W.E.H. Lecky, *History of European Morals from Augustus to Charlemagne.* London: 1869; as quoted in *Animal Liberation,* by Peter Singer. New York: New York Review, 1975.
7. Mark 5: 1-13.
8. Desmond Morris, *The Human Zoo.* New York: McGraw-Hill, 1969.
9. *Ibid.*
10. Carol Adams, *The Oedible Complex: Feminism and Vegetarianism.* Provincetown, Massachusetts: To the Lighthouse Press, 1976.
11. Peter Singer, *Animal Liberation.* New York: New York Review, 1975.
12. *United States Book of Facts, Statistics and Information* New York: Washington Square Press, Inc., 1967.
13. Lyall Watson, *The Omnivorous Ape.* New York: Coward, McCann and Geoghegan, Inc., 1971.
14. *Ibid.*
15. Clarence M. Kelley, Director, Federal Bureau of Investigation, *Crime in the United States: Uniform Crime Reports.* Washington, D.C.: United States Government, released November 17, 1975.
16. Lawrence Meyer, "The Terrifying Increase in Crime," *San Francisco Examiner and Chronicle,* August 24, 1975.
17. Marvin E. Wolfgang, "Delinquency and Violence from the Viewpoint of Criminology," in *Neural Bases for Violence and Aggression* ed. by Wm. S. Fields and Wm. H. Sweet. St. Louis, Missouri: Warren H. Green, Inc., 1974.
18. Kelley, *op. cit.*
19. Claude Brown, *Manchild in the Promised Land.* New York: MacMillan, 1965.
20. Hans Eysenck, *The Inequality of Man.* London: Temple Smith, Ltd., 1973.
21. *Ibid.*

22. Helen Kruger, *Other Healers, Other Cures*. New York: Bobbs-Merrill, 1974.
23. Morris, *op. cit.*
24. *Ibid.*
25. Meyer, *op. cit.*
26. Kelley, *op. cit.*
27. Victoria Hughes Reis, "Taming a Toymaker," *Harper's*, March, 1974.
28. Kelley, *op. cit.*
29. *Ibid.*
30. Wolfgang, *op. cit.*
31. Kelley, *op. cit.*
32. Susan Brownmiller, *Against Our Will: Men, Women and Rape* New York: Simon and Schuster, 1975.
33. Alfred C. Kinsey, *et al.*, *Sexual Behavior in the Human Male*. Philadephia and London: W. B. Saunders Co., 1948.
34. K. B. Davis, *Factors in the Sex Life of 2,200 Women*. New York: Harper and Row, 1929.
35. L. M. Terman, *Psychological Factors in Marital Happiness*. New York: McGraw-Hill, 1938.
36. G. W. Corner, "The Events of the Primate Ovarian Cycle," *British Medical Journal*, 1952, 2: 403.
37. Ruth D. Hart, "Monthly Rhythm of Libido in Married Women," *British Medical Journal*, 1966, 1: 1023.
38. Tiger and Fox, *op. cit.*
39. *Ibid.*
40. Morris, *op. cit.*
41. *Ibid.*
42. Edward Goldsmith, *et al.*, *Blueprint for Survival*. New York: Houghton Mifflin, 1972.
43. *Ibid.*
44. *Ibid.*
45. John Gofman and Arthur Tamplin, *Poisoned Power: The Case Against Nuclear Power Plants*. New York: New American Library, 1974.
46. Ford Foundation Report, *Time to Choose: America's Energy Future*. Philadelphia: The Ford Foundation/Bollingen, 1974.
47. E. F. Schumacher, *Small is Beautiful*. New York: Harper and Row, 1973.
48. Will and Ariel Durant, *The Lessons of History*. New York: Simon and Schuster, 1968.
49. Margaret Mead, *Male and Female*. Harmondsworth, England: Penguin, 1962.
50. Tiger and Fox, *op. cit.*
51. Goldsmith, *op. cit.*
52. Tiger and Fox, *op. cit.*
53. Elizabeth Gould Davis, *The First Sex*. New York: G. P. Putnam's Sons, 1971.
54. Tiger and Fox, *op. cit.*
55. Watson, *op. cit.*
56. Rarihokwats, personal communication, 1975.

57. Anais Nin, *The Novel of the Future*. New York: Macmillan, 1968.
58. Kenneth Patchen, *The Journal of Albion Moonlight.* New York: New Directions, 1961; first published in 1941.
59. James Wright, "A Secret Gratitude," *Collected Poems*. Middletown, Connecticut: Wesleyan University Press, 1971.
60. Louis Aragon, "Manifesto," as quoted in *The History of Surrealism*, ed. by Maurice Nadeau, translated by Richard Howard. London: Collier, 1968.
61. Antonin Artaud, as quoted in *The Savage God*, by A. Alvarez. New York: Bantam, 1973.
62. A. Alvarez, *The Savage God*. New York: Bantam, 1973.
63. Nin, *op. cit.*
64. Valerie Solanas, *The Scum Manifesto*. New York: The Olympia Press, 1968.
65. Jean-Paul Sartre, *The Words*. New York: Fawcett World Library, 1968.
66. Solanas, *op. cit.*

Chapter Five:
HOME REMEDIES

1. M. K. Selmanoff, *et al.*, "Evidence for a Y Chromosomal Contribution to an Aggressive Phenotype in Inbred Mice," *Nature*, 1975, 253: 529.
2. B. Pasamanick, *et al.*, "Pregnancy Experience and Development of Behavior Disorder in Children," *American Journal of Psychiatry*, 1956, 112: 613.
3. A. Zitrin, *et al.*, "Pre- and Paranatal Factors in Mental Disorders of Children," *Journal of Nervous and Mental Disorders*, 1964, 139: 357.
4. Martha E. Rogers, *et al.*, *Prenatal and Paranatal Factors in the Development of Childhood Behavior Disorders* Baltimore: Johns Hopkins University Press.
5. P. Vara, *et al.*, "The Toxaemia of Late Pregnancy," *Acta Obstetrica et Gynecologica Scandinavica*, Supplement 3, xliv.
6. P. Toivanen and T. Hirvonin, "Sex Ratio of Newborns: Preponderance of Males in Toxaemia of Pregnancy," *Science*, 1970, 170: 187.
7. Vara, *et al.*, *op. cit.*
8. Antonio Ferreira, *Prenatal Environment*. Springfield, Illinois: Charles C. Thomas, 1969.
9. J. M. Woodhill, *et al.*, "Nutrition Studies of Pregnant Australian Women: I: Maternal Nutrition in Relation to Toxaemia of Pregnancy and Physical Condition of Infant at Birth," *American Journal of Obstetrics and Gynecology*, 1955, 70: 987.
10. H. Knoblock and B. Pasamanick, "Seasonal Variation in Births of Mentally Deficient," *American Journal of Public*

Health , 1958, 48: 1201.

11. B. Pasamanick and H. Knoblock, "Seasonal Variation in Complications of Pregnancy," *Obstetrics and Gynecology*, 1958, 12: 110.

12. Food and Nutrition Board of the National Academy of Sciences, "The Relationship of Nutrition to Brain Development and Behavior," Washington, D.C., 1973; available free from Food and Nutrition Board, NAS-NRC, 2101 Constitution Ave. N.W., Washington, D.C., 20418.

13. J.C. Sinclair, *et al.*, "Early Postnatal Consequences of Fetal Malnutrition," in *Nutrition and Fetal Development*, ed. by Myron Wynick. New York: John Wiley and Sons, 1974.

14. Neville Butler, "Late Postnatal Consequences of Fetal Malnutrition," in *Nutrition and Fetal Development*, ed. by Myron Wynick. New York: John Wiley and Sons, 1974.

15. G.J. Mohr and P.F. Bartelme, "Mental and Physical Development of Children Prematurely Born," *American Journal of Diseases of Children*, 1930, 40: 1000.

16. Mary Shirley, "A Behavior Syndrome Characterizing Prematurely Born Children," *Child Development*, 1939, 10: 115.

17. C.H. Hendricks, "Delivery Patterns and Reproductive Efficiency Among Groups of Different Socioeconomic Status and Ethnic Origins," *American Journal of Obstetrics and Gynecology*, 1967, 97: 608.

18. Frances Lappe, *Diet for a Small Planet*. New York: Ballantine, 1971.
    Roger Williams, *Nutrition Against Disease*. New York: Pitman Publishing Co., 1971.
    Robin Hur, *Food Reform: Our Desperate Need*. Austin, Texas: Heidelberg, 1975.

19. Ben F. Feingold, *Why Your Child is Hyperactive*. New York: Random House, 1974.

20. Butler, *op. cit.*

21. W.J. Simpson, "A Preliminary Report on Cigarette Smoking and the Incidence of Prematurity," *American Journal of Obstetrics and Gynecology*, 1957, 73: 808.

22. J.R. Zabriskie, "Effect of Cigarette Smoking During Pregnancy," *Obstetrics and Gynecology*, 1963, 21: 405.

23. P.S. Larson and H. Silvette, *Tobacco: Experimental and Clinical Studies*. Baltimore: The Williams and Wilkins Co., 1968.

24. Butler, *op. cit.*

25. E.C. MacDowell and E.M. Lord, "Reproduction in Alcoholic Mice," *Arch Entwick*, 109: 549; cited in *Prenatal Influences*, by M.F.A. Montagu. Springfield, Illinois: Charles C. Thomas, 1962.

26. N.M. Vincent, "The Effect of Prenatal Alcoholism upon Motivation, Emotionality, and Learning in the Rat," *American Psychologist*, 1958, 13: 401.

27. H. Brown and V.E. Davis, reported in *Medical Tribune*,

June 29, 1967; cited in *Prenatal Environment* , by Antonio Ferreira. Springfield, Ill.: Charles C. Thomas, 1969.

28. Ferreira, *op. cit.*

29. C. H. Peckham and R. W. King, "Study of Intercurrent Conditions Observed During Pregnancy," *American Journal of Obstetrics and Gynecology* , 1963, 87: 609.

30. L. W. Sontag and R. F. Wallace, "The Movement Response of the Human Fetus to Sound Stimuli," *Child Development*, 1935, 6: 353.

31. L. W. Sontag, "War and Fetal Maternal Relationship," *Marriage and Family Living*, 1944, 6: 1.

32. J. Bernard and L. W. Sontag, "Fetal Reactivity to Tonal Stimulation: A Preliminary Report," *Journal of Genetic Psychology*, 1947, 70: 205.

33. David Dempsey, "The Noise Plague and a Warning About City Life," *San Francisco Examiner and Chronicle*, November 30, 1975; first reported in *The New York Times*.

34. A. Anthony and E. Ackermon, "Effects of Noise on the Blood Eosinophil Levels and Adrenals of Mice," *Journal of the Acoustic Society of America*, 1955, 27: 1144.

35. L. Salk, "The Effects of the Normal Heartbeat Sound on the Behavior of the Newborn: Implications for Mental Health," *World Mental Health*, 1960, 12: 1.

36. L. Salk, "The Importance of the Heartbeat Rhythm to Human Nature: Theoretical, Clinical, and Experimental Observations," *Proceedings of the Third World Congress of Psychiatry.* Toronto: University of Toronto Press, 1961.

37. Reviewed by Ferreira, *op. cit.*

38. Reviewed by Albert S. Norris, "Prenatal Factors in Intellectual and Emotional Development," *Journal of the American Medical Association*, 1960, 172: 413.

39. Ferreira, *op. cit.*

40. *Ibid.*

41. E. K. Turner, "The Syndrome in the Infant Resulting from Maternal Emotional Tension During Pregnancy," *Medical Journal of Australia*, 1956, 1: 221.

42. D. P. Swartz, *et al.*, "Epinephrine and Norepinephrine in Normal and Abnormal Pregnancy," *Obstetrics and Gynecology*, 1963, 22: 115.

43. W. F. Howard, *et al.*, "Catecholamine Content of the Initial Voided Urine of the Newborn," *American Journal of Obstetrics and Gynecology*, 1964, 89: 615.

44. Ingeborg Ward, "Prenatal Stress Feminizes and Demasculinizes the Behavior of Males," *Science*, 1972, 175: 82.

45. Ingeborg Ward, "Sexual Behavior Differentiation: Prenatal Hormonal and Environmental Control," in *Sex Differences in Behavior*, ed. by Richard C. Friedman, *et al.* New York: John Wiley and Sons, 1974.

46. Ferreira, *op. cit.*

47. Fernand Lamaze, *Painless Childbirth*, trans. by L. R. Celestin. Chicago: Henry Regnery, 1970.

48. Frederick Leboyer, *Birth Without Violence*. New York: Knopf, 1975.
49. Grantly Dick-Read, *Childbirth Without Fear*. New York: Harper and Row, 1944.
   Barbara Gelb, *The ABC of Natural Childbirth*. New York: Norton, 1954.
   Suzanne Arms, *Immaculate Deception*. Boston: Houghton Mifflin, 1975.
   Ina May and the Farm Midwives, *Spiritual Midwifery*. Summertown, Tennessee: The Book Publishing Co., 1975.
50. O. S. Heyns, *Abdominal Decompression*. Johannesburg, South Africa: Witwatersrand University Press, 1963.
51. *Ibid.*
52. Elizabeth K. Wajdowicz, "Abdominal Decompression During Labor," *American Journal of Nursing*, 1964, 64: 87.
53. E. H. Bishop, *et al.*, "Arrest of Premature Labor," *Journal of the American Medical Association*, 1961, 178: 812.
54. Food and Nutrition Board, *op. cit.*
55. See: J. C. Somogyi and F. Fidanza, editors, *Nutrition and Nervous System*. Series of the Institute of Nutrition Research, Vol. 17. Basel, Switzerland: S. Karger, 1972.
   J. C. Somogyi, editor, *Nutrition and Technology of Foods for Growing Humans*. Series of the Institute of Nutrition Research, Vol. 18. Basel, Switzerland: S. Karger, 1973.
56. Donald Oberleas, *et al.*, "Trace Elements and Behavior," in *Neurobiology of the Trace Metals Zinc and Copper*, ed. by Carl C. Pfeiffer. Supplement 1 of the *International Review of Neurobiology*. New York and London: Academic Press, 1972.
57. P. L. Harris, "Vitamin E Content of Foods," *Journal of Nutrition*, 1950, 40: 367.
58. H. H. Gordon, *et al.*, "Studies of Tocopherol Deficiency in Infants and Children," *American Journal of Diseases of Children*, 1955, 90: 669.
59. F. C. Aitken, *et al.*, "Infant feeding: Comparison of Breast and Artificial Feeding," *Nutrition Abstracts and Reviews*, 1960, 30: 341.
60. Joseph Wilder quoted in *Mental Health Through Nutrition* by Judge Tom R. Blaine. New York: Citadel Press, 1969.
61. M. S. Read, "Malnutrition, Hunger and Behavior," *Journal of the American Dietetic Association*, 1973, 63: 386.
62. United States Health Service Report, as cited in *Supernutrition*, by Richard Passwater. New York: Dial Press, 1975.
63. Adele Davis, *Let's Get Well*. New York: Harcourt, Brace, Jovanovich, 1965.
64. Feingold, *op. cit.*
65. *Ibid.*
66. See Beatrice Trum Hunter, *The Mirage of Safety*. New York: Scribner's, 1975.
67. M. Wolfgang and R. B. Strohm, "The Relationship Between Alcohol and Criminal Homicide," *Quarterly Journal of*

Studies on Alcohol, 1956, 17: 411.

68. M. Takala, *et al.*, *The Effects of Distilled and Brewed Beverages: A Physiological, Neurological and Psychological Study*. Helsinki: Finnish Foundation for Alcohol Studies, Publication #4, 1957.

69. Richard E. Boyatzis, "The Effect of Alcohol Consumption on the Aggressive Behavior of Men," *Quarterly Journal of Studies on Alcohol*, 1974, 35: 959.

70. Robert C. Kolodny, "Depression of Plasma Testosterone Levels After Chronic Intensive Marijuana Use," *New England Journal of Medicine*, 1974, 290: 872.

71. John Harmon, Letter to the Editor, *New England Journal of Medicine*, 1972, 287: 936.

72. M. Santas, *et al.*, "Effects of Cannabis Sativa (Marijuana) on the Fighting Behavior of Mice," *Psychopharmacologia*, 1966, 8: 437.

73. H. Kolansky and W. T. Moore, "Toxic Effects of Chronic Marijuana Use," *Journal of the American Medical Association*, 1972, 222: 35.

74. L. J. West, "On the Marijuana Problem," in *Psychotomimetic Drugs*, ed. by D. L. Efron. New York: Raven Press, 1965.

75. Kolodny, *op. cit.*

76. Harmon, *op. cit.*

77. Walter B. Essman, "Nicotine-related Neurochemical Changes," in *Smoking Behavior: Motives and Incentives*, ed. by Wm. L. Dunn. Washington, D. C.: V. H. Winston and Sons, 1973.

78. T. C. Westfall, *et al.*, "Effect of Nicotine and Related Substrates upon Amine Levels in the Brain," *Annals of the New York Academy of Science*, 1967, 142: 83.

79. Barbara Brown, "Additional Characteristic EEG Differences Between Smokers and Nonsmokers," in *Smoking Behavior: Motives and Incentives*, ed. by Wm. L. Dunn. Washington, D. C.: V. H. Winston and Sons, 1973.

80. Ronald R. Hutchinson and Grace S. Emley, "Effects of Nicotine on Avoidance, Conditioned Suppression and Aggression Response Measures in Animals and Man," in *Smoking Behavior: Motives and Incentives*, ed. by Wm L. Dunn. Washington, D. C.: V. H. Winston and Sons, 1973.

81. A. J. Keys, *et al.*, *The Biology of Human Starvation*, 2. Minneapolis: University of Minnesota Press, 1950.

82. *Ibid.*

83. A. R. Holmberg, *Nomads of the Long Bow: The Siriono of Eastern Bolivia*. Washington, D. C.: Smithsonian Institution, Institute of Social Anthropology, Publication #10, 1950.

84. Judge Tom R. Blaine, *Mental Health Through Nutrition*. New York: Citadel Press, 1969.

85. J. Wilder, "Sugar Metabolism in its Relation to Criminology," in *Handbook of Correctional Psychology*, ed. by Robert M. Lindner and R. V. Seliger. New York: Philosophical Library, 1947.

86. Blaine, *op. cit.*
87. H. L. Newbold, *Meganutrients for Your Nerves*. New York: Peter H. Wyden, 1975.
88. Richard Passwater, *Supernutrition*. New York: Dial Press, 1975.
89. *Bhagavad Gita*, Chapter 17, verse 10.
90. J. S. Walters cited in H. L. Newbold, *Mega-nutrients for Your Nerves*. New York: Peter H. Wyden, 1975.
91. John D. Fernstrom and Richard J. Wurtman, "Control of Brain 5-HT Content by Dietary Carbohydrates," in *Serotonin and Behavior*, ed. by Jack Barchas and Earl Usdin. New York and London: Academic Press, 1973.
92. Reported by Demsey, *op. cit.*
93. R. G. Green and E. C. O'Neal, "Activation of Cue-Elicited Aggression by General Arousal," *Journal of Personality and Social Psychology*, 1969, 11: 289.
94. Demsey, *op. cit.*
95. A. P. Krueger, "Preliminary Consideration of the Biological Significance of Air Ions," in *The Nature of Human Consciousness*, ed. by Robert Ornstein. San Francisco: W. H. Freeman and Co., 1973.
96. Barbara Brown, *New Mind, New Body*. New York: Harper and Row, 1974.
97. Robert E. Ornstein, editor, *The Nature of Human Consciousness*. San Francisco: W. H. Freeman and Co., 1973.
98. G. J. Bloch and J. M. Davidson, "Behavioral and Somatic Responses to the Antiandrogen Approterone," *Hormones and Behavior*, 1971, 2: 11.
Dietrich Blumer, Discussion of "Hormones and Behavior," in *Neural Bases for Violence and Aggression*, ed. by Wm. S. Fields and Wm. H. Sweet. St. Louis, Missouri: Warren H. Green, Inc., 1974.
J. M. R. Delgado, *Physical Control of the Mind*. New York: Harper and Row, 1969.
Murray Goldstein, "Brain Research and Violent Behavior," *Archives of Neurology*, 1974, 30.
Issue devoted to drug treatment for human aggression: *The Journal of Nervous and Mental Disease*, 1975, 160: #2.
K. Junkmann and F. Newmann, "Mechanism of Action of Progestogens Having an Antimasculine Effect on Fetuses," *Acta Endocrinologica*, 1964, Supplement, 90: 139.
Birger Kaada, "Brain Mechanisms Related to Aggressive Behavior," in *Aggression and Defense*, ed. by D. Clemente and D. B. Lindsley. Los Angeles: University of California Press, 1967.
Ursula Laschet, "Antiandrogen in the Treatment of Sex Offenders: Mode of Action and Therapeutic Outcome," in *Contemporary Sexual Behavior*, ed. by Joseph Zubin and John Money. Baltimore: Johns Hopkins University Press, 1973.

253

Kenneth Moyer, *Substrates for Aggression and Aggression Control.* New York: Raven Press, 1976.

F. Neumann, "Antiandrogens," *Research in Reproduction,* 1970:, 2: 3.

Elliott S. Valenstein, *Brain Control.* New York: John Wiley and Sons, 1973.

Appendix I:
HOW TO HAVE A GIRL

1. David M. Rorvik with Landrum B. Shettles, *Your Baby's Sex: Now You Can Choose.* New York: Dodd, Mead and Co., 1970.
2. Donald Schuster and Locky Schuster, "Speculative Mechanisms Affecting Sex Ratios," *Journal of Genetic Psychology,* 1972, 12: 245.
3. J. Rock and D. Robinson, "Effect of Induced Intrascrotal Hyperthermia on Testicular Function in Man," *American Journal of Obstetrics and Gynecology,* 1965, 93: 793.
4. Schuster and Schuster, *op. cit.*
5. Iline Wittels and Philipp E. Bornstein, "A Note on Stress and Sex Determination," *The Journal of Genetic Psychology,* 1974, 124: 333.
6. Joan Healy and Patricia Van Houten, Letter to the Editor, *Lancet,* 1970, 7672: 574.
7. R. T. Ericsson, *et al.,* "Isolation of Fractions Rich in Y Sperm," *Nature,* 1973, 246: 421.
8. "Selecting a Sex," *Newsweek,* January 7, 1974.

Appendix II:
FEMALE PRIMACY & THE MALE MUTATION

1. Jerome Cobb, "Philogyny," *The Village Voice,* September 14, 1972.
2. Elizabeth Gould Davis, *The First Sex.* New York: G. P. Putnam's Sons, 1971.
3. Esther Milner, *Human Neural and Behavioral Development.* Springfield, Illinois: Charles C. Thomas, 1967.
4. E. J. W. Barrington, *Hormones and Evolution.* London: The English University Press, Ltd., 1964.
5. *Ibid.*
6. Adelle Davis, *Let's Eat Right to Keep Fit.* New York: Harcourt, Brace, Jovanovich, 1954.
7. Barrington, *op. cit.*

Laurel Holliday, MA, has published two previous books, co-edited a women's magazine, and run a small publishing company for five years. She is currently living in the country, enjoying occasional forays into the city for speaking engagements, and celebrating the birth of a new publishing company, Bluestocking Books.

Her other new book, *Heart Songs: The Intimate Diaries of Young Girls*, is also published by Bluestocking Books.